CAUSES FOR CONCERN

First published in 2006 by
Liberties Press
Guinness Enterprise Centre | Taylor's Lane | Dublin 8
www.LibertiesPress.com | info@libertiespress.com
Editorial: +353 (1) 402 0805 | sean@libertiespress.com
Sales and marketing: +353 (1) 453 4363 | peter@libertiespress.com
Liberties Press is a member of Clé, the Irish Book Publishers' Association

Trade enquiries to CMD Distribution
55A Spruce Avenue | Stillorgan Industrial Park | Blackrock | County Dublin
Tel: +353 (1) 294 2560
Fax: +353 (1) 294 2564

ISBN 10: 1–905483–09–0
ISBN 13: 978–1–905483–09–9

2 4 6 8 10 9 7 5 3 1

A CIP record for this title is available from the British Library

Cover design by Liam Furlong at space.ie
Index by Sharon Corcoran
Set in Garamond

Printed in Ireland by Colour Books
Baldoyle Industrial Estate | Dublin 13

Causes for Concern

Irish Politics, Culture and Society

Michael D. Higgins

For Sabina, Alice Mary, Michael, John and Daniel

CONTENTS

ACKNOWLEDGEMENTS

Many people assisted in the putting together of this book. Brendan Halligan suggested the project. Seán O'Keeffe and Peter O'Connell at Liberties Press undertook the task. I would like to thank both Seán and Peter for all their hard work, particularly Seán, whose assistance in making choices of the pieces for inclusion and whose assiduous attention to detail on the final draft were invaluable in bringing this selection into being. Michael Treacy and Deirdre Clancy were involved at all stages of assembling the material. Noreen King, Daniel Villanueva and John Higgins provided invaluable assistance with the preparation of the electronic manuscript.

I would like to thank all of the editors of previously published work who facilitated this collection, and in particular Niall Stokes, who responded to this project with the characteristic generosity I recall from my *Hot Press* period. I would like to express my gratitude to those who assisted in typing the articles in their first form, in particular the *Hot Press* pieces, including Betty Dowling, Margaret Shiel, Eileen Hayes, Judy Dunne and Louise Carmody. I want to express my deepest thanks to Declan Kiberd for finding time in an extraordinarily busy academic life to read the manuscript and provide a foreword. For his professional help, good advice and much-appreciated friendship, I have become even more indebted to Jonathan Williams.

Finally, I would like to thank my family – Sabina, Alice Mary, John, Michael and Daniel – for all their assistance, in so many different ways, both at the original time of writing and in the preparation of this volume.

FOREWORD

Although these essays and talks arise from disparate occasions, there is in all of them a marvellous willingness to link intellectual analysis to the life of the emotions. Michael D. Higgins writes and speaks always from the pressure of a felt experience. His moving accounts of his parents' arduous lives in a newly independent Ireland depict the disappointments of a people who once said 'revolution or death' and then faced the death of their own revolution. The poverty and the fragile solidarities of that world are evoked with a beautiful restraint, as also are the casual cruelties committed by a stressed people. Yet the communal values to which everyone subscribed seemed to allow a greater scope for the elaboration of a personality than does the material wealth and 'personal freedom' of our own era. In all of his pieces, the author here offers a very individual enunciation of a collective vision, a world of citizens rather than consumers, of characters rather than egotists. Some readers may be surprised that the man well known as a radical socialist emerges from these pages as something of a critical traditionalist, very much on the model of his beloved teacher William Clune. That man, who knew the Latin name for every flower but also the principles underlying psychoanalysis, was 'going back as well as forward'.

In an age when the great ideological battles between capital and labour have been pronounced to be over, Higgins is one who has kept ideas at the centre of political life; in a time of technocracy, he offers vision; and while others run for office on the basis of competence, he insists on an ethical perspective.

He began as a sociologist whose study of the gombeenman in Ireland exposed a dark secret of community life. His essay superbly exposes the 'literary' nature of much of the sociology produced by outsiders on the subject of rural Ireland, even as it stakes high claims for the sociological accuracy of artists like MacGill and O'Flaherty. The study of clientelism is by now regarded as another classic, demonstrating how a brokerist politics privatised what should have been a state activity, thereby preventing the poor from organising themselves or articulating a shared programme. Politics, reduced to simulations of private charity, could never in that form be a substitute for organised justice.

Higgins became an early critic of the functionalist methods borrowed by many Irish sociologists from British and American counterparts: in essays here, he is quite scathing of the ways in which they rejected the world of process and narrative for one of stasis and quantification. His own best work was done on the cusp between sociology and literature, and he will, we must hope, in the fullness of time write down his many brilliant intuitions and analyses of deviance and normality. For the world of his childhood taught him that the so-called eccentric is often simply that person who has a deeper than average understanding of what passes for normality, and that the broken people of a society are often the ones with most wisdom to teach.

A rich and long political career as a Labour TD for Galway West led to a successful appointment in 1992 as Minister for Arts, Culture and the Gaeltacht. While some of us lamented the fact that this took Michael D. Higgins away from academic life, our compensation lay in the fact that he brought imagination into politics. (He read his way through more than one novel by Thomas Mann during a particularly extended set of debates on land inheritance.) His political speeches carry many literary echoes, even as his writings have the urgency of passionate speech. He spoke of trees and birds at a time when people ran the risk of destroying their natural environment.

Democracy for this man is the dissemination of a common culture as widely as possible among a people audacious enough to imagine their own present and future. It is not to be confused with ease of access by trained technocrats to this or that managerial elite. At its core is an educational ideal based on the principle that learning is life-long but never quantifiable, a process rather than a product, a humanistic challenge rather than a technical qualification. In a land that now has more lawyers than priests, and whose telephone salespersons invade private space far more arrogantly than did any cleric of the old order, these essays give us a measure not only of the world we have lost but also of the world that we might yet win.

Declan Kiberd, October 2006

Introduction

The Limits of the Possible

It was Brendan Halligan, former general secretary of the Labour Party for many years, including the period when I was chairman of the party, who brought Liberties Press and myself together. He and they were aware of different pieces I had written, chapters that were scattered or articles published in disparate places, and they were interested in bringing some of them together. While the pieces were written at a particular time, and often addressed to a specific context, they felt that they would show a particular perspective on events that crossed three decades or more. A selection was made of a number of pieces, and for the most part they have been included as they were originally written.

My own interest lay in assembling fragments, as it were, from a life lived in public, and chosen to be so lived. From my earliest days in school, I have been interested in writing. The form of this writing has changed; what has remained constant is my respect for narrative and the indomitable urge to narrative that defines all cultures.

It has been my privilege to be a public representative for a number of decades and also to have been a university teacher. The pieces that follow draw on these experience, and also on my column in *Hot Press* magazine, which appeared from 1982 to 1992. In addition, there are some speeches included from the many I have given over the years within the Labour Party. Rhetoric may be out of fashion in an age of spin, but I attach an importance to it. The decision to stand on a stone wall and to be faced with the joint challenge of getting those present to listen – and, more important, of assembling something substantial to say – is a demand of public rhetoric quite different from that of writing. The printed version of a speech will always disappoint those who can recall the tension and passion of the moment of delivery. Nevertheless, there are some topics where, perhaps, the substantive matter is still worthy of recall in printed form.

The reflective consequences of an impulse to write or perform in public are not automatically benign in every respect. In the pieces that follow, there are at times attempts to address the contradictions of my own life and to make a connection to the wider contradictions of the times. I remain convinced of the importance of possibility, of that which can be envisaged but has not yet been attained, and the empowerment of the contradiction that ensues, as well as the disappointing failure, with regard to the achievement of ideals, which one may have to endure.

What follows is not a biography. Neither does it purport to be fully representative of my work over the years. It is a sample of pieces written or delivered in different circumstances. Yet there are common themes that may be discovered and are, I hope, of interest. The atmosphere, too, in which they were received differed from decade to decade.

Some of the pieces will recall the controversies of the times. What strikes me now, after so much has been uncovered in institutional settings that were previously closed or authoritarian, is the manner in which other areas of life have become less accountable and even more authoritarian than the institutions upon which the light was shone.

I began in public life at a time when an extraordinary authority was claimed by an institution that at times abused this authority. Today, the economic sphere is more unaccountable, and far greater in its demands for authoritarian submission – be it in the circumstances of working life, education, or fundamental freedom – than any church in recent centuries.

The pieces which follow were written by, and show the emergence of, somebody from a small-farm background who saw education as an escape, or a release. There is a price to be paid for such an ambition. While something might be gained, there is also a loss in the dissociation involved. Again, too, there is the burden of meeting the demands of others, which are predetermined in the educational realm. While meeting the standards that are set in any discipline is a stimulus to intellectual work, such a requirement can also become a stifling burden, leading to imitation, rather than an opportunity for creativity or the production of original work.

Most of my life has been lived in cities, yet when I came to write poems in recent times I found that those experiences retained in the memory from a life lived in rural Ireland were what prevailed.

There is no escape from life consciously lived, and the enhancement of life comes through others; it is this which offers an illumination of that which transcends the immediate and is possible, even if not always achieved.

It may be that, in time, I will write about, or seek to impose a tenuous narrative on, all the events and people to which the pieces which follow refer. For the moment, these pieces are simply laid out, as stones might be laid out on a return from a day at the beach. Those who read the pieces may need to resubmit them to the water of memory for them to return to their original appearance.

In returning to these pieces, I was moved by the great gift of friendship I have received from so many people. What follows are descriptions of what was, after all, shared – or a yearning for what might be shared. They are, then, pieces written in anticipation of or against the flow of the extreme individualism that emerged from the 1980s, that invites us to have hearts of stone when there is so much for which we should weep. In this changed world, it is that much more important for us to do creative work, the stuff of celebration.

Michael D. Higgins, October 2006

PART I

THE PERSONAL IS POLITICAL
AND THE POLITICAL IS PERSONAL

PERSONAL REFLECTIONS ON THE HUMAN CONDITION

Personal Reflections

While I was born in a city, my memories of it are confined to the first five years of my life. Nevertheless, there are images which I retain, such as the pleasure of being brought up past Janesboro to the public park in Limerick. That memory, however, fades into insignificance when I consider the implications for all concerned of the leave-taking that was involved in the breaking up of our family.

This book is not a biography, but I have decided to leave pieces, even pieces of a biographical kind, stand as they were written, be it in a journal, as a chapter of a book, or for a lecture. The circumstances of the pieces are thus left intact. In some of the pieces, I was encouraged to recall or recover a particular time or set of experiences, and did so for the purpose in hand. Such a biography as I might attempt in the future would probably be thematic and structured more generally, if not chronologically.

I have been struck by the strength of the images from my early life. It is such images that have surfaced most easily in the poems I have written. In the three collections, *The Betrayal* (Salmon, 1991), *The Season of Fire* (Brandon, 1993) and *An Arid Season* (New Island, 2004), I drew on such images as the journey to Mass, of 'relatives assisting', the ambience of the men's gallery in the church, and such experiences as long Sunday afternoons spent in County Clare, when the dominant sound was that of Mícheál Ó Hehir commenting on the GAA match of the day.

The intimacy of the relationship with animals has surfaced in all three of my collections, be it the proximity of one's head to the udder of a cow in the first collection, to the soft silk of a donkey's ears in my most recent collection. That said, there is an undercurrent, too, in these works of a sense of loss, and of considerable loneliness. This makes its way into some of the pieces which follow, which were written or given so much later.

After secondary school, I worked briefly in a factory at the Shannon industrial estate, but on 6 January 1961 I was called to the ESB as a Grade A clerk. It was a final chance to leave. On the following day, I accepted, and became staff number 26373, in a safe job.

On 21 January, I thumbed to Galway. The last of my three lifts was from a very kind Brother, who explained to me that such places as Newtownsmith and Newcastle were places in Galway city. I moved into my first digs, and began my acquaintance with landladies at a house with the name 'St Walburgas'. I was not familiar with this saint, but I came to admire the particular cultural contribution that the Galway landladies made to Irish life. Most of my own life in the following years was influenced, protected and tolerated by the O'Connor family, with whom I stayed.

It was not an uneventful period, but the detail has to wait for another work and another time. The ESB was moving towards the end of rural electrification, which was marked with 'switch-on hoolies', at which the Parish Priest would reveal the new light for the parish, the families of which had committed themselves to a minimum of one plug and two bulbs, which could include a Sacred Heart lamp. I signed in every morning in an attendance book, which was ritually removed at about ten past nine. After that, one had to sign the late book; a surfeit of signatures in this book could lead to an extension of one's probationary period.

In the ESB, I was struck, and am still moved to this day, by the loyalty of the staff to each other. However, after two years, the generosity of a patron made it possible for me to resign my job, leave, go to England for the summer, and on my return attend university. Galway would become my home, and while I would depart from it for periods, I would always return.

The experience of a person such as me in a university, in this period, was a mixed one. On the one hand, the numbers made it possible for rich friendships and rewarding relationships with those who taught to develop. Eccentricity was perceived as an aspect of lost or missed genius rather than as a fault. There was too, however, the feeling of strangeness, the demands of the efforts to belong. These, however, were minuscule in comparison with the effort required to immerse oneself in the postgraduate settings of English universities, where one could be expected to be asked to tell the story of your own people with exactly the same curiosity as had been addressed to the Nuer, or the Xhosa.

What happens in education is crucial in the life of the person, and it defines the values of the society. In some of the pieces that follow, I was trying to address the issue of what would be an appropriate ethos and curriculum for education in a country such as Ireland at that time.

MY EDUCATION

I was born in Limerick in April 1941. I left Limerick with my brother on 15 August 1946. My father had become very ill, and it was felt that my mother, whose brother had died just a month or two earlier, wouldn't have been able to handle us at that time. What had begun as a temporary removal from Limerick city to Newmarket-on-Fergus, County Clare, became a quasi-permanent move, and I lived in Newmarket-on-Fergus until I was nineteen.

> When we set out together to find
> our new home,
> I suspect
> we cared less
> for the broken heart of our mother
> who had let us go
> than for the wander
> of the journey
> in a black Ford Eight
> though fields
> at twilight.
>
> It is that wonder
> that brings me back
> to the age of five,
> not any great grief
> I should have felt
> or tears I should have shed.
>
> And then, we were
> together,
> a source of curiosity,
> a legacy from tragedy
> that had given a childless pair,
> an uncle and an aunt,
> two instant children,
> brothers
> so alike
> we could be twins.
>
> *from 'Brothers'*

I remember quite clearly the black Ford 8 car. Its registration was IE 3283. It had been bought by an aunt of mine who was a nurse, and during the war it had been stored in a shed and kept in perfect condition. I remember being driven to the house in Newmarket-on-Fergus. It was a very interesting arrangement, because my father and his brother and sister had been involved in the War of Independence, and, in the Civil War, my father had been on the republican side and my uncle on the 'Free State' side, and my aunt was in the middle, as an ex–Cumann na mBan member. Both my uncle and aunt were unmarried and they had acquired two instant children. I was effectively reared by my aunt and uncle, with intermittent visits by us to Limerick city when it was possible, until the age of about thirteen, when we were all reunited briefly again in County Clare. Then there was a kind of a scattering, with my sisters going to England and my brother and myself being educated at St Flannan's College in Ennis.

That parting was a tough decision for my mother, and I was very influenced by it all my life. She had been reared in Liscarroll, County Cork, living over a shop and going away to secondary school. It was a quiet life with aspirations towards respectability and then there was the development of these aspirations in the early days of her life with my father in Limerick. My father's business collapsed and then came the encounter with poverty.

> She stood straight then, and, in a long leather coat,
> After her mother died she packed her case
> Left and joined him a full decade after
> The Civil War. And she had loved him
> In her way. Even when old Binchy placed a note
> Behind the counter in his shop
> In Charleville that when all this blackguardism
> Was over, there would be no jobs
> For Republicans in his firm, or anywhere else,
> For that matter.
>
> Now bent and leaning towards the fire,
> With blackened fingers holding the tongs,
> She poked the coals; and we knew
> It best to leave her with her sorrow
> For her lost life, the house she'd lost,
> The anxious days and nights,
> And all that might have been.

We ran outside and brought in turf
And did our lessons and vowed that we would listen
To what she said, of cities where always
There were voices for company, and churches
Close by, if never cheap.
We would listen to her story
And vow that, for her at least,
We, her children, would escape.

from 'Dark Memories'

One of the most powerful things I learned much later was that education wasn't just a series of years succeeding each other – primary, secondary, third-level, teaching or whatever. I have spent my whole life learning from people, listening to people, often very broken people and people with extraordinary stories, not necessarily stories of success. There is in the line 'All that might have been' a sense of loss and a sense of urgency, too; that you have one shot at life and that maybe opportunities have passed. I know that my mother's aspirations were for those respectable things – for a house, for simple things – and that tells you something about her. I am not interested in judging as to whether this was a form of quiet snobbery, a desire for security, or a result of her upbringing. It is more important to say that this was her story, and I am interested in the democratic right of everyone to have their story told. That is what makes me write poetry. In the poem 'Dark Memories', when I said we 'did our lessons', I deliberately used that phrase because it is the one I find buried in my own memory. Education was less about releasing anything in yourself than about getting these things done, but I had the extraordinary fortune of having a marvellous, holistic primary teacher in a two-teacher school in Newmarket-on-Fergus, a man by the name of William Clune.

William Clune defeated time because he was going back as well as for-ward. He knew the names of plants and bushes in Latin, Irish and English and, on sunny days, he used to take the whole school to the top of a hill to show them the history of the local area. He had an integrated approach to everything before that word was invented. He was a man with an extraordi-nary sense of history in his own life too, because his brother was Conor Clune, the Volunteer who had been shot just before the founding of the State.

He was a man who loved the wonder of children, and he had some extraordinary ideas, which I am sure couldn't be proved. He had an idea, for example, that if you tried hard enough and used your concentration, you could go back through not only your own memory but other people's memories to remember an Irish word. He was a Jungian. Everything that I was later to encounter about Jung and consciousness, he was in fact practising in his own way in the school yard. There was not one person who came into his school yard from any background, with shoes or without, who wasn't respected as a carrier of wonderment. It was the central value of his pedagogic technique.

We all went barefoot to school at that time, not because we didn't have shoes or boots but because that was what was done. This was in a time before tarmacadam, and I remember the sensation of the chippings on your feet as much as I remember the beet dropping off the backs of lorries, beet which we would then eat.

What I do not suggest, however, is the romanticising of these enriching physical sensations to the exclusion of the social side of things. I know the experience of grass between your toes and I know that a fern will cut you and I know where butterflies gather and I know about mosses. I can remember all these sensations very clearly, but I also remember when my aunt and uncle's house was caving in, and youngsters going past the house saying 'We haven't broken windows in our house' and firing stones at the old couple and their nephews who were living inside. I remember the quiet cruelty of it: it is dishonest of people to take the quietness and richness and complexity of natural settings and use them as a mask for the cruel social divisions that prevailed in rural Ireland. I was very glad to escape from that poverty. It was only after a lot of healing that I was able to reach back through these memories and rediscover again the colour and sensation of a fern, or a moss or a grass. I really do not have much time for people who try to perpetuate a kind of pastoral nonsense about rural Ireland.

By the time I was able to relate to him, my father had been terribly wounded by life. He was a person who believed in a republic in this country. All his energy had been used up before I could know him. He had slept under reeks of turf and in dugouts, and he had developed a very bad bronchitis problem. He was on the run in the War of Independence; he was on the run again in the Civil War and had been arrested. He was unemployable; people didn't speak to him when he came home from the Curragh to Newmarket-on-Fergus. He started his business in Limerick city and was successful. What

I got from him was a sense of how right it is for people to have both a dream and the courage to hold on to it, even at a price.

My mother was very different. She loved books and, on our visits to and fro, I read everything she had. I remember going through all the Annie P. Smithson books and I got a love of learning from those. It has been my great love since about the age of twelve.

My mother played the violin, but I have no training in music and I have regretted that all my life. Even if you could get access to a musical instrument, you have all those intangible barriers, like bogus critical categories, standing between you and the love of life and the world. Much of what I have encountered in criticism is of little value, and yet, when a great critic illuminates something, I am so grateful that I could almost weep for his or her insight.

My uncle and aunt dedicated themselves to us. There was nothing they wouldn't have done for us, but they had difficulty explaining why we had come to them. I found it very hard as a youngster to deal with the illness of my uncle, who was bedridden. I looked after him a great deal and I often think about how insensitive very small children are to the needs of people in that situation. It was a one-room-slated, two-room-thatched house with no toilet and no running water. I felt sure that, if an Irish God had created the world, he wouldn't have invented woman with a bucket at the end of each arm. My aunt was one of the women for whom electricity came too late to straighten their backs. Life was very hard for my aunt, less so for my uncle, I think. In my book *The Season of Fire*, I have a poem called 'Katie's Song' in which I give her the affection that I feel I should have given her then.

Oh Katie, I remember
when your writing carried a flourish
and the lightness returned
to your fingers
as you smiled the magic
on the schoolbooks you covered,
satchelled ambassadors
twixt home and school,
our steps to the future.
Your fantasy
compensation
for a life
of lesser things.
Oh Katie, I would sing your song

25

if now I could recover
more
than your moments
of intimacy
and fantasy,
two threads that did not make
alone
the garment of your life.

On a sometime Sunday,
I recall
your playing with magic words.
You dressed yourself
with such unusual care
that the violence of my question
as to where you might be going
did not dislodge you from your dream.
You were not going to any haggard
that afternoon.
You were, instead, intent on strolling
in a pleasure garden
and you told us you had an appointment.
We, whose thoughtless demands
defined
your every action,
could not understand.

And when you died,
after calling us for an hour,
your summons from the fields
not heeded,
not perceived,
your anxious tones
faded,
alone,
at a distance
from children not your own
moved to an unbearable anxiety.

Oh Katie, I am making my way
along a lane of hazel.
I am stretching

for the fire of the senses
that will bring me back
to where I can stand still and shiver
and weep
at all the love
you earned
never paid
by a child afraid,
in iceberg times,
to throw his arms around
the plump frame
of the maker
of his bread
and magic.

from 'Katie's Song'

I went to St Flannan's secondary school in 1955. We were all escaping. The teacher's children were heading for teachers' jobs, more were heading for the civil service, and an odd one or two were heading for third level. There was a sense that you were on your way to somewhere and you were grateful for it. The great aspiration within the institution was that it had been placed on this earth for three things: *one* to win the Harty Cup, *two* to win the gold medal in Greek, and *three* to send priests to the diocese. These three great reasons for existence in the world tended to inform everything. As well as that, there were the usual single-sex brutalities and cruelties.

I met the odd wonderful individual teacher. There was a Canon Maxwell, who, if he hadn't given his life to the Church, would have been in the Royal Shakespeare Company. When he was teaching Shakespeare, he would act out all the parts – he was Iago one minute and Bassanio the next. There was another man, called Martin Kirwan, who loved English poetry as much as he despised Irish poetry, but even in his prejudices he was enthusiastic. However, there are subjects in which I was literally impaired, and I really think that this is a problem that must be addressed. If someone is not successful as a communicator of information, which teaching requires, we should find a different opportunity for that person within the education system. It is very wrong to leave such a person in the classroom year after year. Despite all that, I got over 90 percent in seven subjects in the Leaving Certificate – 'a great Leaving', as they would say . . . .

My brother and I worked in factories in Shannon, and then there were different offers, culminating in the ESB in Galway. I remember going out on the road and getting a lift and asking where Newtownsmith was. I was a Grade 8 clerk there for six pounds, fourteen and threepence a week, paying three pounds ten for digs, living madly out of the rest of it and still sending some money home. I made my way through university and studied commerce and economics for one degree and English literature and language and sociology for another. I studied at Indiana University and Manchester University and then I came home and began teaching at third level.

I am pre-grant and pre–milking machine, and that explains a lot about my life! I have enjoyed teaching, but I have hated structures. I dislike the idea that we are 'processing' large numbers of people through the system. I feel wrecked as an educator and as a teacher by what is happening at the present time – the pressure, the strain – and for what? I feel violated by the suggestion that all of what I believe in about education should be thrown aside so that the transitory requirements of industry should be forced onto the educational process. I think it is an example of fatalistic and inferior thinking.

What influenced my choice to go into politics more than anything I read was the waste of humanity that accrues from stopping people from developing their potential. Nobody should have to struggle so hard for an education. Nobody should be without proper housing. Women's lives should not be shortened by poverty and need. There could be a marvellous humanistic endeavour around all the practical subjects in which I did my postgraduate work. I lectured in monetary economics for a while, but I never believed that all the people for whom my father struggled to have independence existed for monetary economics, but that monetary economics was a technique that existed within economics to serve a social purpose. I met Dr Noel Browne in 1967 and I heard him give a talk in Galway. He spoke about the importance of those people who had had training giving back to society. I object to people saying you should have an amnesia about where you came from so that you can get on with your own personal mobility. We are supposed to wipe out all of what we have been trained to see, and we are supposed to have some kind of vulgar individualism, but some of us see that as something people liberated themselves from in the eighteenth century.

Now, at the age of sixty-five, I can repeat what I wrote at the age of fifty-one: I feel that my education is just beginning. I am starting to see ranges in language that I didn't see before. I am re-reading existentialist literature. In these tough times, I regard it as very challenging to live within categories of constructive pessimism. We may need to paint with the colour black for a while before we earn the right to use the rich colours. I had no opportunity

28

to study physics, yet I love debates about relativity and time. I get excited about new discoveries in biology. I would love to have several lives to pursue these things.

I can truthfully say that there are about a dozen books that have influenced me in my life, but there are so many *people*. I have been very lucky to meet people in different parts of the world – people who have been not only towers of strength in themselves but great sources of strength to others. I think that my entire life was changed by my wife, Sabina Coyne, my partner, whose commitment to the Stanislavsky technique in her acting formation made for me a connection to the power of reflection, meditation and awareness. It was from her that I heard for the first time the phrase 'sense memory'. I feel it is a very partial achievement to use the past to defeat the present. I remember when I was teaching sociology, looking at the Lenten pastorals of the old days and of the new days, and one of the things that they had in common was the sense that, if you could march yourself out of the present and into the past, from the city into the rural areas and from industry into the farm, you would be in a kind of golden age. I feel that I owe it to this alleged golden age to describe life as it was, with all its humanity, because it is the complexity of our humanity that is important.

The magical thing about being alive is the fact that you can weep as well as laugh, and there has been such little space for weeping and healing in Ireland. It is such a nonsense to say 'I had a wonderful childhood.' Life is complex and I think that people should be able to release both the joy and the sadness that is in them, expressing the dark side as well as the bright side of themselves. I would he horrified to meet a street full of orthodontically cheerful people. I would say 'Let me get a bus, quick. . . . ' I shared my early life with my brother but that too would end, as I wrote in my poem 'Brothers':

You were better at all these
practical tests
of strength
and judgment, too.
For me, the image of escape
distracted
from the tasks of place.
The books I loved
were instruments
for the breaking of the bars

and a run
towards the light
and a new life
back
in the city.

At times, on the bar of a bike,
I vowed
to bring you
where I presumed
you wished to go.
It was through pain
I realised
that our journeys
would be separate,
alone,
requiring different skills.

And I sought my brother
in a hundred others
for whom
my heart warmed
at shared
hopes
and fears.

Every embrace a compensation
for the lost moments
of feelings
buried beneath
the boulders
of other expectations
of duty
and respectability,
of fear
and dust
and sweat
and a life reduced
to rehearsal
for the decency in depth
that was the legacy
of our family.

Back from the tomb,
Christ saw brothers
everywhere.
The stone rolled back,
he never returned
home
but embraced every stranger,
brothers all
in the light
out of the dark.

from 'Brothers'

from My Education, edited by John Quinn (Townhouse, 1997)

EDUCATION FOR FREEDOM

THE DELIVERY

I have delivered my children
to school
in the half-grey light.
Always,
the half-grey light
reminds me
of anxious arrivals,
temporary releases.
Hurried half-kisses
furtively offered,
must be sufficient
for that time
of the offering up.

Leaving
I question my complicity.
No blind faith any longer
moves me.
I am the deliverer
of what were my children
to the Chapel of Fear
for sacrifice.
I weep full tears,
Alone.

There are few subjects as important as education. For some, it is the route to escape; for others, ascent along a meritocratic ladder; for others, a prerequisite for the acquisition of wealth; for so many, a bad memory; for those fortunate to have encountered inspired teachers, a warm memory.

Yet it is central not only to our existence and our ability to be human but to the development of that capacity for future generations. Put simply, the interaction between education, economy and society not only has an immediate importance but determines the reproduction and shapes the responses to change in society.

Yet on that interaction, there are so many questions that rarely get asked. When parents send their children to school any morning, how much are the parents allowed to know about that to which they send them? How democratic is their education? How possible is it for teachers as professionals to review and renew their capacity in their subjects? Can education be joyful? Is it democratic or republican to reject political and social literacy m the widest sense, to refuse to teach political and social studies in the curriculum, while piously looking for a committed citizenry? Above all, is education to be allowed to facilitate changes in the direction of that more human world we have scarcely dreamed of, or is education condemned merely to react to change, as interpreted by narrow vested interests? I have been asked all these questions in recent times. My response is: let us begin such a Great Debate in education as will engage these and other questions.

Recent decades have shown a great imprecision, and an even greater distrust, of language. I sense, regularly now, a feeling that all meaning is arbitrary, that concepts such as democracy, equality, freedom, justice and rights are as often employed as terms of abuse as they are as tools of understanding. Indeed, one could go further and say that understanding the world has declined as an intellectual project by comparison with controlling the world, or of imposing on the world a single, usually economic, version of itself.

Freedom has been defined and reduced to market freedom. Equality has been pilloried as the pursuit – and a jealous pursuit at that – of sameness. Justice has been sacrificed again and again as it is limited and equated with legal process. Individuals and families, indeed whole societies, have been destroyed in this distinction. Democracy itself has been limited to the few occasions when parliament is elected. It has been excluded almost, it seems at times, as a moral principle from the social and economic world. In foreign policy, theories based on democracy and right have been replaced by a theory of interest. Democracy has not been allowed to extend into, and permeate, our lives.

Yet in a time of broken words and uncertainty, the irrepressible search for authenticity – of self, of class, of nation, and of humanity – continues. Within that search, I believe that the role of education is crucial and must now be debated in a context that is sufficiently wide to question all those themes that have been evaded until now.

Indeed, it ill behoves a country such as Ireland – which now calls itself a

33

republic, and which was established through the courage of those who had so much less than most of us – to be content that the prevailing version of ourselves must constitute, in educational thinking, the borrowed, failed ideas of our former coloniser, founded on their concession and legacy, reformed on their failed initiatives. Why not make a start even now at something original and creative?

To begin with, some basic principles: I have learned with pain to recognise the difference between schooling and education. I have had to face the reality that, as a parent, I could not be clear as to whether I was delivering my children to a public school, a national school or a denominational school. I realised that, even in the systematic evasion of the question of control, a great rejection of democracy and republicanism was involved. I wrote the poem with which I opened in a black moment, when it struck me that, far from joy displacing dreariness, which so many recall, children in the future were to be made the pawns of a new version of education which denied creativity as strongly as it demanded from even the earlier levels of education the dehumanising values of Friedrich von Hayek, borrowed by Milton Friedman, and used as tools of oppression by the administrations of Margaret Thatcher and Ronald Reagan, and brought home to Ireland from the British jumble sale of ideas by the insecure followers of acquisitive greed.

No one could be as long as I am in politics without noting the unequal distribution of resources that has affected access to education. Let me emphasise one fundamental point until a movement commences aimed at enshrining education as a right: we will never redress the inbuilt inequalities of our system.

Beyond the issues of control and access, there have been even fewer opportunities to discuss the curriculum. It is in this latter neglect that perhaps most is revealed. Curriculum provokes such questions as: What is being taught? For what purpose? For whose benefit? It exposes the connections between society, economy and education. Even well-intentioned people have become so worn out in their efforts to extend the quantity of education that they never reach the issue of the quality or content of education.

Some writers recently have gone so far as to assert that education, because of the volume of spending involved, must justify itself in meeting the needs of the economy – and the domestic economy at that. The shabbiness of such arguments is exceeded only by the silence of those who are yet to speak. I do hope that the challenge and example of such educationalists as Dr Pádraig Hogan is emulated. His paper 'The Sovereignty of Learning, the

Fortunes of Schooling and the New Educational Virtuousness' is a seminal contribution. May it and the efforts of parents, teachers and administrators force the pace and give us the adequate education debate we need.

Such a debate will have to be inclusive rather than exclusive. There will have to be respect for the opinions of all on such questions as: What is democracy in education? What is authoritarianism in Irish education, and in education in general? How can democracy be made to prevail? There are some who are happy to have education run in an authoritarian way. Let's hear from them. Theirs is a most unusual view: to be content to have education function as an autocratic, undemocratic institutional structure within a formal democracy and a rhetorical republic.

Of course, it is never put like that. In educational matters, there is an official or formal transcript, but there is also a separate transcript of practice. Quiet capitulation and moral acquiescence prevails, but, I ask, where in the world have patriarchy or authoritarianism as personality traits disappeared by a quiet evolution, other than by being named, acknowledged and then, by democratic decision, abandoned? The silent who morally acquiesce are victims in charge of future victims, handing on from generation to generation their moral acquiescence as a substitute for participatory citizenship.

This silence must be broken. The challenge to those who have been silent up to now on the shape of education in the future is to confront those who see education in the future as enjoying a minor functional relationship with the prevailing economic prejudices of the day and, let's admit it, to economic ideas that have failed, and that have often been based on exploitation. In this usage, 'prevailing economic prejudices', I make the distinction between such and the theoretically grounded antecedents of such aberrations that exist in the history of what was once called political economy. This discipline was, in the classical period of economic thought, seen as an instrument of a moral purpose. a philosophical purpose.

I was asked to give this lecture not long after I had been assisted in the making of a documentary film on the UN Conference on Environment and Development in Rio de Janeiro. In preparing for that task, I had gone back to material from authors such as Gregory Bateson and Fritjof Capra. I recalled being struck by the starkness of the choice they provoked, when I wrote in 1972 of such writers. They quoted the assumptions of the Idea of Progress, based on such propositions as: 'It's us against nature.' The alternative assumption was: 'It's us in symmetry with and as part of nature.' The first assumption was enforced through colonialism and imperialism. In my own schooling, it was represented by the modernisation model: the ideological glasses placed on all of us scholars from the so-called developing world who studied in the US in the 1960s and which had the effect of blinding us to the reality of our own story when we returned home from the metropolitan centre of thought. The second assumption was, and is, a fundamental of the thinking of Eastern thought, influencing the rising ecological consciousness of the present. At Rio, even the most tough-minded followers of the old idea of 'progress' were forced to admit that development was not open-ended in an ecological sense. In the same period as the reassertion of ecological responsibility, the feminist movement has made even greater advances. In the south of the planet, where four-fifths of the planet's population are allowed less than one-fifth of the world's resources, aid, trade and debt are being explored by a new generation of economists, social scientists, political scientists and lawyers, who have been educated often in exile, and are tortured at home, but are close to the needs and democratic aspirations of their own people.

The formal rhetoric of the UNCED never engaged this new and creative thinking. This disjunction had less to do with the distinction between head and heart than with the difference between the 'public transcript of powerful nations and the public transcript of dependent nations', as the political scientist James C. Scott put it. The private transcripts were there too, with all their ringing challenge

Let me say a little about this concept of transcripts. Scott gives the story of Aggy as recounted in Albert J. Raboteau's *Slave Religion: The 'Invisible Institution' of the Antebellum South*. Aggy's daughter has been beaten for a crime of which she was innocent. Aggy is forced to look on, but, left alone in the slave living quarters, she is visited by the governess, Mary Livermore, and Aggy bursts out: 'Thar's a day a-comin'! Thar's a day a-comin'! . . . I hear the rumblin' ob de chariots! I see de flashin' ob de guns! White folks' blood is a runnin' on the ground like a ribber, an de dead's heaped up dat high!'

Those who dominate have a public transcript for public consumption and a private one for consumption in the security of their own company. George Orwell's dilemma, recounted in 'Shooting an Elephant', is used by Scott to illustrate this. The dominated too have a public transcript; it is one of deference. Scott quotes the old Ethiopian proverb: 'When the great lord passes, the wise peasant bows deeply and farts.' The dominated also have a private transcript, and they well up in themselves frustration, rage, a memory, and a legacy of wrong and exclusion. The dam breaks on all these emotions at the moment of liberation, or even of rumour of the possibility of liberation.

I wonder how many private transcripts there are buried beneath the formal public transcript: of deference that is demanded from institutionalised education and those who have been forced to exist within it? How many speeches have been rehearsed in silent rage and, to the untold damage of those who composed them, never been delivered? How valuable it would be if the Great Debate began with a great breaking of silence on all the issues, including the ones I have listed.

When, in *My Education*, I said, with enthusiasm, 'I feel that my education is only beginning', I seemed to strike a note of resonance with a very disparate but open-minded community of listeners. What I had in mind was that I was, in a curious, maybe even desperate, way attempting a kind of search for a fantasy home where true education was possible. Let me say immediately that I do not believe it is possible, sufficient, maybe even desirable, that I should know whether such a home in the sense of a settled place, or a defined period of time, ever existed – and, if it did, where it was located and how I might make my way there. My life has been enriched by uncertainty that, even if it has brought pain, has also brought openness, my battered philosophical suitcase.

What might be more appropriate, it seemed to me, was to attempt a journey along a curve – a heroic journey that, if completed, might bring one home even in dream, or an old psychic harmony, to a harmonious unity, where one could experience the shared breath of the planet. But then again, 'home' might turn out to be a formidable and challenging illusion.

When one is a young scholar, one is always made insecure – the peasant not ready for the parlour. When you are an older scholar, you are seduced towards becoming secure: an institutionalised piece of furniture in the parlour – cynical, but, in my own case, also desperately anxious to begin again and again and again, radically rooted in the experience and history of one's human companions and their concerns. The quest for authenticity in life and language is sure to bring pain, and can make no certain guarantees, only a possibility, of a moment of joy, of celebration of the divinity of total, undivided humanity. Yet this is the fundamental quest.

On my journey along the curve of old questions and books revisited, authors that I would like to call, with respect to G. I. Gurdjieff, meetings with remarkable ghosts, came forward. Among the most important was Hannah Arendt. I encountered her through Melvyn A. Hill's *Hannah Arendt: The*

Recovery of the Public World. In that volume, I was intrigued by both the cover photograph of Hannah Arendt with a cigarette perilously close to the hair above her left ear: a gesture of addiction, anxiety and vulnerability – or was it employed as an aid to concentration? And Glenn Gray's chapter 'The Abyss of Freedom and Hannah Arendt' also made a great impression on me.

The photograph revealed in Arendt's face the terrible problem of choice and individuation. The phrase 'the abyss of freedom' encapsulated for me the central moral issue of the twentieth century. In her uncompleted final work, Arendt drew a distinction between thinking, willing and judging. The set of lectures on the first was completed. Preparation of the second set of lectures caused her great problems, and she died before the lectures for the third topic were completed. For her, freedom was exercised through thinking. But that was not enough.

For educational theory, the lesson is that we have to educate for both the integral personality and the social self. Arendt asserted that, if we were to avoid the impasse, the moral loneliness and angst, of the isolated ego, we must be 'able to do what we ought to will'. In this is a powerful agenda for education. We are called to act as well as to will. Our action, as Arendt develops it further, is also social or communal, not isolated.

Between the photo and the article too, I felt a sense of pain, a pain I have come to know of the private person impelled across this bridge of consciousness to the realm of the public. Arendt wrote in *The Recovery of the Public World*: 'Even those among us who, by speaking and writing, have ventured into public life have not done so out of any original pressure in the public scene and have hardly expected, or aspired, to receive the stamp of public approval . . . these efforts were, rather, guided by their hope of preserving some minimum of humanity in a world grown inhuman while, at the same time, as far as possible, resisting the weird unreality of this worldlessness – each after his own fashion and some few by seeking to the limits of their ability to understand even inhumanity and the intellectual and political monstrosities of a time out of joint.' What a contemporary challenge that is to all those in education.

I feel here that what is at stake is, maybe, more than the solipsistic agony of a self alone, fashioned out of will. There is the as-yet-unchallenged burden of knowing, a stage beyond thought, will and judgement, a stage where instinct and the heart force on the rational an impulse to action that makes it not only uncomfortable, but impossible, for thought to be a mere spectator in the game of life.

G. Glenn Gray acknowledges, too, Arendt's category of contingency. He gives as example the experience of the artist who succeeds by willing success, often against failure. She or he has seen success in achieving the finished symbolic object in their mind's eye.

How long, I ask, can we live in a political system where the institution of education is precluded from taking responsibility for political and philosophical, critical thought, and yet at the same time another more generally consumed institution, the media, frequently equates public life with venality, corruption and self-seeking? Why not make it possible for millions to be educated in ethical, political, philosophical choices and let them all sweep into debate, to participate, to initiate and to create change?

Is it not the protection of unquestionable certainties that lies at the root of this cancer of exclusion and alienation? Have we seen what a democratic education would be, even in our mind's eye? We will always be strung out on the challenge of a world in which, by one excess, we could be consumed by a reality, never known, or on the other, we could perish by our being repelled from the world. As I was preparing this lecture, I saw a documentary on Thomas Merton. How well Merton understood the poles of the dilemma and, more importantly, the need to recognise the challenge they pose by their existence.

Education is inescapably located in a context of continually challenging forms of life and unresolved philosophical challenges. It is *not* some form of commodity or utility which we can measure in terms only of quantity or setting, although any government that condemns pupils to lesser involvement, and teachers and pupils to insanitary and drab buildings, is disqualifying itself from being described as a democratic administration.

Back from Rio, I could find not one significant theme from ecology, feminism, egalitarianism, cultural pluralism in the framework for the Great Debate in Education. Yet the values of anti-social, aggressive, individualistic, greed-based values of Thatcher–Reaganism were there beneath a thin veneer of 'corporate speak'.

Rejected entirely was any debate, so central to educational theory, on the nature of creativity. It is crucial if we accept creativity as a social, rather than inherently a private, attribute, that we make it a central informing principle of the curriculum. Otherwise, we are left with privately purchased units of child improvement, imposed on children outside the school day. How well I remember it! 'The piano will stand to her', and the role of parents sending, delivering, collecting and, of course, paying. Worst of all, children whose parents cannot afford it are excluded from all the developmental potential of the arts.

In a world where the impact of science and technology in the interests of an economics of acquisitive greed has done so much ecological damage, where consciousness itself is inadequate, and language being emptied of meaning, must we not demand that our children's creativity and humanness be allowed to flower, so that, in the next century, our planet will be peopled by those who think holistically and have been allowed to develop the 'mind of peace' informed by hearts where love, and the will to take on the responsibility of interdependency, can reside? Any education towards freedom requires that future children, and ourselves – returning, continuing, retired students – have the freedom to go on past the rut of our existence and the thought imposed on us, or deprived from us, or not dreamed of yet.

I want now to list some personal themes about which I would love to hear during the Great Educational Debate. What is the difference, I ask myself, between a pedagogy of fear and a pedagogy of love? The son of a peasant, I have often felt like a migrant in the metropolis as I made my way past the excluding and often intimidating signposts of postgraduate seminars – in three university systems. What little excitement there was in the sharing of knowledge, or even the commitment to such a project, what minimal patience, what absence of generosity. In another culture – that of post-dictatorship Nicaragua – I saw and tried to learn that powerful generosity of defining education as the sharing of stories and dreams, of respecting energetic curiosity, and above all of education for true participation and effective citizenship, from such people as the brothers Ernesto and Fernando Cardenal. And I have wept for all the children who have been humiliated, mocked and, in the past, beaten and made insecure by such systems as have substituted the agenda of order for the aims of leading out the inner light of each person. This, for me, is neither idealistic nor sentimental. It is an issue of rights, rather like the abolition of slavery. It is an insult to the intelligence to suggest that an authoritarian regime is a necessary condition for effective administration in education.

A pedagogy of love would eschew fear as a principle of education. We are far from a general beginning, not to speak of the completion, of such a project. To be accurate, it has been begun in brave and isolated places, and has been sustained unevenly, and against the odds.

What are the prospects then of education for peace? Of educating for participation? Of educating for creative co-operation? What is the likelihood of our becoming critical participants in the debate on the connection between science, technology and society? What will be our opportunities for constructing a curriculum where there could be respect for the right of all peoples to tell their story and have their dreams regarded with respect?

In Ireland, formal, if not intellectual, independence, having been gained, has not been allowed to surface. It has been buried or evaded by lesser people – people who are terrified and timid, threatened by clerical displeasure or seduced by meritocratic individualism. They drifted on with educational directives – illegally, some would say – in the twentieth century, happy with the colonisers' nineteenth-century sop, and later with their outmoded, outdated version of education. That they sacrificed democratic education, or education for democracy, did not – and, some would say, does not – bother them.

Now, their heirs ask us to forget the world and settle for the real but limited project of being citizens of a European Union based on economic requirements, rather than the great transcendental challenge of being human in the most international and interdependent sense of that term. They ask us to be useful to a dying economic system, rather than inviting us to be allies in building a new, just, peaceful, interdependent, international economic and social order. We must surrender our lives and our children's lives to dying and dead ideas. We must surrender our capacity to produce ideas and will new, creative versions of society.

Most recently, education has been constituted as a commodity. A teacher is to become an executive. A university president is to envisage himself or herself as 'the chief executive of a multi-million-pound company', I read recently in a Dáil speech.

If neo-utilitarianism gives content to the public transcript of education, and if the alternative (private, up to now) transcripts do not move quickly to confrontation, there will be a terrible harvest to reap – and it will not be within the same terms of discourse, perhaps thinly veiled, that are available now.

I have consistently supported the late social historian and socialist Raymond Williams's proposals for curriculum reform in his day. For English conditions, he suggested, for example, a curriculum would include:

1   Extensive practice in the fundamental languages of English and maths.

2   General knowledge of ourselves and our environment.

3   History and criticism of literature, the visual arts, music, dramatic performance, landscape and architecture.

4   Extensive practice in democratic procedures and practice in the use of libraries, newspapers and magazines, radio and TV programmes and other sources of information, opinion and influence.

5   Introduction to at least one other culture, including its language, history, geography, institutions and arts, to be given in part by visiting and exchange.

I recall the even more ambitious aims of the renowned philosopher of education Quentin Hoare, who felt that Williams's reforms required a socialist transformation of teachers and society that Williams, he felt, neglected. Hoare gave four distinguishing marks for a socialist approach to education:

1   Critical, as opposed to conservative, tradition; it would stress education as the development of critical reason in the child, questioning alternatives to all existing reality.

2   As opposed to the Romantic School, it would embody a full acceptance of the social character of humanity, rejecting forever the notion of a pre-social dimension of human existence.

3   As opposed to rationalisation, it would insist on the active nature of children's participation in the learning process and contest the mechanist concept of education as the transmission of fixed skills.

4   As opposed to democratic tradition, it would be dialectical, treating all human reality as radically historical, refusing to consider programmes outside man's capacity to execute, emasculate or refute them.

That was all so long ago. It may surprise some of you to hear that I would protect education's freedom never to be forced to serve any particular ideology. Rather, I would want it to be free to develop critical thought in the best sense of that term. I would be with Raymond Williams rather than Quentin Hoare.

Since that time, other themes have arrived, including the ecological challenge and the threatened loss of the human population of whole continents such as Africa, their position, exacerbated by the AIDS crisis, made fragile by the $55 billion transferred each year from South to North. We are now facing the choice of a new relationship to the planet and each other. We can educate for a regression to brutal self-interest or we can educate for peace and true security, for openness. What is required now is a critical capacity developed within an educational system where creativity is made central.

We should not despair. We should remember Bertrand Russell:

Meantime, the world in which we exist has other aims. But it will pass away, burned up in the fire of its own hot passions; and from its ashes

42

will spring a new and younger world, full of fresh hope, with the light of morning in its eyes.

If we engage the connections between science, technology and society, it is possible for us, even yet, to become a symbolising rather than a symbol-abusing species, and to experience the joy of our humanness, made immanent. Let us choose the pedagogy of love and allow the pedagogy of fear to fall away from our institutions, our practice and our personalities.

Let us make education a right, accessible through one's entire life. Let us have real democracy, elective and accountable, not only in a geographical sense, but in a community sense. Let us elect our representatives for educational accountability from within the sectors involved and from outside. Why should we settle for less, unless we are conceding democracy itself?

The new dawn of which Russell wrote will only be possible if we refuse to surrender education to the passing fad of neo-utilitarianism. In this new century, we will be asked to be many things but, above all, we will be most useful to the human family and ourselves if we are holistic.

I am mindful of the issue of resources for education. I have supported and will support the political fight for adequate resources and their direction, in particular, to areas of disadvantage. But we do not have to choose between activity on that issue and related issues, such as in-service training and renewal, and we can no longer neglect the debate about the very nature of education itself.

In conclusion, may I say that there is too much that is covert in Irish education. There is far too much piecemeal decision-making. The antipathy to intellectual ideas, to philosophy and theory in education, and in the social sciences in general, must be ended. For example, so many within teaching, and so many parents, would welcome the control functions of education and their responsibilities for enhancing and releasing creativity being set in tension, and such tension being critically examined.

It is a time for courage, a time to demand and to ensure that, in our country, education will never again be allowed to destroy the wonderment of a child; rather that, heroically, we will begin to make our way back to that wonderment and live in peace with each other and our planet.

If educating towards freedom means discomfort, let's choose it, consciously, as an alternative to giving away the control and content of education. We are not asked to pay the price of Aggy the Slave. We can and should exercise our democracy and, by making education genuinely democratic, at last set out on one of the obvious heroic journeys of an authentic republic.

Within that great national journey, we can all make personal journeys to wholeness, people in solidarity within a great movement of planetary and social healing.

Let me end as I began, with a poem written from the broken pieces of my own life, a poem for my youngest son. I dedicate it to parents, teachers and satchel-kickers everywhere.

THE COLLECTING

As my eyes peel the playground,
I am distracted by sounds that are chaotic
celebrations of release.
The harness of satchels
is being tossed
with a disrespect
hard-earned.

The bag, discarded,
is placed in perspective
by an involuntary kick
from a stranger
who had not invested it
with the intimacies
of welts and warm shoulders.
It is the peopled yard
that attracts
the backward glance.

The classrooms, abandoned,
linger in empty silence
until morning
when the breath of authority
will, again, define
their arbitrary purpose.

Their long shadow
captures the first words,
'I've a pile of homework.'
We drive on homewards
with the wedge of school between us.

One day children will come to school and the day will begin with music and they will learn in relaxation. Fear abandoned, love will define the pedagogic process. We must make that day.

The Open Word Guest Lecture 1992, broadcast by RTÉ

Education and Democracy

The issue of the connection between democracy and education is as old as philosophy itself. It is of such basic importance in revealing the nature and assumptions of society that it is very often hidden. To mask the issue is a profoundly ideological stance and is one of the hallmarks of conservatism populism or totalitarianism.

In the Irish Republic, the very name given to the state raises a further dimension. Does the use of the term 'Republic' imply a commitment to democracy in a processual sense, i.e. as requiring continual definition and assertion, above all extension into the institutions and day-to-day behaviour of society? Or is the allusion to democracy in our constitution qualified, conditional, even perhaps rhetorical? The answers to such questions are not merely academic: they tell whether we live in what at best might be called 'bad faith' or, perhaps more accurately, with an illusory notion that rhetoric is reality.

As a political spokesperson for some years in the field of education, among others, I have often been astounded at not only the unwillingness but the downright hostility shown by various ministers for education, urged on by conservative officials, open and closet, modulated and extreme, to facilitate a debate on the purposes and functions of education.

'As always, very interesting' is the recorded remark of the present incumbent to my last efforts to force such a debate. It reveals the suave dismissive attitude, the anti-intellectualism that pervades Irish politics. Indeed, the estimates speech of July 1989 singled out demographic change as the dominant, if not single, indicator upon which educational provision will be based.

This emphasis on the quantity of education and its cost, as opposed to a consideration that might also include the purposes of education in conditions of change, or the content of education and its implications, is one that is not solely a ministerial or departmental one. I have observed it in those forced by circumstance to deal with both ministers and the Department of Education. The teaching trade unions, parents' organisations, even reformers, are forced into a discussion, the terms of which are the quantity of education rather than its quality and content.

The Irish educational system is not democratic in terms of access, control, curriculum, social impact or organisational structure. Just a few words

46

about each of these. The work of Patrick Clancy, Damian Hannan and others has penetrated even Leinster House. Yet their conclusions that not only is third-level entry selective by income group but that the basis of class selectivity is laid at second level has produced nothing by way of a policy initiative to level opportunities.

In what is to me one of the most valuable pieces published in recent decades on the subject of educational policy, Kathleen Lynch in 'Dominant Ideologies in Irish Educational Thought: Consensualism, Essentialism and Meritocratic Individualism' (*Economic and Social Review*, Vol. 18, No. 2, January 1987) clearly showed that egalitarianism was never an option favoured by the Department of Education in Ireland.

In fact, in terms of control, education in the Irish Republic is often the very antithesis of democratic accountability. Those who pay for it are excluded from policy and administration to a large degree. Those who wish to use it for purposes of mental domestication, of inculcating docility, hold an unaccountable power. Is it democratic to claim a transcendentally based authority in education? Obviously not. It is also, I believe, an abuse of the human right of the child, as Dr Desmond Clarke has convincingly suggested in his book *Church and State*. Indeed, different ministers of education have been careful to give guarantees that Irish education will never be publicly controlled, beginning with Eoin McNeill and going right down through John Marcus O'Sullivan to the modern period. The social impact of Irish schooling has been to rationalise privilege, most notably by bogus tests of ability. Such tests are class-biased in content and therefore present various challenges.

A tension sometimes emerges between those who believe in meritocratic individualism and those who believe in what I have come to call amoral familism. An example might illustrate what I mean. Having come through the not necessarily educative experience of securing points and an adequate examination performance may not guarantee in itself entry to that wing of the Irish legal profession controlled by the Incorporated Law Society, which allowed itself the luxury of debating at Council level the pros and cons of reserving places for sons and daughters of the legal profession.

I recall equally hearing details of a university medical school's discussion of reserving places for the offspring of the medical profession. Did Irish republicans die for such things?

But my primary purpose here is to address the neglected issue of the content and purpose of Irish education. In November 1983, Una Desmond of the ASTI asked me to speak on a related topic. Nothing has changed. In fact, in many respects matters have got worse.

But to revisit my reflections of some years ago. I had been invited to concentrate on 'The Role of Policymakers in Education' as part of a general consideration of curriculum development and reform. My first reaction was to consider the content of the debate on education in Ireland at policy level as it has been represented in statements by policy-makers at public and Oireachtas level.

It is impossible not to be struck by the emphasis on the requirements of schooling, as opposed to the content of education, that such statements reveal. Although Raymond Williams suggested that it should be the purpose of policy to keep the learning process going for as long as possible in every life, such a suggestion, and its implications, has taken second place in what I have read about the provision of buildings, enrolment figures, management structures and discipline. Indeed, the question must be asked, even of those who correctly challenge the limited access to education, have they sufficiently considered the content and purpose of that to which they suggest more people and children should have access? My final preliminary observation is that questions about schooling that are as yet unresolved or that serve as the basis for present conflict are often invoked as an absolution from taking the general question of the nature of education seriously.

Traditional sociology texts have usually included a chapter on 'the functions of education'. The language itself gives the game away. The conservative emphasis of such texts took the existing social structures and arrangements for granted and saw no problem in defining the overall purpose of education as the reproduction of the existing society. Thus the 'socialisation' aspect of education was emphasised. Following socialisation, which was perceived as basic training in the 'rules' of society, acculturation into the ideas and symbols of the existing order, it was assumed, followed easily. Intellectuals were seen as being formed in the schools, and culture was defined within such confines. With rapid social change providing what was perceived to be a new, troublesome context, the traditionalists have been forced, with obvious distaste, to respond to a new utilitarianism. Having been absorbed themselves into a society that they accepted as 'natural', having left it unanalysed, and having failed to make it the subject of critique, they brace themselves to become more modern. They capitulate to the demands for more narrow skills, and allow their classrooms and lecture halls to be the cost-free training and recruiting halls of a capricious and haphazard world of work.

I define such a set of responses as constituting the under-labourer model of the role of education. The needs of the society in general and the economy in particular are regarded as a given and left unquestioned. Education is perceived as being determined by these needs. The consequences for uncritically placing education at the behest of the given economic structures and social forms are only too obvious. The worse features of the society are fed into the educational experience as 'natural'. Sexism, authoritarianism, ridicule, fear, repression, aggression, selfishness, distrust of others, hero-worship, the apeing of the privileged are all, at times, part of the formal curriculum, and are nearly always presented as – and excused as – a cultural inheritance. The authority figures from outside flit like demons through the corridors of the education system. This model of the connection between economy, society and education is a subtle form of imprisonment, an imprisonment that will erode the mental and spiritual depth of the person more perversely than any incarceration.

In recent years, professionals have, it seems, succeeded in developing an alternative idea that education can, by structuring its demands from the needs of the classroom, and what are perceived as the requirements of personality development, carve out a neutral model of the connections between society, economy and education. The activity of education, it is suggested, has generated a specific process, an identifiable set of experiences and rules. The proponents of such a model, however, have not had the motivation, or perhaps the capacity, to develop a critique of the economy or of the society in which they 'function', to use their own narrow term.

Then, too, there is a view that education, far from being predetermined, is itself a determining process. From the political right, and a section of the left, has come the suggestion that change in society can principally be brought about through education. There is no doubt that conservative and authoritarian interests have held obstinately to their opportunities to capture hearts and minds, and have brought forth the response that they must be dislodged and replaced by their opponents. I reject this deterministic model in its simpler versions and favour a fourth way – a critical model of the connection between education, the economy and society. The proposals of Quintin Hoare in his article 'Education: Programmes and People' (in Martin Hoyles's *The Politics of Literacy*, 1977) seem to me to provide an exciting and open alternative. The following summary quotations give the spirit of his approach:

As opposed to the conservative traditions, it would stress education as the development of critical reason (in Marcuses's sense of the word) in the child – a questioning attitude towards all existing reality.

As opposed to the romantic school, it would embody a full acceptance of the social character of humanity, reflecting for ever the notion of a pre-social dimension of human existence.

As opposed to rationalizers, it would insist on the active nature of the child's participation in the learning process and contest the mechanical concept of education as the transmission of mixed skills.

. . . it would be dialectical, treating all human reality as radically histori-cal, refusing to consider programmes outside of men to executive, emas-culate or refuse them.

Perhaps I should briefly, and perhaps crudely, summarise the positions Hoare rejects in favour of a critical perspective. The conservative emphasis on 'high culture' has had attached to it sets of values which were not con-fined in their influence to the private schools in which the most archaic and anti-human practices could flourish. These schools pioneered the distinction between 'intellect' and 'ability', and their poorer relations aped them and accepted their lesser designations. The romantic movement, with its focus on individual self-realisation, was a most exciting development but, unfortunate-ly, accepted a definition of the experience of education and life as a private rather than a social activity.

The democratic position has concentrated on equality of opportunity defined in a particular way. Everybody must have an equal opportunity, get-ting on the bottom step of the merit-determined escalator. The escalator, its origins, destination, defects and merits, are accepted without question. For me, the critical model offers the best achievements of these views, and much more. This model opens up prospects for education as an exciting experience for life and fulfilment. Of course, to begin to consider a broader view, one must get beyond questions of cost and value. Educational expenditure can-not be quantified like other social expenditure, such as road sanitation and housing. Education's content is its most important aspect but has been neg-lected for decades.

That neglect is all the more dangerous at a time when changes in the definition of work are urgently needed. No longer will there be a sufficient number of status slots to which the merit escalator can deliver its human packages. The social world of the future will be structured along the dimension of access to information. The learning world has already moved back into the home to a large degree, through the use of computers and computer games.

The question of access to education has, of course, drawn forth significant work from Irish scholars such as Damian Hannan, David Rottman, Patrick Clancy and others. Our exclusion of citizens from education is scandalous. Unfortunately, the public is now being fed questionable academic rationalisations of limited access. The recent publication of studies stressing ability gives urgency to the need for a public debate. Unless you make allowance for the factors that exclude access, that cause drop-out, that infringe on the learning situation – such as bad housing and unemployment – ability studies are partial and distorting. My general conclusion from the earlier access studies is that we are reproducing the current system of privileges and exclusions.

The early discussion on models of the connection between society, the economy and education impinges on the social order of the school. Briefly, if the educational model is an under-labourer one, the social order of the school will be attuned to keeping order, to competition, to the transmission of information and culture in the most bearable conditions to the greatest number. It will be hierarchical, authoritarian and competitive, and will foster individualism. If a critical model prevails, it will be democratic and participatory, encouraging the experience of democracy in the institution and in the learning experience. The ambivence of the former concentrates on unquestioned answers, the latter on spontaneous questions.

I want to repeat my suggestion for inclusion of political and social studies at second level as a full examination subject. The case for it is so obvious that it should hardly need to be stated. We would all be appalled if a young person did not have an elementary mental map of where she lived. We allow no opportunity for young people to acquire a map of their society, their state. Such a subject should offer an introduction to forms of society, forms of state, different philosophies, ideologies, the role of women, development studies and war and peace. I could not stress sufficiently the contribution this subject would make to the elimination of alienation among the young. I see political and social studies as replacing civics but I do not see it as a challenge to home economics, as there is a valuable body of sociological themes that can be strengthened and expanded in that discipline.

It would be very remiss of me if I did not refer to the manner in which badly devised university requirements dominate the second-level curriculum. This colonisation should end. How can it be defensible to visit on those you exclude from third level the requirements of that from which you exclude them? I see an urgent need for the integration of the arts into the curriculum, not to enable isolated recreation later but to build the experience of the arts into the normal formation of young people.

These changes have yet to be campaigned for at the political level. There are powerful interests who will oppose any such change. Politicians to date have not considered the curriculum argument sufficiently seriously – although in 2007 Citizenship will become part of Social and Political Studies for the Leaving Certificate for the first time.

In the end, what is at stake is freedom and joy. We are not condemned to lose this battle. We can lose it only by inaction through fear, ignorance or lack of conviction. To paraphrase Brecht: 'To never say never makes the impossible tomorrow morning's task.'

Patrick McGill Summer School, entitled 'Education, For What and For Whom?',
Glenties, County Donegal, 15 August 1989

CITIZENSHIP

THE SPACE OF POLITICS RECOVERED

Recent calls for a national conversation on citizenship are to be welcomed –
but will amount to nothing if the discussion does not fundamentally challenge how Ireland is evolving as a society. It is not enough to call for an
increase in voluntarism as the gap between rich and poor widens across the
country. The policies of the current government, embedded in inequality,
tend towards making genuine inclusive citizenship impossible.

One of the most discernible and alarming trends in contemporary society is the acceptance of politics, society and the economy as separate spheres.
Increasingly, economic discourse is perceived as having nothing to do with
social critique or a discourse of ethics, but as being governed by a mechanis-
tic pseudo-rationality. Neither is the phrase 'political economy' used commonly in policy debates. The economy is generally free from political direction and left to find its own level, driven by a free market, which is assumed
to be beneficial. Poverty is thus seen as an aspect of social policy unhinged
from economic policy. This is despite the obtrusive presence of monopolis-
tic tendencies and the unrestrained concentration of ownership, which in fact
delivers economic exploitation.

The demand to remove decision-making over the economy from the
political sphere is reflected in efforts to keep matters such as public expenditure, pay for the lower-paid, borrowing, and so on, outside public scrutiny.
This is the new 'unaccountable' economics: an economics that regards the
public as a mere component of a self-regulating economic system.

The individualism of the marketplace now extends its tentacles into the
political sphere, creating a privatisation of political experience. If, in the past,
citizens agitated in the public space for the right to participate in the state,
society and economy, today it is as consumers, in the isolated cocoon of the
private sphere, that they calculate their market value. Their demands surface
not through the exercise of citizen power but though the interface of consumers with the market. At the same time, politics itself is reduced to a contest of competing populisms: it becomes mired in diminished public trust
and viewed as corrupt and disengaged.

From such a broken linkage between economy and politics emerges a society that is characterised by fragmentation, alienation and disillusion. I believe, in fact, that we are drifting to a final rupture between the economy, politics and society. If this happens, the ensuing conflict will not be mediated through trade unions, political parties or social movements. With the wealthy getting wealthier and the poor getting poorer, this rupture will be a naked confrontation between the excluded and the powerful, between the technologically sophisticated and the technologically manipulated, and between consumers and the consumed.

There are likely to be few shared norms of citizenship experience which will serve to mediate this conflict. Today, the norms of a shared life have little opportunity to be articulated and debated. Public participation is falling in every institution of civil society. Society is often pathologised and feared as endemically crime-ridden and threatened by 'the other'. Even technology, abandoned to the marketplace, is adding to the schism, creating new classes of information-rich and information-poor, of literate and illiterate, of participating and excluded.

A case must be urgently made therefore for a new and vibrant citizenship that can vindicate such values as solidarity, community, democracy, justice, freedom and equality, and give them practical expression. At the heart of this conception is respect for the life of the person as having a shared public value beyond the narrow consumer power of the individual. Such an approach to citizenship stands for the right of every citizen to participate in society and to have the opportunity to develop their personal and social selves in conditions of freedom and communal solidarity.

We should see ourselves as sharing and using the economy and technology to achieve our values. We should see ourselves as the makers of history, not its pawns or passive victims. We should see ourselves and those who are yet to be born as constant and potential creators of advancing forms of human society – forms that are more ethical, more just, and more communal than has been either experienced or envisaged to date.

This is the greatest and most exciting challenge at the beginning of a new century: building a democratic citizenship in a just economy and with an ethical politics and an actively participative civil society. The practical achievement of such a society must be a central goal of government. A vision of ethical citizenship can infuse every area of policy prescription. For example:

§   Basic needs in income, health, housing, social welfare, education and culture are provided as a matter of right, the minimum to ensure participation, inclusion, freedom, personal development and celebration.

§ Education is accessible and democratic in structure: the citizen is not simply a consumer seeking to purchase a private commodity.

§ Workers have rights to organise and participate in the economy and society in ways that go beyond the personal assertion of economic and social rights.

§ The information society and technology serve citizens, enabling them to communicate and participate as never before.

§ In urban planning, citizens' use of the safe public space is assured over minimal concessions from a speculative market.

§ In the field of security and justice, an active theory of citizenship builds bonds of security that stand in stark contrast to today's peddling of purchased safety. It works to develop an understanding of deviance, a critique of law and a spectrum of care and social control, taking into account not just the rights and duties of citizenship but the need to belong.

In every area, therefore, it is possible to promote a policy response which is different from other managerial models, traced from a theory and process of citizenship rights.

As the economy grows, such a citizenship requires that all be enabled to participate in that growth. More importantly, it stresses that the purpose of growth is improvement in the welfare of the citizenry. It will be necessary, too, to end the myth that redistributive measures are inimical to economic growth. There is real evidence that the opposite can be the case.

The choice is clear: a citizenship rooted in a democratic agenda, socially inclusive and politically accountable, with an economy viewed as instrumental, or a citizenship founded upon a populist consumerism, where rights are defined by purchasing power, society is modelled as a conflict zone, and the political system is construed as a place of corruption. The alternative is a recipe for violence that will inevitably accompany the collapse of political discourse, the rejection of ethics and politics as sources of guiding principles in life, and the succumbing of society itself to an unaccountable market.

Address delivered to Trinity College Politics Society, 3 November 1988

The Challenge of Building the Mind of Peace

Asserting the Humanistic Vision

I am very conscious of the honour of receiving a prize established in honour of the work for international peace and justice of the president of the International Peace Bureau from 1974 to 1985 – Seán MacBride, former Irish minister for external affairs, Nobel Peace prize–winner, joint founder of Amnesty International and initiator of the World Court Project to declare weapons of mass destruction illegal.

When I was introduced, reference was made to the different zones of conflict which I visited and of which I have written. It encouraged me to think again of what it has meant to me to come so close to so much death, suffering and anguish too, of those who were forced to look on at the death, mutilation, malnutrition, the disappearance or incarceration of a loved one.

I am, however, also conscious of Hans Magnus Enzensberger's essay 'Tourists of the Revolution' in his book *Raids and Reconstructions*. In the essay, he quotes the poem of Herberto Padilla, entitled 'The Travellers'. Let me quote but a single stanza which I have always considered to be a terrible warning:

> They come in the clothes of the affluent society,
> a thorn in whose side they are, whose 'unreliable'
> elements they constitute,
> fitted out with academic titles,
> writing books for the Department of Sociology
> of the best Universities
> (which underwrite the cost).
> They get their visas in a jiffy,
> are informed about anti-war campaigns,
> about protests against the Vietnam War, in short;
> they are treading the righteous path of history.
> While they lounge in the shiny seats
> of the international airports,
> each flight they take, an illegal act,
> they feel pleasantly subversive,
> their conscience is clean.
> They are the comfortable travellers of the wave of the future,

with Rolliflex cameras, perfectly suited
for the tropical light,
for underdevelopment;
with information charts for objective interviews,
if however (of course) something less than impartial,
for they love the struggle,
the guerrillas,
the *zafras*,
the hardships of life,
the vulgar Spanish of the natives.

Enzensberger's use of the poem was, in part, to draw our attention to the mistrust that is encountered by those who have moved between two social systems. I always wished to think that Padilla's poem was both too general and too harsh. In that wish, I was expressing a fear that moving into and out of zones of conflict carried with it a responsibility that could never be fully discharged.

Fikri Sonmez, the tailor of Fatsa, whose trial, with six hundred others, in Amassya I covered in Turkey, died in prison. Marianella Garcia, human-rights lawyer, whom I met on my first visit to El Salvador, is dead after being tortured. The Jesuits who briefed me in San Salvador have been murdered and mutilated. I do not know how many of those who crossed the Sahara to the Wall with me are alive. Above all, I remember the children: the little boy who cleaned shoes in a society without social security in militarised Turkey, the children of Francisco in Managua who, he writes me, are hungry because he has been unemployed since Doña Violetta Barros de Chamorra abolished his job . . .

To look at bodies abandoned on a rubbish tip, to write the details of torture, are experiences that cannot ever again be obliterated. To risk a gaze at such wounds of humanity is to choose to be changed forever.

The conservative can exist in comfort only by averting his gaze. To choose to know is to risk being presented with a dilemma. That dilemma, put simply, is that, once one knows, you can, from that moment, live only in the bad faith of guilty silence or act.

Many choose not to know. Such a position constitutes an ideology. It also creates a vacuum into which can be placed prejudices, rationalisations of racial domination, exploitation, sexism, homophobia, status and privilege. Others have knowledge kept from them. The majority in the self-styled Developed World have knowledge mediated, made conditionally and partially available to them.

57

When Noam Chomsky gave the Bertrand Russell Memorial Lectures at Cambridge University in 1971, he entitled them 'On Interpreting the World' and 'On Changing the World'. The only adequate relationship to zones of conflict, visits to refugee camps, the sharing of the experience of those who struggle, must include an act of interpretation and an agenda for change, however inadequate these may be. To opt for a merely personal reflection, to recoil – understandable as this might be – may be profoundly reactionary.

I have, in recent times, been struck, too, by the related challenge to peace movements. It is no longer sufficient to make the ethical case for peace, to assert the moral superiority of such a position. It is necessary to interpret the conditions that have made possible the acquiesence of so many, in so many different cultures, at so many different times, in constitutional arrangements that have sustained and reproduced a systematic, pervasive and corrosive violence.

As we end the twentieth century, can we conclude that those who have been given the intellectual opportunies have exercised them in such a way as to create a moral temper that would make war, torture, exploitation and cultural manipulation objectionable, if not impossible? The peace movements must develop even more their critique of how fear is embedded in what has been called the 'socialising institutions' of family, education, workplace, state and, even, community.

The peace movement will, in the twenty-first century, be a focal point for those who not only will commit themselves to a reflexivity that is unbounded but who will also be demanding the new forms of participation that such a radical critique will demand.

There are now more and more intellectual workers willing to engage in the wider agenda of building the economic, social, cultural and political infrastructures of peace. They are, however, in a minority. Most certainly, they do not hold power in the mind-moulding institutions. Yet, by constructing new networks, by utilising the new technology, they can create patterns of influence, magnets for those whose humanistic impulses cannot be quenched. If I was somewhat intimidated by Enzensberger's use of Padilla's poem, I was shaken by Chomsky's quotation in his second lecture, 'Changing the World', of Jan Myrdal's powerful passage in *Confessions of a Disloyal European*:

> The unconscious one does not betray. He walks secure through life. But we who are a part of the tradition – the Europeans – and who carry on the tradition – we have betrayed – with awareness, insight and consciousness. We have carefully analysed all the wars before they were

declared but we did not stop them. (And many amongst us became the propagandists of the wars as soon as they were declared.) We describe how the poor are plundered by the rich. We live among the rich, live on the plunder and pander to the ideas of the rich. We have described the torture and we have put our names under appeals against torture but did not stop it.

The quotation ended with the unforgettable indictment of moral cowardice:

> Now we, once more, can analyse the world situation and describe the wars and explain why the many are poor and hungry but we do no more. We are not the bearers of consciousness. We are the whores of reason.

The peace movements have expanded consciousness. The future now requires getting beyond that achievement to a wider agenda of action.

Let me stay for a moment with the personal impact of a statement, admittedly too general, such as that of Myrdal. The distrust that a peasant in the South might bear today is mirrored in the distrust that the unemployed and the poor within the North might feel towards those who express solidarity abroad but cannot see the case for it at home.

It is so obvious that a holistic approach is now essential. It is also clear that it will be necessary to demystify social behaviour and institutions and to do so in new conditions of image and symbol manipulation. Isn't it strange that today few would risk a direct justification of war for naked economic reasons? It would be presented as unavoidable for a greater and common good. However, there is scarcely any objection when market economics are stated to be an essential prerequisite for democracy.

There is no great intellectual repudiation of the obviously anti-human suggestion that children should die for the purity of market economics rather than economics serving the welfare of children as a tool of public policy. Where, now, are those who rushed to correctly condemn statism and distorted Marxism for the fallacy and related oppression of reification? Imagine our ending the twentieth century without the intellectual courage or capacity to question a de-peopled economics. Imagine a public morality that places the economy as a transcendent entity above the human inhabitants of nations and the international community.

There is an urgent need to reconstitute the orientation of the social sciences. There is a public need for moral courage, for rage, agitation, organisation and struggle in favour of the humanistic project.

How possible is this? It is far more likely to come from those in the South, such as Marcos Arruda in Brazil, and those like him, than it is from the North. There is a spareness and a rigour in the work of those who are in their daily experience dealing with issues of debt, trade and aid that is singularly missing in so many – there are brave exceptions – scholars in the North, stuck in the interstices of institutions that acquiesce in the anti-democratic order of things rather than questioning it. Indeed, the unemployed, the poor, the exploited, the South within the North, have so much more to gain from the Arrudas and those like him.

Nevertheless, it is necessary to get beyond a simple conflict with the existing order of things. It is worthwhile, necessary and possible to change the relationship of science, technology and society as that relationship has been constructed by the powerful. Within each component of that connection, there are dynamics that can be utilised to engage those who hold power. A reflexivity can be instituted that could encourage and engage those interested merely in transcending the inevitable collision of their interests with a violent social response, with all its consequences, even in their own interest. I do not reject lightly the capacity of those who now operate on poorly understood assumptions to change. Yet, neither am I naive, and I suggest that confrontations with an empowered, conscious, critically aware majority, well organised, will be of immense assistance in the revision of the thinking of those who hold and, consciously or unconsciously, abuse power.

If such a view be a tolerant one, it can be contrasted with the unique intolerance that now prevails in the western world. I have been appalled at the intolerance and near-hatred which has informed the actions of those who are now claiming a victory over all forms of Marxism and state planning. That intolerance goes beyond any condemnation of the excesses of statism. It is of the character of a general condemnation of all state-led initiatives. Those who live within such systems must suffer, it appears, as civilian victims of a demonology that masquerades as an international policy.

What is striking in the coverage of current international conflict is the disrespect for complexity and context and the penchant for demonology. In such an atmosphere, those who favour peace are sometimes labelled 'soft'. Indeed, it is not accidental that during the Gulf War the resources of the media were used to turn homes into arcades where video war games were played endlessly.

This situation will continue until we accept the need to have an articulate public with access to political and social studies, including a central module on building the mind of peace. Knowledge of the map of power, of the location of decision-making that affects one's life, are basic tools for participation in any meaningful version of democracy. Without it we have but an illusion of democracy. We do not will it that way.

Our existing reality is suffused with violence and aggression. We do not will it that way. We acquiesce in it. Analysing the basis of that acquiescence is our single greatest intellectual challenge.

Let me make, in summary, some tentative suggestions. In recent times, I have often asked myself – perhaps a naive question – as to whether it is possible to aspire to a universal ethic that would at once transcend the specific postulates of different cultures and receive such popular acceptance as would place it above all interests – private and public, national and international, communal and corporate. Gandhi believed in such an aspiration.

To speculate on the answer to such a question today is insufficient. It simply defines the distinction between optimism and pessimism. It is necessary now to forge such a universal ethic out of the most imperfect material in a workshop into which fewer and fewer will venture.

That universal ethic cannot be of the character of an absolute. It might be more appropriately envisaged as the cohesive element in an unfinished mosaic. It is the material which will enable different cultures to join and enrich each other in an unending process of creative enrichment, a mosaic of infinite expansion and resonance.

To venture in search of this element, this source of a true and lasting peace, constitutes a heroic mission restated for our times. It requires a journey within and beyond the person. That journey will require the shedding of the burdens of patriarchy, exploitation, commodity fetishism, ethnocentrism, racism and violence of all forms, including, particularly, that violence that obstructs the emergence of a new world order and that, overtly or covertly, denies the various stories of our planet a right to be heard.

It is no longer sufficient, I repeat, to offer ethically superior gestures in favour of peace and against war. It is essential that we offer a critique, a map, that would show how it is that so many potentially good people acquiesce in acts of war, terror, economic exploitation, patriarchy, wilful torture, forced famine, degrading job destruction, poverty and exclusion.

We have, as Raymond Williams put it, allowed ourselves to become the target, not the arrow. We are the victims of images rather than being their creator. It is of the utmost importance that the process of mystification of power relations be exposed, that we enable a popular reflexivity to come into being.

If we are to heal ourselves at the end of this century so as to become a symbol-using and empowered congeries of communities, we must emancipate ourselves from the condition of being a symbol-abused species.

To assert the right of every story to be told is not as simple as some may think. We must never forget that violence which greeted the publication of the MacBride Report on a new World Communicative Order, a violence which drove an individual from his position, if the institution of UNESCO was to survive.

The right to tell one's own story, to hold one's dream of freedom, of more secure and loving relationships, is daily threatened. These threats are often couched in a language that masks the intent of such new and powerfully distorting techniques of colonialism and domination.

One of our most urgent tasks is to restore to ourselves the integrity of our symbols, our language, our relationships, our mythopoeic longing for wholeness and the right to share in a form of consciousness free from all fear, insecurity and aggression.

What then would constitute an agenda for the recovery of our capacity to get beyond the morass of armaments thinking, of barren abuses of language in such phrases as 'the peace dividend', for an affirmation beyond the existential depression that is so manifest? Such an agenda will involve institutional reform, including the urgent reform of the United Nations. It will require an extension and reassertion of human rights. It will require a dissemination of power.

Before we get to this necessary practical agenda, however, there are assumptions which have to be addressed, assumptions that may have to be let go – such as the association of rights with territory or property.

The twentieth century will end, and the twenty-first emerge, with the figure of the migrant at the centre of things. Contained in the essence of the migratory experience are relationships to time and space that have, up to now, been seen as the experience of a minority which, for most policy purposes, could be neglected without cost.

The neglect of the migratory experience has meant that the nature of intellectual life has become distorted in its assumptions of the sedentary, of the systemic, of the power and possibility of tradition.

At the heart of migration lies the transience of things. It is that transience that explains both the risks and the neglected benefits of having chosen, or of having been condemned to break the inherited links to space, time and cultural certainties.

The migratory experience is one of pain. That fact has been document-
ed again and again. One issue immediately suggests itself. It is that of the
rights of migrants. If migrants are to possess rights as both human persons
and collectivities, their rights attach less to place, nation, race or, indeed,
property, than they do to persons, individually and collectively. The appalling
destruction of the phrase 'human rights' as a term of abuse, hurled by one
state at another, is made possible in part by the distortion of locating rights
conditionally in space, culture or property.

The migrant's experience cannot be reduced to the learned assumptions
of the point of origin or the point of destination. It is an experience born of
the flux of things, not only precariously balanced between the learned past
and the anticipated future, but creative in itself of something new and different. Migrants are at once the carriers of fear, wonderment and hope.

From that flux is created a unique capacity for tolerance. It is of the
nature of transience that absolutes are left behind, that truths are varied and
tenuous, all to be tested against the requirements of the human group and
person on the move.

The importance of today's displaced people and migrants is, in part, that
they represent all our future possibilities for renewing and reshaping the
human composition, the human contribution to the planet.

From an observation of the migrant's world of transience, a problem
observed can become an empowerment. For the migrant also gains from the
letting go of boundaries, barriers to seeing, cognition, understanding, action
and historicity. The migrant regularly reinvents the world within the flux of
time and space, as we all must learn to do now. This means letting go, and
renewing and replacing institutional certainties, systems of logic, patterns of
thought and cultural security blankets. It is not accidental that the artist often
foresees what the politician will labour to learn. It is very understandable
when one recognises how often exile is chosen, even if only symbolically, by
the artist as a necessary condition for creativity and celebration of the
humanistic impulse.

If we are to learn tolerance and establish it as a general value, it must
include then the commitment to hear a multitude of stories, to share a
panoply of dreams – as migrants have always been called upon to do – stories of the home left behind, dreams of the destination, food for disappointment perhaps, only to be replaced by a dream held in indomitable hope of
the return home.

I have often felt the experience of migration in my own life in another sense of not belonging. As a participant in the intellectual and political world, I have been made conscious of how little sharing there is of insights, what little companionship in struggle, what little celebration of creativity – or what the authoritarians call madness. It is rather a matter of intellectual property being traded, becoming the stuff of joint ventures in derived and dead theoretical flourishes and conceits.

The migrant in the academy has to forget his or her own story. Like all migrants, he quickly comes to know that imitation from close observation is the most important tool in the possession of those who would belong, and would put an end to the alienating terror of transience.

We are always under pressure to forget, develop amnesia, throw aside our own past, the experience of our class, the story of our nation, our myths that transcended the boundaries of time and space. Let us never forget the difference between the conscious shedding of the irrelevant, so that one might choose to stand like Lear as 'a poor, bare, forked animal', and to be stripped of identity. The former is a celebration of a form of freedom, the latter a violence most often delivered with subtlety.

'Keep yourself nice, Winnie,' Beckett's character tells herself in *Happy Days*. How many institutions of learning could take it as their motto? And yet to them I owe the opportunity of dissenting as I do.

We are fortunate that there is in the human mind an indomitable capacity for subversion of everything that impedes truth. That is the strongest case for academic freedom. There are both threats and opportunities in the academy. They change all the time. They cannot be avoided except at the price of despair or intellectual capitulation.

Academics are in a better position than most to observe how bad faith is being exercised, how subjects that might liberate are sold out and made manipulative, how language itself is emptied of meaning. The confusion in recent times of individualism with personal freedom is a singularly striking example.

To assert freedom, to support the impulse towards freedom, to live and die for that impulse, is one of the higher values in human experience. What, then, are the consequences of equating this with stripping the human person of any impulse towards solidarity and interdependence?

What does it tell us of the communicative order when Havel and Thatcher both speak of freedom, the one of personal liberty, the other of the unrestrained power of the market. To misquote Jerry Rubin, who in his day said, 'How can I say I love you when cars love Shell?' How can we speak of freedom after von Hayek, Friedman, Thatcher and Reagan have spoken of freedom?

The truth is that we have been robbed even of our vocabulary. Academics are both victims and perpetrators at times of a unique form of fear, a fear of authenticity. Their very existence, at times, seems to require a slavish adherence to the fallacy of the possibility of an objective and neutral relationship to the human condition. It is, of course, a pathetic pretence, an aspiration to the status of the physicist who might argue that a scientist can stand detached from the consequences of his or her research.

The recent UN Conference on Environment and Development, which took place in Rio de Janeiro, seemed to draw an acknowledgement from world leaders that the future of the planet had been put in jeopardy by actions that had, until then, been seen and promulgated as the every essence of development, of a progress against which nations, their governments, their leaders and their citizens had been judged and categorised.

At Rio, there was no reflection on the Idea of Progress, or its most aggressive offspring – the modernisation paradigm – that dynamic of colonialism and imperialism. I found not one scholar either who went back to Bacon's famous, or infamous, remark: 'I lead to you Nature and her children in bondage for your use.' The imagery of domination, of patriarchy, of exploitation, was frighteningly prophetic. From Bacon, through the Idea of Progress, passing on via the World Bank and the International Monetary Fund . . . the core assumptions survived intact from Rio.

It became clear to me that not only was there an ecological crisis, there was also a general crisis of consciousness, and within it a specific crisis of language. Not only were the assumptions which led to the ecological crisis left unexamined; it was assumed that, simply by putting a new word, 'sustainable', before the word 'development', a solution to the uncontrolled ingress of ecological despoliation could be found.

At Rio, too, there was little reference to the production and sale of armaments, and none at all to the intricacies of the aid, trade and debt relationships that link the North and the South – why not be candid? – intricacies that link the exploited with the source of their destruction, the exploiting multinationals.

Would it not be a powerful point of convergence between North and South if the Idea of Progress was rejected as a source of ecological disaster, exploitation, domination and cultural ethnocentrism? Would it not be exciting if scholars lifted the yoke of the modernisation paradigm from scholars of the Third World?

The economic power of the multinationals is so great that such questions could not even be posed. Yet it most happen. The Idea of Progress will be abandoned. Movements of reflection between and with the person will emerge. The debate on gender will move to one of considering the continuum of the male in the female, the female in the male. Yet we must remember that we also live in a world of need, of basic necessities, which demands a response now, for which an evolution in consciousness offers insufficient hope. The agenda must include not only the insights of ecology and psychoanalysis. It must create an entirely new economics and social science.

It would be wonderful to report that this consciousness was present among the non-governmental organisations at Rio, that it was the difference between the Global Forum and the Conference at Rio Centro that was a division between heart and head. To put it like that is simply to keep alive an old organicist fallacy.

The truth is that, apart from the work on the Alternative Treaties, the issues of economics, trade, debt and aid were at times and in many places as unwelcome in the Global Forum as they were at Rio Centro. In the latter, they were consciously obstructed, in the former, neglected, regarded as tedious, or rejected as materialistic.

Why should one have to choose between ecological concerns and issues of trade, debt and aid? Of course, a holistic scholar would regard such a choice as absurd. Between 1979 and 1986, Brazil, host to UNCED, paid more than $100 billion, as much as the total amount of its debt, in debt service. Last year, more than $50 billion was transferred, as a nett figure, from the South to the North. In 1983, the figure was $43 billion. In 1987, it was $38 billion. Since 1983, the North has been extracting more and more from the South, at the very time when the threat of famine and malnutrition is increasing.

We will, in the future, have to be many things: ecologists, economists, sociologists, scientists, poets and lovers. We do not have to replicate the constricting specialisations of the broken world that is dying. The old solidarities *will* be renewed. The symbol-using species will realise itself only when individualism has been made a dark memory.

Address delivered on being presented with the Seán MacBride Peace Prize by the International Peace Bureau in Helsinki on 30 August 1992

PART II

MAKING SENSE OF SOCIAL CHANGE

THE PEASANT TRADITION AND THE BETRAYED REPUBLIC

THE ORIGINS OF IRISH SOCIOLOGY

In the 1960s and 1970s, the opportunities for postgraduate studies in the social sciences existed for the most part in the United States, and they were appreciated by students such as myself in the almost-complete absence of such provision in Ireland.

At Indiana University, where I studied, Latin Americans, Asians and Africans were introduced to a positivist orientation in the social sciences – a structural-functionalist sociology. The assumptions of the method were based on a nearly unquestioned empiricism. Yet there was one brilliant phenomenologist in the Department. He was Norwegian, and could be relied upon to have access to the materials of such writers as Alfred Schutz in their original German. There was one Marxist theoretician, or rather theorist on Marx. The world was ready for quantification. Consensus could be assumed, and conflict was to be ignored. Radical students might quote C. Wright Mills's *The Power Elite*. Some might become involved in protests against the Vietnam war, but any who did so put their student visas at risk.

After my return to Ireland, I worked on a study of Galway docks and dockers. The dockers' lives were from another world compared to the one of structural-functional abstraction which I had left. Their lives were ones of comradeship, division, exploitation, and the continuing struggle against the de-casualisation of labour.

In 1968, I was in the Manchester University postgraduate programme. It was an extraordinary time in British anthropology. In the 1960s, many African countries achieved independence. I recall Erskine Childers, the late distinguished United Nations official, historian and journalist, describing to me a few years before he died the flag-lowering and flag-raising ceremonies. The British flag was lowered in darkness, and as the lights came up the new flag was raised. As this happened, the BBC commentator would say: 'And a new country takes its place among the free countries of the world – free to make its own mistakes.' When Erskine Childers objected to this phrase, he was fired from the BBC. 'Amnesia at Midnight', he had intended to entitle the book which he was preparing before his death.

From this period at Manchester University, I gathered an interest in migration studies, both theoretical and practical – an interest I still retain. After independence in so many African countries, British anthropologists came home. In the years to come, urban studies would absorb their interest, but for that period at the end of the 1960s, there was a rich debate on theoretical work such as migrant networks in urban situations and circular migration.

If, in the Midwest of the United States, the emphasis was on the convergence of social science and the physical sciences in terms of method, at Manchester the emphasis was on observation studies and ethnography. In Manchester, I met Peter Gibbon, who later joined me briefly as a visiting colleague at University College Galway. With him, I wrote of patrons, clients and brokers, and the phenomenon of the Irish gombeenman.

Our critique of the modernisation model of development drew a predictable reply from those within the modernisation school of economics, who produced what I might now call a hagiography of credit and the banking system.

The advocates of the modernisation model had little patience for the diverse sets of complexities that existed within Irish rural society in particular, or for the conflicts which these complexities threw up within different forms of boundary – territorial, linguistic, ethnic and social.

The crude ethnocentrism of evolutionistic models was of course superficially attractive. Not only could it carry all the old rationalisations of colonisation, political suppression, social exclusion and cultural manipulation, it could also offer a model for the future. Economic backwardness constituted the features of those who had to be helped from their social, cultural and economic attitudes into modernity.

This model, whether through the idea of 'progress', 'modernisation' or 'globalisation', retains so many elements of rationalisation, of domination, that it in effect strips rationality itself of moral force.

It was clear to me from my own experiences that what I had been reading in those structural-functionalist studies, which emphasised consensus, did not fit with what I had come to know, or felt I knew. I found reality in the literary accounts – and an abstracted unreality in the formal sociological accounts.

It was Peter Gibbon who introduced me to the theoretical literature on transactionalism. This led us both to locate some empirical material but, much more importantly, literary material that could be used within a new perspective to challenge the assumptions of modernisation theory, which was sitting like blinkers on Irish social science.

While the early writing by Gibbon and me was challenged by the linear theorists within the modernisation school of development, these people failed to refute the facts as presented. Their inability to deal with the literary material illustrated – and still illustrates – the great loss suffered by Irish sociology in not having a method that enables it to draw on qualitative as well as quantitative material. The piece which follows on the gombeenman in literature drew correspondence on parallels from such countries as Japan.

I recall, too, that in this period Irish social scientists were largely neglecting the State as a subject of critical analysis. With some exceptions, few were following us into clientelist studies as an area of theoretical enquiry. While this approach may have more limited utility, contemporary conditions, dominated by such realities as tribunals of enquiry into political and administrative corruption, particularly in the area of building land, mean that the more general approach of transactionalism could still yield a rich theoretical harvest. I am absolutely convinced of the usefulness of such an approach in trying to understand, for example, politics in some African countries where 'good governance' is being prescribed as a model from outside.

One may well ask why the tools of anthropology are not being used to source models of governance from deep African experience and memory. More controversially, perhaps, one might argue that making a critique, and moving past the clientelist structures that are located within such societies might be a more viable project than seeking to impose economistic versions of 'good governance' drawn from entirely different historical and social circumstances. Indeed, such impositions are often being recommended to elites that are not connected to the broad mass of the people, do not take account of the reform of the State that has to occur, and pay scant attention to indigenous political decision-making structures. The models drawn from transactionalism – from the literature on patrons, clients and brokers – are, I suggest, much richer in possibilities for study.

Over the years, I have become convinced that some strange intellectual inferiority complex has led some Irish scholars away from the rich truth of the narrative and into the readily distorted, and superficial, quantitative realms and away from rich veins of qualitative hypotheses. These of course were never 'either, or' choices. Both qualitative and quantitative methods are necessary. It is a fact, it seems to me, that Irish literary writers have been much closer to the full gamut of Irish life, including its conflicts and cruelties, than any post-hoc analysis of a quantitative kind. I would further raise the question as to the use of a singularly quantitative method in fields that are not really appropriate for quantification. The pieces that follow are some of those written from the sociological perspective which was not chosen.

It was Orlando Fals Borda who wrote of the ideological glasses through which all of us studying our own people are forced to look. That we have chosen to keep the glasses on our face is particularly regrettable. The attempted colonisation of intellectual life is, of course, never-ending. If, in the sixteenth century, it was attempted with the imposition of a standard form of grammar, today it is successful in the presentation of a single paradigm of intellectual life that justifies an extreme version of market unaccountability.

When I reflect now on what has been extrapolated from the ideas of the classical founders of sociology, the subject I taught, I feel that it is the projected consequences which Max Weber saw for the version of society emerging, and being imposed uncritically, that represents the greatest threat. Formally free, we drift to unfreedom. Consumed in our consumption, we become neurotic. No longer knowing our real needs, we accumulate more and more. Anxious to protect our possessions, we subscribe to the politics of fear, and the social becomes a distant memory or an abstraction.

Since our environment is threatened by our unlimited consumption, we lack the integrated scholarship that can address the loss of symmetry in our lives.

The Limits of Clientelism

Towards an Assessment of Irish Politics

The introduction of clientelism into Irish political science discourse took the form of an explanation of 'anomalies' which the Irish political system exhibited in comparison with Western European democracies. These anomalies included

> . . . the character of both the major parties as vertically integrated inter-class alliances; a lack of serious ideological differences between these parties; a comprehensive localism in national politics; a statistically attested, extremely low degree of public confidence in the ability of ordinary citizens to collectively influence local or national governmental action; an absence of interest groups or public campaigns in national politics; the dominance of national and local politics by the personal clienteles of politicians; and the constant recurrence of corrupt practices in local government.[1]

These features of 'Irish political culture' came to be perceived as 'anomalies' precisely because of the acceptance of modernisation theory as the dominant mode of explanation in Irish political science in the 1960s, and all of these anomalies are ascribed by Basil Chubb – the first comprehensive critic of Irish political-legal institutions in the modern period – to the operation of patronage and brokerage.[2] Chubb attributed these anomalies in an otherwise modernised state to residual tradition:

> For generations, Irish people saw that, to get the benefits the public authorities bestow, the help of a man with connections and influence was necessary. All that democracy has meant is that such a man has been laid on officially, as it were, and is now no longer a master but a servant.[3]

The principal work within the patronage/brokerage model of political relations that succeeded Chubb's pioneering study of the largest political party in an Irish constituency in the period prior to and during an election was Bax's study of a constituency in the Munster region in the south of the Republic.[4] Bax went further than Chubb and asserted not merely that patronage and brokerage were the principles underlying Ireland's political anomalies but that they were the means by which the vertical integration of Irish society had been accomplished in the last hundred years. Landlords of the last century had functioned as patrons and brokers and had been succeeded by professional politicians mediating between citizens and the new interventionist measures of the state. Following Scott, Bax asserts that the interaction of such factors as poverty, fragmentation of power, strong parochialism and particularism in the relationships of social life create a context applicable to modern Ireland in which machine politics may flourish. Added to these factors, Bax notes perceptively the consequences of the Irish electoral system, proportional representation with a single transferable vote in multi-member constituencies, which sets politicians from within the same political party in competition with one another for votes:

> The main point of my argument is that machine-style politics is the outcome of a paradox in Irish political culture: on the one hand, strong and traditional party loyalty, on the other, extreme pragmatism and self-interest. This cultural paradox is maintained by the implications of a peculiar electoral system which functions in a predominantly pre-industrial society of small farmers who set great store in face-to-face relations and who have a strongly particularistic attitude.[5]

Bax's study is a very close and detailed examination of processes in a rural Irish constituency, and his summary of how the politician is evaluated amplifies Chubb's original suggestions and goes much further, to locate Irish political process firmly within the context of brokerage:

> Having high centrality and being well-known in one's area is important in order to play a brokerage role, but it is usually not enough. People must not only know the would-be politician, they must also know that he has the qualities to manipulate persons and situations successfully. In other words, he must have built up credit with the population. 'You must show what your grapevine is worth', as a politician put it to me.[6]

The other significant study of Irish politics in rural areas is that of Paul Sacks.[7] Studying political behaviour at the opposite end of the Irish Republic from Bax but in the same time period, he too explains machine politics as he found it in terms of peasant political culture: 'It is the countryman's act of ideas about the nature of the political process that makes machine politics possible in Ireland.'[8]

Clientelism is adequately reported, then, as an important feature of Irish political behaviour. That has been one of the major contributions of the late sixties and seventies to Irish political science. Much less satisfactory have been the attempts to explain or assess clientelism in terms of its origins, mechanisms of survival or transition, or consequences. The formulations to which we have referred take 'peasant political culture', 'the rural–urban dichotomy', or a variant theory, 'centre–periphery relations', as the explanation of anomalies or paradoxes in Irish politics.

In 1974, Gibbon and Higgins assessed the utility of the new empirical studies on patron–client ties.[9] That work discussed the form of the patron–client approach as a development within political anthropology. Case studies were presented of patronage and brokerage in historical and contemporary society, the adequacy of the relationship between patronage, tradition and modenisation was examined, and the weakness of existing formulations was discussed. We were led to conclude:

> In modern transactionalism, these descriptive categories are replaced by others of precisely the same [i.e. essentially descriptive] status: 'action-sets', 'quasi-groups', 'social networks', 'factions' and, of course, patron–client and patron–broker–client relations. Social structure is again conceived as an aggregate of these relations. Its existence in both cases is only at a purely empirical level, and is given no theoretical determinacy.
>
> In consequence of the absence of any complex abstract conception of social structure which could account theoretically for evenness and unevenness within the totality, the diachronic conceptualisation of the societies in question must inevitably take the form of the movement from one substantively unitary and untheorised aggregate of sub-structures to another. Any particular change must therefore be conceived simply in terms of temporal succession rather than determined structural transition, and change in general must be conceived in the form of a recession of simple linear and individually untheorized steps.[10]

I feel now that we could go further than suggesting such a limitation in theoretical terms. Patron–client studies have, even as descriptions of political systems, made claims that cannot be sustained. Confined to behaviour within the electoral arena, they explain but a part of that behaviour. Electoral confrontations consist of more than the confrontation of clientist machines. Methodologically, of course, they rely on a reconstruction by actors of what such confrontstions are about which is often illusory. The concentration on apolitical culture has fostered the assumption of a voluntarism that does not exist. What is missed altogether, as a consequence, is the coercive, exploita-tive character, over time, of such relationships.

This is not the place to go into the origins of these relationships, but the point should be made that they pre-date the extension of the franchise in 1918. It is worth quoting one letter to a local newspaper in 1910 referring to the local politicians of the day, and written by a founder of the Rural Co-operative Movement:

> All the local appointments are in their gift, and hence you get drunken doctors, drunken rate collectors, drunken JPs, drunken inspectors – in fact, round the gombeen system reels the whole drunken congested world, and underneath this revelry and jobbery the unfortunate peasant labours and gets no return for his labour. Another enters and takes his cattle, his eggs, his oats, his potatoes, his pigs, and gives what he will for them, and the peasant toils on from year to year, being doled out Indian meal, flour, tea and sugar, enough to keep him alive. He is a slave almost as much as if he were an indentured native and had been sold in the slave market.[11]

Noteworthy in this quotation is the clear exploitative character of the relationships between the gombeenman representative and the people. The gombeenman, as broker, shopkeeper and moneylender, was the effective ruler of large tracts of western Ireland in the period between about 1870 and 1930.[12]

In order to appreciate the role of clientelism in modern Irish politics, it will now be useful to look at some examples of how it actually works.

All over the Republic of Ireland at any weekend, elected public representa-tives will travel throughout their constituencies, stopping for brief periods at public houses and hotels, which usually display notices in advance of the times of their visits, to meet their constituents, or hear 'confessions', as it is called. The more usual name for such meetings, however, is clinics.

A private room is provided, and clients will be organised in rotation, with the same rigour as might be expected in the waiting room of a dentist or a doctor. Such meetings will be held on Friday evenings, all day Saturday, and sometimes after the last Mass on Sunday. On Monday, the representative will attend local-authority meetings. County councils usually meet on Monday afternoons, and city councils on Monday evenings. Ancillary bodies, such as health boards or education committees, meet in the afternoon, to enable the permanent staff to attend. On Tuesday, the representative leaves for the Dáil in Dublin, and remains there until Thursday evening, when he or she will return to the constituency, and the cycle will recommence. While in Dublin, the representative will deal with the previous week's cases, ringing up government ministers or their private secretaries and writing approximately two hundred letters to constituents. The deputy will occasionally enter the Chamber for debates on legislation or an estimate for a government department, but will usually attend at Question Time, where questions of local interest will be answered. When the official report on Question Time is printed, he or she will tear out the pages which carry an account of the question answered from the record and post them to the local newspaper back in the constituency for publication.

About twice every month, the deputy will attend a meeting of the Parliamentary Party. Details of the week's legislative activity will customarily be given by the Chief Whip, and an opportunity may be taken for voicing the feelings of those back home in the constituency on the impact of particular legislative or administrative measures. Ministers may be chided too for not communicating decisions made by their departments which affected the constituencies of deputies concerned, who would have used such information in the local press. Any provincial paper in Ireland in any week carries reports of questions raised in Parliament, decisions of the state departments communicated by ministers to fellow party members, reports too perhaps of after-dinner speeches in the constituency by visiting ministers outlining new state measures, and advertisements giving the intinerary of public representatives.

At the weekend 'confessions', the deputy will write details of all the cases in a notebook, called by some his or her 'prayerbook'. The prayerbook will be placed beside the phone in his or her room in Parliament, and the deputy will shout the details of the cases into the phone for the civil servants in the different departments of state. He or she will preface all calls with the title 'Deputy'. This is to ensure deference and adequate attention, and a good reply. Failure to deliver these will be communicated to the minister in charge of the department involved. A simple request for the name of the civil servant answering the call can, as a deputy put it to the author, put 'the fear of God' into the person answering.

Councillors in Ireland will have a less extensive circuit to cover than deputies. Their schedules will be organised, their meetings will be face-to-face encounters at any time of any day, and frequently they will act as intermediaries in making appointments to see the deputy. They do not have the resources of free postage, secretarial assistance or salary that the deputy enjoys. The problems brought to them are usually local ones and deal with the services provided by the local authority of which the councillor is a member. Councillors collect travelling expenses for attendance at council meetings once a month and for attendance at committee meetings which they go to as nominees of their council. They usually use such meetings as occasions for clearing their books of the cases they have collected. These cases may have to do with planning housing needs, home-improvement grants, and loans for building and repairs. These are described by Sacks in his study of machine politics in Donegal, although planning applications are of more importance in the usual month's work of a councillor in a typical county council than Sacks reports from his fieldwork.[13] The activities we have outlined for deputies have been described as brokerage activities by both the recent major studies.[14]

The activities of councillors have been called the activities of a broker's broker. These descriptions fit the behaviour well, and political scientists are in agreement on their appropriateness. They are not in agreement on the source of such behaviour, its functions, what it tells us of the political system, or its consequences.

We have presented a necessarily very simplified description of the activities of councillors and deputies. It is appropriate to look at an example of the behaviour of the clients of both. In every small town and city in Ireland today, the number of applicants for local-authority housing exceeds the supply of such houses. The houses are allocated on the basis of need laid down by an act of the Irish Parliament, the Housing Act of 1966, and this Act is administered by the county or city manager. He or she is the person who allocates the house, who decides that one person's needs are greater than those of another. Nevertheless, there is a widespread belief that the elected members can influence such allocations. Thus, every weekend, women put their children in prams and pushchairs and head for the clinics of their local deputy. The author has found that women outnumber men by six to one in the presentation of housing difficulties.[15] Today in Ireland, mediation on such difficulties as housing is regarded by some men as unmanly and as being a woman's business. Many women may leave the same area of bad housing and wait in the same queue for the same politician about the same needs. Their presentation of their case will be an individual one about their needs, and not about the principle of the gap between the number of houses needed and those provided. Being without adequate housing is perceived as an individual problem that might be resolved by the mediation of the politician. As numbers of children expand and length of time on the housing list grows, the person will be likely to be housed in any event. The councillors of the local authority will be informed of the allocations by way of a list. The applicant will be informed that she is being housed.

She is likely to be congratulated on her good luck by several politicians, and she may choose to select from among the many congratulations her most effective mediator, as it appears to her rather as pious people who have stormed heaven, though many intermediaries select a particular saint as being particularly efficacious for a particular job.

It is not proposed to give many examples. Suffice it to say that the mediations consist of the presentation of a need to a broker. Next to housing might be the need for a medical card. Another usual source of requests is the delay of the state and local bureaucracies in answering the letters or forms of those in need, who may suffer by such delays. This latter point can be expanded upon briefly to fill out our bird's-eye view of the interaction of brokers, their clients and the agencies of the state.

In Ireland, employment in the public service was in the past – and even today is – seen as something of an achievement. It represented a form of mobility in a social sense and involved the shift in symbolic and real terms from a rural to an urban lifestyle. The safe, permanent and pensionable aspects of such positions have always been emphasised. In recent times, such appointments have been the subject of competition. In the early days of the Irish state, there had been numerous allegations of corruption, some well-founded.[16] An aspect of the service that may be of more importance than that accorded to it so far has been the practice of promotion consisting of being moved away from the public. The most senior people are in the most remote, most inaccessible offices. Those who pull the hatch in the public offices to deal with the public are frequently young and inexperienced. Unlike England, for example, few Irish state offices have an open-plan lay-out. They consist of stark rooms where the public stand and wait, or sit on a form made of wood, until their names are called, or the hatch opened, when their turn has come. Zimmerman has commented from his data on Dublin on how the treatment of the public in public offices can lead to those in need seeking the assistance of a clientelist politician.[17]

In the urban area of the constituency most familiar to the author, the bulk of enquiries from constituents relate to housing. Of such requests related to housing addressed to the author in his capacity as a public representative, most people simply ask for an appointment to be arranged whereby they can get to see the officer to whom the processing of housing applications has been delegated.[18] I feel that the perceptions held by public servants of the public, the manner in which their promotion consists of being allowed to escape from 'them', the public, has been underemphasised as a factor facilitating the recruitment by clientelistic politicians of clienteles in Ireland. Apart from such a service as getting an answer more speedily and with more respect than their clients, clientelist politicians, in the opinion of the author, rarely objectively influence a decision. They create the illusion of assistance, however. Crucial to the creation of this illusion is the ability to acquire information on central and local state decisions. The great competition today is for the pieces of communication that convey state decisions. To know good news in advance is a great advantage. To prevent bad news, such as an unfavourable decision on administrative or legislative measures, from getting to one's constituency is, incidentally, one of the basic necessities for political survival. To acquire a list of any kind that can be used before one's competing councillors or deputies powerfully assists in creating the illusion that one is a person with real pull. To accomplish this is known amongst clientelist politicians as 'pulling a stroke'.[19] The councillor who pulls a stroke is at first the source of objection but over time becomes a source of envy and indeed admiration by fellow councillors and even the media. One councillor in a local authority studied by the author carries the nickname of 'Stroke' and feels rather flattered at being referred to in the local press by his nickname.

This councillor acquired his reputation by appearing to pull off unexpected coups in securing a nomination for the council elections in apparently hopeless circumstances, then later in positioning himself at national conferences near prominent front-benchers likely to be 'on camera' and, therefore, in his eyes, cornering publicity, getting to speak at Youth Conferences at the correct time for radio coverage, and so forth, However, capturing publicity is but a minor aspect of 'pulling strokes'. It more usually consists in acquiring information in advance of official communications.

Competition between councillors is often characterised by inventing strategies for acquiring information before anybody else. One deputy in a neighbouring county to that under study has been known to have informants in hospitals and homes for the elderly. Recently, he sympathised with the relatives of a patient who had died before the relatives had been informed of her death. Sometimes the currency of such clientelist relief activity is devalued, when more than one councillor competes, to the extent of writing a letter claiming exclusive credit for representations to the same client.

Councillors see all lists of decisions taken by the council's executive as the raw material of their practice. For example, the names of all recipients of regular payments recorded in the manager's order book have to be made available at meetings. This book, referred to by Chubb as a mechanism of accountability, is a veritable well of potential clientelist options for the electors.[20]

To engineer special access to a list is to pull a real 'stroke'. Such was the case in 1976, when a former member of the Cabinet visited the Housing Office of one of the local authorities under study by the author, and by a mixture of cajolery and subtle intimidation secured a list of housing allocations before the local representatives had received their list. The legislator in question was not a member of the local authority but was a local deputy. He had been promoted to the Cabinet. He was able to congratulate all the 'lucky' recipients of houses three days in advance of his political rivals, and even his fellow party councillor henchmen. His actions became known when his letter went to the client of a competing deputy of the opposing party – a Fine Gael deputy.[21] He was further embarrassed by his sending a congratulatory letter to the wrong family. Two families on the housing list had the same surname.

The assistant county manager handling the confrontation resulting from this was straightforward and told the aggrieved councillors that he could only, if they wished, discipline the official who had given out the list. Nobody, of course, wanted to go this far and lose the co-operation of all the remaining staff in the local authority.

One source of 'strokes' is provided by telephone installations, for example. Recently, a minister for state required all new telephone installations in his area to be communicated to him. The same minister has congratulated all the elderly recipients of fuel under a Health Board's free fuel scheme on having got coal, and suggested that, if they need the second allocation possible under the discretionary provisions of the scheme, he was the man to get it for them.

One could elaborate. Suffice it to say at this stage that every action of the state, of the local authority and of related agencies generates a source of clientelist communication. They help create the illusion of assistance.

We have been speaking of 'big strokes'. 'Little strokes' are pulled by major party activists who are not elected members but who can become activists at election time, those referred to by Sacks in his study as 'cadres'. These range from being elected to officerships of residents' associations in an election year to manipulating the agenda of such associations to include 'demands' known to be already in the process of being met by some local or central state decision. Elected members feed information on anticipated works so that the demand from residents' associations can neatly anticipate the work and enable credit to be generated for the clientelist politician the party activist favours.[22] Contacts of local politicians also inform the representatives of funerals and events in the community which must not at any cost be missed. They achieve their own centrality by, as we have said, taking over positions in community associations. This extends to the Church. Processions and public religious events are very important occasions for the contact people. They ostentatiously take positions as ushers, stewards, and so on. They have a real importance too in blocking demands from the community when their party is in power and such demands cannot be met, and bringing such demands forward when their party is not in power.

Viewed superficially, one could see in community involvement a plethora of good will and generosity as citizens come forward for public service. In practice, a calculated takeover of a clientelist kind is being staged. Success is rewarded by the party in power, and defeat is penalised, by the giving or withholding of support for positions within the party organisation itself.

Having presented a description of some councillor activity, we now finally turn to an analysis of the part played in this by the local state executive. County managers could wreck the operation of such clientelist practices as we have described by writing to applicants for various services directly and expeditiously. Why do they not do so? The answer lies, in addition to bureaucratic inertia, in the quid pro quo of the council meeting. Councillors could, if they so wished, insist on a measure of accountability and information that could make life difficult, or at least tedious, for the manager. This does not happen. The long-established principle – so long established that it is an expectation of normative status, in Bailey's terms – is that members cooperate with formal nods in the direction of accountability by way of information, and the manager in turn consults and communicates in a way that makes a clientelist system possible, that leaves its procedures intact.[23]

It has happened that managers and representatives have differed.[24] In such a confrontation, the clientelist network of the member is at risk, to the degree that the member's prospects of re-election can be damaged. However, managers and councillors usually do co-operate. What has impressed the author after a few years of observation is the degree of understanding that does exist as to the parameters within which the rules of collision and collusion operate. 'Strokes', for example, are rare and innovative. Their novelty shakes the system of understood co-operation with the executive. If tolerated, other councillors may add them to their repertoire of clientelist performance. If they go too far, their one-off nature is emphasised in the executive response, which gives a gentle reprimand that this is not playing the game.

At first glance, it may seem useful to seek to understand such interactions, to explain them by a model such as that which Bailey[25] has developed. We could elicit a model of normative rules and contrast it with the pragmatic rules of operation of clientelist politicians. We could examine how co-existence was achieved. Such a model as Bailey's is limited in what it can explain. It gives us an understanding of the logic of the competing sets of rules of the forms of competition that comprise the game of public interaction. It deals only, however, with those public interactions that the competing sets of rules draw forth. Perhaps these limits to Bailey's model are the limits of clientelism in general, as an explanatory system within political science. It tends to ascribe an innocence, a neutrality, certainly at least a non-coercive non-exploitative milieu, to interactions such as those we have discussed, all of which are based on a vulnerability of some kind.

Political life in Ireland consists of routine interactions at clinics, as we have described them. Occasionally, however, issues obtrude themselves on the centre of the political stage, and by examining the handling of one such issue by politicians we can encounter clientelism as a process. The following is a case study from the author's notebook.[26]

There are along the west coast of Ireland two or three natural oyster-spawning areas. One of these was claimed as their private property by the descendants of a landlord. The landlord in turn based his rights on a charter given some hundreds of years earlier by the British Crown. In the present century, sporadic attempts had been made to dislodge the private owners in favour of the local community's desire to supplement their small farm incomes by part-time dredging. The Irish state had faced this issue at a public inquiry in 1960, at which the claimants to the oysterbeds and the local people confronted each other. The outcome of the semi-judicial inquiry was that the claimants to the beds were given a licence under new legislation, to which conditions were attached. These conditions concerned maintenance and a commitment to farm the beds. In acknowledgment of the new legislation, the claimants gave up whatever claim they were making by inherited property rights on the beds.

The descendant of the landlord to whom such a licence was offered, however, very shrewdly formed a company with one thousand issued shares and had the licence allocated to the company. She was free to sell the shares in the company at any time, and the new owners would have the licence as an asset of the company whose shares they bought. This happened in 1980, when four Breton mariculture farmers and businessmen bought shares in the company for an undisclosed sum.

In 1980, the state law on fishing was changed, and attempts were initiated to establish a policy for mariculture development. Central to such a policy was the question of who would initiate such development. The state agency allocated the task of developing the fishing industry had basically three choices: it could get involved directly and organise the new industry with demonstration farms, so as to show how the new technology could take a new form of livelihood from the sea and then set about diffusing such an example, through the community; it could assist local groups already formed in their attempts to move into this area; or it could give assistance to those who controlled and had access for oysters and other shellfish products to the lucrative European markets. Such interests were of Breton origin in the example we are discussing.

The first option was never really considered by the agency owing to the hostility that direct state investment has traditionally provoked in the main political parties whenever a private commercial alternative was available.[27] The second strategy involved the mobilisation of people at a community level and was perceived as unwieldy and slow by the agency's personnel, who were largely scientific, technical and clerical in work orientation. The third strategy, of dealing with those who had market knowledge, some special expertise and a reputation for hard work, was chosen. In defending their decision, the agency would later contrast such traits with their opposites. They saw the local community as having no knowledge or interest in the rational development of a mariculture industry. The locals were perceived as having no interest, as being divided amongst themselves, and as having a record of idly looking at such existing natural resources as they had access to without utilising them. They would of course now benefit, it was suggested by the Bretons. Work would be available in the re-seeding and maintenance of the beds which the Breton owners would develop, with grants from the Irish government and the European Community.

The local communities were confronted with the news that the oyster beds had, as they saw it, been sold to foreigners. They were invited to a meeting by the State Fisheries Agency to hear of the plans of the new owners to develop mariculture with state assistance in a way, it was suggested, that would benefit everybody. The meeting was arranged through a local community activist, who was later to regret providing any assistance whatsoever and who had done so out of deference to the state agency. At the meeting, it was quickly pointed out that more than three hundred families in three parishes made a living from part-time oyster dredging and that the oyster beds should be developed for such people. At this point, the local people walked out, leaving the representstives of the state agency and the new owners without an audience to whom they might explain their plans.

There followed a series of meetings over six months which were to reveal significant aspects of clientelistic practice. The local people from the very start elected a committee, the secretary of which wrote to all the public representatives in the area asking them to attend a briefing; later, their support was sought for the different strategies adopted by the locals. Present also at most meetings was a legal adviser, who pursued the possibility of the conditions of the licence not having been fulfilled. His contribution at every meeting was based on rational-legal grounds.

The meetings were taking place just before a general election. The area involved is part of a constituency that would elect five members of parliament in the forthcoming election, owing to a constituency revision. At the time of the agitation, it returned four deputies. These four included a member of the Cabinet, a former minister, a government backbencher and an opposition deputy from the Fine Gael Party. The minister did not take a direct interest in the early meetings. A former minister who would be running in the newly drawn five-seat constituency, however, had to take an interest since he was 'coming in' to the constituency.[28] The former minister took an occasional interest. It is important to bear in mind that, at this time, a change in leadership in mid-term had divided the Fianna Fáil government party into two factions in practically every constituency. The minister for state we have referred to belonged to the faction in power. The former minister belonged to the previous leader's faction.

Each had a contact in a local councillor. These two local councillors, one in each faction, belonging to the same district, would be in competition for a nomination for the general election. Both saw the issue as one that could bring them credit in two ways: at the selection convention of their party and, if they were chosen as the candidate, as an issue with the electorate.

At the first meeting attended by all the local politicians and political hopefuls, the legal adviser outlined the principles of the case. This presentation was dispassionate, and a strategy for action logically followed from it that consisted of the minister for fisheries being forced to say whether he would act in accordance with powers the legal adviser asserted he had. However, the doubt as to whether the minister would have sufficient grounds to act as the legal adviser suggested was to be crucial for the politicians.

They began by pledging support. The government-party representatives, whose party claims a virtual monopoly on true nationalism, spoke of the travesty of foreigners obtaining rights against the local people.[29] The councillor on the side of the faction in power lived near to the site of the oyster beds, was the newest arrival on the political scene and had, it transpired later, fewer branches of the government party supporting him for the forthcoming selection conference. All these factors affected both his language and his performance. 'I'm a republican, as I said at a party meeting, and no way do I want the people to give in to the Frenchmen', he told the first meeting.[30]

What followed cannot be dealt with in detail. A meeting with the minister for fisheries was requested. In this, the local minister of state and his factional councillor supporter gained credit by getting the minister for fisheries to meet the local people at 8 AM on the morning after a formal dinner which he was attending in the constituency. The meeting was arranged close to the site of the oyster beds. The government party had a belief in a certain earthiness towards the public that consisted, if we might be paradoxical, in the minister looking out at the sea towards the oyster beds with his own eyes. After this, he was addressed by the committee chairman, the secretary, the legal adviser and the politicians. He would do whatever he could. He was sympathetic but was promising nothing.

Much time passed. Nothing was heard from the Department of Fisheries. The Breton owners of the oyster beds, however, used this delay to carry out some work on the beds in question and thereby eroded the legal case on the condition that those who held a licence from the state should carry out development work, the nub of the legal adviser's case. The local committee quickly put a picket on the pier. Minor scuffles took place but the government-faction councillor, who had been quick to participate in this radical action and was now giving speeches of his willingness to go to jail or, as he hinted, to go on hunger strike until the locals' demands were met, gave a speech calling for peace, in particular because the confrontations were taking place on a Holy Day of Obligation, a day when Roman Catholics attend Mass by obligation, in addition to their Sunday obligations.

Meetings were now being held every Saturday evening. Difficulty was being experienced in keeping up morale, something vital for the continuance of the picket. No news was forthcoming from the minister for fisheries. The local representative of the small Labour Party got his party leader to ask a question in Parliament as to whether the minister for fisheries intended to act in accordance with the powers he held to secure the livelihood of the three hundred fishermen involved and their families. The reply was given by the Labour councillor[31] to the local press, who carried it in one of the local newspapers. The headline 'BRETONS WIN IN WAR OVER FISHERY' appeared in its first edition. The local paper has a country edition sold over a wide area and which appears on a Thursday. It has a city issue, which carries a few different pages and is distributed on a Friday. Immediately after the headline appeared, the Cabinet member, who had remained in the wings until now, rang the newspaper for details of the Parliamentary Question and to suggest that there must be some mistake. This call came from Dublin and was the first of many during that day. A request was made to have the story excluded from the city edition. This was refused. At the last moment, however, a statement arrived from the minister saying that, on the basis of the information available to him, he had given this reply, but he was open to new information if it was provided. Meanwhile, in the constituency, the fact that this story had now replaced the story in the first issue of the paper was being used by the local councillors from both factions of the government party as a basis for a rumour that the Parliamentary Question had never been asked, and that the answer quoted in the paper had been concocted by the Labour councillor; anger was thus being channelled towards the paper, which, it was suggested, was not on the people's side.[32]

At the subsequent fiery meeting, the photostat of the question was produced by the Labour councillor, but this was still insufficient to convince many that the minister had said what he had said in Parliament. A delegation was chosen to go to Dublin and meet the minister. Here, the government-faction councillor was most active. His friend, the minister of state, could get the delegation a place to meet, and anything else they needed. When the delegation arrived at the grounds of parliament, it was met by the local deputies. A meeting was held and was attended by the former minister and his councillor friend, both from the faction of the former leader of their party. Had we not best be careful to see how strong our case was, they asked. What did the delegation want the minister to do? Had not work been carried out, and did this not indicate some form of compromise?

The minister for fisheries was accompanied at the meeting by the secretary of the fisheries department. The case, well known at this stage, was presented by the legal adviser. The minister asked the secretary to speak. He felt that the grounds of the locals' case were weak. Intention to invest money, preparation of a plan, and the preliminary work carried out before the picket could perhaps satisfy the conditions of the licence. This was contested hotly by the legal adviser and the Labour councillor. The minister intervened. He could only go according to the advice given to him. The secretary quoted the attorney general. The minister again spoke: Was this latter not the man paid to tell him and fellow ministers what he could do? At this stage, the exchanges were too much for some of the delegation, who suggested that the minister had gone back on his word. The minister would end the interview if this tone continued, they were told. Would he act and make it a test case on behalf of the people of the state, he was asked by the legal adviser. He would have to have permission of the Cabinet because this would involve a lot of expense. Time was up, and the meeting ended with a promise that an answer would be given on the action he would take, one way or the other, within a fortnight. The councillor of the faction in power got off the bus on the way home to ring the television network to claim that he had led a delegation to the minister for fisheries and was confident all would be well. He had left the bus to call the television station, gone on in a car, and later on had flagged down the bus to tell the occupants they had 'been on the news'. He had pulled another stroke by upstaging in particular his fellow party councillor and competitor for the nomination in the general election.

Time went by; the election atmosphere was growing. The Taoiseach was giving hints of a forthcoming election.[33] A rumour gathered ground that maybe the local people would not vote at all in the election. Meetings were now becoming dispirited. The Taoiseach was due to visit the constituency to open a hurley factory and a sports recreational centre. The suggestion was made that he be met. Earlier, the government-faction councillor had suggested contacting the Taoiseach at the funeral of the wife of a local deputy which he had been expected to attend. This had come to nothing. Some locals spoke of picketing the Taoiseach's visit.

The minister of state was most active now. A telegram arrived. The

Taoiseach would make time to see a delegation in his hotel before a celebratory dinner for his party faithful. The delegation waited in a special room while, behind the scenes, the two factions of the government party argued as to who from the party's hierachy should be allowed into the room.

The Taoiseach arrived, accompanied by the minister for fisheries and the minister of state. The by now standard speeches werc made. The Taoiseach asked a few questions about the original landlords of the area. He jokingly asked: Had they not been burnt out, and if not, why not? Amusement was shown by the party faithful present. The Taoiseach had the reputation, part of his rise to power within his party, of being not only a millionaire but 'a great republican'. 'Ye want me to make my mark in history. Is that what ye want?' he asked. The Cabinet member on one side of him winked at the people in the room. 'Yes, Taoiseach,' she replied. 'Well, I happen to believe that the resources of the country should be used for the people,' he stated. He would go to the site of the oyster beds in the morning and then make a statement. The chairman produced a little carrell of oysters wrapped in seaweed and presented them to the Taoiseach. 'Will I get them every year?' he joked, as he handed them to his private secretary to be brought away.

On the following morning, the Taoiseach was met by a cavalcade of cars, and some posters along the way made the case of the fishermen. A large crowd of onlookers had gathered as, on the previous night, a local meeting had been summoned in anticipation of good news circulated by way of rumour by the minister of state. The Taoiseach looked out to sea, at a map, and repeated his statement of the night before to the press. There was some apprehension that nothing had been decided. Negotiations were in progress and he could say no more, the minister of state whispered to a few.

Time went by, and no announcement was forthcoming. In fact, negotiations were in progress with the Bretons. Like a bolt from the blue came the announcement from the Fianna Fáil councillor of the previous leader's faction that the Bretons had agreed to sell their interest to the state, that what was important now was to have a plan for development, and he would help in this, as he had in the negotiations behind the scenes. He was able to tell the newspaper the good news through his good friend the former minister.

Consternation on the part of the minister for state and his councillor friend greeted this announcement. At the next meeting of the committee, he attacked the councillor who had made the announcement. The councillor, however, had arrived early, and under the excuse of pressure of another meeting he had left just as the minister for state arrived.

In future, the minister of state would not issue any statements except to the committee. The matter was not settled. The negotiations were still in progress. The publicity could be dangerous. Earlier, the councillor from the opposing faction had said four options had been presented to the Bretons, one of which was an ultimatum that he was not free to disclose; the meeting ended.

Meanwhile, the general election had been declared. A selection convention had seen the former minister help his councillor friend get a nomination at the expense of the minister of state's friend. At the final meeting, a letter was read by the secretary of the local committee saying that an agreement in principle to buy the oyster beds had been made. The minister of state and his councillor and other politicians attended. The councillor was now working for his friend and, in a brief speech, he suggested that thanks were due to two people in particular, the Taoiseach and the minister for state.

Not revealed at all, and not presented as the concern of anybody, were the terms of the deal. Concern was expressed that it should be made clear that the oyster beds were being bought for the people of the four parishes and not for everybody in the state. Who would invest anything if that were so?

Details are not formally available, but it appears that the Bretons accepted the deal on condition that they would be paid compensation at a rate of three times their original purchase price, that an alternative site up the coast would be found for them, and that the state agency would ensure their trouble-free introduction into such an area. An issue involving the public or private ownership of the sea bed or its public and private development, which might have served as an opportunity of state development, for political organisation by the community around a common goal for the confrontation of public interest and private gain, was thus turned into material for a clientelist exercise and a competition between local brokers.

From the weekend activity we have described, and the behaviour elicited in the handling of a community issue, we are now perhaps in a position to make some observations about the consequences of clientelism. These parallel to a very great degree those noted by Graziano for southern Italy.[34] Some are based also on observation of behaviour within the work-rooms of parliament and the accounts of deputies to the author as to how they handle their constituency work.

(a) Clientelism has led to the privatisation of state activity. It thus robs the state of any innovative role in a policy sense. Decisions are presented as the outcome of personal interventions, and not as policies put forward and debated or decided in an accountable way.

(b) As we have seen, it disorganizes the poor in that it serves as an impediment to their aggregating their demands or mobility in horizontal associations for the prosecution of such demands. We can see too that it is the vulnerability of the poor, their dependency, that makes clientelism a possibility. To explain, for example, such clientelism by analogy with the theological worldview of the poor is to seek to explain one epiphenomenon in terms of another. Common to the source of both is the structural fact of poverty.

(c) Clientelism has had a particularly disorganising effect on attempts to mobilise women in pursuit of common goals. This is exacerbated in Ireland by the low participation of women in the industrial workforce and their being thus deprived of the opportunity and experience of collective action of a trade-union kind, for example.

(d) In so far as even its prizes are illusory and fictional, it creates a consciousness of having lost out to somebody with better circumstances or more pull, and thus increases the resentment of members of the public.

(e) As it disorganises the poor, so it works against those whom they elect. Those representatives who come from business and commerce give the tedious obligation of spraying their constituency with communications to their office staff within their business. Representatives who must compete with this from their own resources, and with the meagre facilities of the Dáil, are quickly bogged down. The representatives of business interests are freer in terms of time and other resources to get on with influencing state law and state administration for the benefit of their class.

(f) We have noted how clientelism secures the collusion of the bureaucracy, local and national. This too has its effects which damage the legitimacy of the state. Such collusion has taken the form of officials answering representatives' letters in duplicate – so that one copy can be sent to the client, the other filed – and treating representatives in a manner different from the public. The effect of this is to lower even further the confidence of the citizenry in the state, and it serves to recruit those made to feel inferior by state officials to clienteles of politicians.

(g) For the political parties, clientelism has provided a particular problem. The parties may seek to react to changes in the economy, Ireland being a small, open economy, by a series of policy innovations. These may find their way to the annual conference of the parties and to the monthly meetings of their national executives, but there they stop. The elected representatives

91

will confront such policy innovations with the jibe that policies are all right in their own place but they, the representatives, know best how to get elect- ed.[35] We can add a set of generalisations as follows: policy differences are minimised as the central bureaucracies of the political parties have their influence eroded by clientelism; the small Labour Party, struggling from time to time to achieve an ideological identity, has been faced with the co- opting of its members into clientelism and, by association, into positions completely at odds with its policies; clientelism thus makes stagnant any pol- icy and ideological development.

(h) In so far as clientelism may be successful in mobilising votes, it has encour- aged the embracing by candidates of populist positions and has recruited, both at national and, particularly, local level, candidates who are committed to reactionary positions and who seek office to obtain personal commercial benefits for themselves and others.

(i) Clientelism has conversely repelled and even excluded many who feel a repugnance to what they have come to expect of political office.

(j) Related to these last points, the legislature has come to have a preponder- ance of clientelist politicians, ill-equipped in educational or motivational terms for the drafting or scrutiny of legislation and the achievement of accountability in public finances. It thus contributes to the provision of an elaborate pseudo-democratic façade to a non-accountable state.

(k) Finally, there are some consequences that we can note as arising from the effect clientelism has on public expenditure. It is enormously wasteful, as the pre-election expenditure in the recent election of 1981 demonstrated. In the weeks prior to the election, expenditure not authorised by the Dáil was announced in several constituencies with the intention of promoting the electoral prospects of the outgoing government's candidates, who were informed of the forthcoming expenditure by letter for publication in their local press.[36] Local government was thus faced with the reality that, while it could seek to assess local need and hear the views of local representatives, such an exercise was to be ignored and the requirements of clientelism to take precedence. Later, these local authorities would have to raise funds for projects on whose location they were deprived of any opportunity of expressing an opinion.

One fact impresses above all: clientelism is exploitative in source and intent. Its resources in the past included the control over real resources in terms of land credit and job opportunities. Today, its resources are illusory. We cannot, however, see any neat progression from patronage to brokerage. In a previous study, we showed that what is involved in gaining a victory in a political confrontation in a constituency is the force of the resources one can bring to bear, and these will be of a patronage kind if necessary.[37] However, we now turn to the political-science construction of the events we have been describing.

As to the consequences of clientelism in Ireland, little has been written. Schmitt is alone in suggesting that clientelism softens the impact of the state in so far as the authoritarianism of Irish culture is mediated by the opposing trait of personalism equally strong within the culture.[38] Such an assertion is not of the status of an explanation. Neither is that of Russell, who draws an analogy between the theological world-view of the peasantry and their political world-view.[39] Such an assertion takes the form of explaining one part of the culture in terms of another, while ignoring the structural underpinnings of both that have elements in common, namely poverty, insecurity and dependence. It can hardly be held to absolve political scientists from getting back beyond political behaviour to elements of political structure. Does clientelism as a conceptual apparatus help us to relate to the major issues of change in Irish society? I feel that its utility is limited to an explanation of interaction. It is a very limited perspective that describes complex contemporary dependencies, rather than explaining them in terms of origins or consequences. It is, of course, not accidental that the brokerage approach would recommend itself to Irish scholars. Its evasion of class relations fits well with the major tradition of Irish sociology and social anthropology that took as its point of departure *The Irish Countryman* of Arensberg and Kimball.[40] Indeed, class analysts have had to struggle against an ahistorical emphasis that has characterised every attempt by the many intellectual tourists that Ireland's 'simple society' has attracted.

The problems that the concept of clientelism does not solve for us in Irish politics consist of the interaction between economic and social change and politics. In the decades before Irish independence, for example, Ireland's tenants became tenant proprietors. Monetisation of rural Ireland was completed, with an elaborate range of commodities forming the basis for shop debts. Welfare payments of the modern period had their antecedents in a range of poverty-relief measures. Emigrants' remittances expanded following the post-famine emigrations.

All these changes had political effects that are not adequately conceptualised in a simple rural–urban dichotomy. Indeed, it is interesting to note that Irish economic theory had its own conceptual equivalent in the notion of the dual economy.[41] This approach contained the essential principle of there being a developed and an undeveloped region of the Irish economy.

Economic backwardness, like the system of peasant political values, was envisaged as a failure of penetration.

If it does not fit easily with historical change and adjustment, neither does the clientelist approach enable us to answer crucial contemporary issues in Irish politics. The degree of accountability within the Irish political system cannot be fully assessed from this perspective. If the content of brokerage be mythical influence, then, apart from showing how people are fooled, the model leaves major questions untreated. The structure of power or influence on state decision-making, for example, is left unexplained.

The suggestion is contained in Irish brokerage studies that the entire structure of politics is being explained. But is it? Is the state itself explained? Can legislative decisions be traced as outcomes to a brokerage system? The author is engaged on a study of one of the consequences of the clientelist character of Irish politics – the contribution it makes to the sustenance of the illusion that state decision-making is accountable in Ireland. It is hypothesised that clientelism is a characteristic of electoral activity which has the consequence of providing representatives to assemblies that create the myth of accountability.

The Irish political system is highly centralised, with the civil service providing assistance to the Cabinet (chosen from the dominant party) alone. It can be shown that, even in the weekly meetings of the party in power, little opportunity is provided for a contribution of any substantial legislative kind.

At the county level, Irish politics is administratively centralised to a unique degree by European standards. The county manager holds effective power of administration, which consists of relaying state decisions down to county level. The manager, however, is anxious to deflect the scrutiny of the public from such a concentration of power and creates an elaborate form of 'consultation' through the statutory monthly meetings of county councils. The councillors, anxious not to appear as powerless to the public, initiate enquiries on matters of routine administration which are promptly answered by the county secretariat in duplicate: one copy for the councillor' s files, one for the client. When the councillor becomes a member of parliament, he is already socialised into this collusion in illusory accountability. The consequence is that no real accountability exists in a general sense at national or county level. The accountability is in a formal compliance with the constitutional requirements. It has no public-participatory dimension.

A clientelist approach to Irish politics leaves many of the most significant problems unexplained. Its empirical character ignores structural determinants. What is required is a more general theory that can handle the relationships of economic and political change of an even and uneven kind, and that can include a critique of the state.

Elsewhere, I have raised the issue of whether within 'strong' or 'weak' transactionalism the patronage/brokerage approach has real utility.[42] The case studies examined suggested some support for 'weak' transactionalism. However, anomalies remained. First, patronage was not replaced by brokerage universally: for example, credit bondage in rural Ireland endured. Secondly, the survival of patronage did not represent anything 'traditional' but rather was anchored to commercial relations specific to a commodity economy. Finally, while brokerage replaced patronage in general terms, in one of our case studies patronage relations were the more effective in assuring a favourable outcome.

I am convinced now that further research aimed at close examination of the basis of dependency, and of the economic relationships of rural Ireland and their related effects, is a more fruitful intellectual project that will lead to an explanation of patronage and brokerage rather than to arid empirical description.

In conclusion, I am left with the questions I raised some years ago about political theory in Ireland. How adequate is modernisation theory for the general understanding of the major changes I have referred to? Changes in Irish society contradict its essential linear and evolutionary pretensions. Gibbon and I raised two general issues in concluding our first study of patrons and clients six years ago. The first was the adequacy of modernisation theory:

> In the Irish case, 'progress' appears in actuality to have taken the form of the combined and uneven development of different modes of production, combining a diversity of elements from classical 'feudalism' and classical 'capitalism', which, while ultimately deriving their co-presence from the dominance of successive forms of metropolitan capitalism, cannot be regarded as transparent 'expressions' either of its developmental principles or of any sociological description of its rationalistic properties.
>
> In Ireland, at least, neither the economy nor the state developed through a progression of simple evolutionary stages, nor did changes in the rest of the social formation appear to 'correspond' directly to changes occurring in the 'essential' sector. In our case studies at least, the clue to transitions in patronage–client relations should be sought not in

any general theory of modernisation but in some theory which is able to grasp the specificity of particular forms of uneven economic and political development and their determination.[43]

The second issue we raised was as to whether it was possible to amalgamate political anthropology with a different (i.e. non-evolutionist) theory of social change while still retaining its characteristic subject-matter and methodology.[44] Modern transactionalism's substitution of 'actual behaviour' concepts of social networks, for example for functionalism's categories, such as 'role' or 'status', condemns us to remain at the level of description.[45]

These general issues remain. I am convinced that the clientelist approach seriously sells us short and distracts attention from the real basis of economic exploitation, political domination and ideological manipulation in Irish society.

From Private Patronage and Public Power: Political Clientelism in the Modern State, Christopher Clapham (ed.), Cambridge University Press, 1982

The Gombeenman in Fact and Fiction[1]

Writing from Cork on 2 December 1880, Bernard H. Becker had this to say of the subject of this article:

> During my stay in Ennis and Limerick, I succeeded in holding somewhat protracted conversations with three landed proprietors, three of the largest land agents in Ireland, two bank managers, an influential lawyer, three leaders of the people, and one probable assassin. Through the discourse of all of these – varied and contradictory as much of it necessarily was – I could see distinctly one ugly shadow, as of an old man filthy of aspect, hungry of eye, and greedy of claw, sitting in the rear of a gloomy store looking over papers by the light of a miserable tallow dip. From the papers the figure turned to a heap as of banknotes, and there was in the air the chink of money. For the name of this grisly, and terribly real spectre, is 'gombeen'; which, in the Irish tongue, signifies usury.[2]

This was not the first reference to the gombeenman. De Bhaldraithe, for example, has instanced the reference in the *Times* of 18 October 1845:

> The word 'gombeen' simply means an extortioner, but the sale of meal or oats was the usual method of evading the usury laws by exacting enormous interest.

The Oxford English Dictionary gives Coulter's *The West of Ireland* (1862) as the earliest usage. This, as De Bhaldraithe has shown, is not correct. The same writer has shown that it is from a confusion of two words, *gaimbi* (interest) and *gaimbín* (a small portion) that the word 'gombeen' in English comes, and that the Irish word *gaimbín* now has three distinct usages.[3]

However, it is the actions of the gombeenman that interest us. It is the view of the writer that an examination of these will illuminate some issues in political science, economic history, sociology and Anglo-Irish literary criticism. Specifically, the novelty of brokerage referred to by recent writers on Irish political life is suggested to be the logical flaw of a false theoretical position, rather than a historical fact within economic history. The writing on the origins of credit institutions will be shown not only to present an apologia for such institutions in the twentieth century but also to reach back to rescue the gombeenman from previous and present opprobrium.

The gombeenman's activities reveal also the myth of a harmonious rural community established as the received version of Irish rural life in the 1930s by Conrad Arensberg and Sol Kimball.[4] The use of literary evidence as a subversive voice of truth will be made when the formal economic history has become so apologetic that it seeks to rehabilitate a figure of general opprobrium of which writers from Carleton to O'Flaherty and O'Donnell were unsparing.[5] The structure of literary patronage will be seen as an obstacle to the establishment of social typifications in the work of Liam O'Flaherty. The depiction of the growth of the acquisitive impulse presented in the same writer's brillant story 'Two Lovely Beasts', published in 1946, will be referred to as suggestive of a whole range of nuances in the ingress of the cash-nexus economy to an island economy, a subject still the interest of Peadar O'Donnell almost thirty years afterwards.[6] The rehabilitation of the gombeenman occurs in a context of ideas which has sought to present uncritically an image of Irish history as the shared experience of disaster. The present article is a small contribution to the case for interdisciplinary treatment of historical themes but, more importantly, to the presentation of successfully hidden contradictions of Irish rural society from the nineteenth century to the foundation of the present state.

The principal source of evidence of the activities of the gombeenman in the second half of the nineteenth century are the letters by Coulter and Becker to their respective journals, *Saunders's Newsletter* and the *Daily News*.[7] Coulter's correspondence was published in 1862 under the title *The West of Ireland*, Becker's in 1881 under the title *Disturbed Ireland*. Coulter's examples are taken from the western counties, while Becker's letters are written from the south and claim to be written from an experience of both the southern and western counties. He is not specific in his locations as Coulter is. Coulter's letter from Castlebar, County Mayo, is a very useful description of the precise practice and circumstances of the gombeenman's activities:

> The system of borrowing money from loan offices and 'gombeen' men is universally practised in this country; and as the rate of interest charged is enormously high, the unfortunate people who resort to this mode of obtaining money are constantly in a state of embarrassment, which an unfavourable season develops into one of distress. A 'gombeen' man is one of the peasant-class who has contrived to accumulate some money, which he tuns to account by lending to his poorer neighbours at usurious interest. For instance, suppose a loan of £1 is asked, the borrower

only receives 17s. 7d – 1s. being stopped for interest, 3d for the price of the card, 2d for the IOU, and 1s. for the first instalment. Nineteen shillings must then be paid back to the lender in weekly instalments of one shilling each, and there is besides a fine of one penny in the pound imposed for every default in the weekly payment. Shopkeepers are also in the habit of selling meal and guano to the country people on credit, and charging high prices. The giving out of guano in this way is practised by some land agents, who sell quantities of it to the tenants in spring, the debt thus incurred to be paid at Christmas, and the price charged being seventeen and eighteen shillings per cwt. for what is selling in the market for cash at fourteen shillings per cwt. When the tenants come to pay their rent, this private debt is first demanded, and the landlord's rent must afterwards be forthcoming.

The result of this practice is injurious in many ways. Heretofore, the farmers did not know what artificial manures were. They used seaweed, mud, and lime mixed, and farmyard manure, which they collected laboriously and industriously throughout the year. Now, however, the facility of obtaining artificial manures engenders laziness and idleness. The small farmers will say: 'What is the use of killing ourselves collecting manure? Sure, won't we get a cwt. of guano for sixteen or seventeen shillings, and no carting, or working, or trouble at all?' Accordingly, instead of consuming their own straw, as formerly, in turning it into manure, they sell it to the large farmers for that purpose, and buy guano, which, with the imperfect mode of tillage that they pursue, is by no means beneficial to the land. When a farmer sowed an acre of potatoes with farmyard manure, he obtained in ordinary years a good crop, and had 'soil' suited for grain in the following year, besides improving the land. Guano, on the contrary, forces a crop for one year, leaving the land almost useless for grain. Then, when the crop manured with guano chances to fail, which was universally the case last season in this part of the country, the cultivator loses not only his crop and his labour, but some £4 an acre which he has expended in the purchase of artificial manure; whereas formerly, in case of failure, he lost only his crop and his labour. Another point to be remarked is that, while these people are very chary of spending their money when they have to pay in cash for their purchases, they are so improvident that they will accept credit to any amount; and the facility afforded them by shopkeepers and sub-agents of obtaining guano 'on time' induces them recklessly to incur debts which they must pay. The result of this is to be seen in the number of decrees for small sums which are obtained against them at every quarter sessions by shopkeepers, gombeenmen and others to whom they have become indebted. At Castlebar, there were but few decrees obtained at the last session, but at Westport there were a great many. At Swinford also there were over four hundred undefended decrees; and it is expected that at the present sessions there will be double that number, the sums sought to be recovered varying from £1 to £3.

Some essential features are revealed by this account: the high rate of interest, the manipulation of innovation as a basis of exploitation (the guano of the nineteenth century becomes the modernisation grant of the twentieth century), the ignorance of the precise rate of interest, the use of court decrees, and the small amounts involved. This last seems to be important since the survival of the gombeenman's activity after the establishment and extension of the banking system was made possible by his readiness to advance small sums on very weak security at high rates, the banks concentrating on more secure debtors for larger amounts with a more regular, if exploitative, rate.

In the same letter, Coulter also adverts to another feature of the gombeenman's practice – the attempt to retain in outer appearances the characteristics of the general peasantry. He writes of Derrycoosh, County Mayo:

> Words fail to convey an adequate idea of the filthy and disorderly appearance which this village presents. So bad it is, that a road is actually in course of construction for the purpose of avoiding the abominations of Derrycoosh. And yet, squalid and miserable as the place looks, I am told that it is one of the most independent villages in Mayo. It can boast of several gombeenmen, who possess from three to six hundred pounds apiece. I saw one of the wealthiest of these persons as I was passing through the village. He was dressed like any ordinary peasant, and his house was one of the worst-looking in the place, having most of the objectionable features of the others, with this additional one, that the windows were stuffed with straw.[9]

We are also told of the extent of these practices and the manner in which the formal legal process was invoked, with the shopkeeper or land agent seeking priority for the recovery of his debt:

> The extortions of the usurers, who are to be found in almost every country town, also press very severely on the unfortunate people whose necessities force them to have recourse to those harpies, for the mass of the people are absolutely ignorant of the commercial value of money,

and though they feel the burden, and sometimes sink under it, they do not really know how atrociously they have been 'fleeced'. Fifty, sixty, seventy, eighty, and one hundred percent are frequently charged by these money-lenders. Here are two illustrations of the system. A farmer applies for the loan of £5; he receives only £4 15s., and has to repay the.sum nominally borrowed at the rate of £1 1s. per month for five months. In other cases a shilling in the pound is deducted in the first instance on lending the money, and interest is charged afterwards at the rate of six pence per pound per month until the loan is repaid.

I leave it to your readers to calculate for themselves the rate of interest which is charged in these cases; but there are several instances in which the interest levied exceeds 100 percent. The money is advanced generally without risk to the lender, for he always takes care to have two or three names on the IOU, and is able to recover the amount at any time he pleases. If the debtor appears to be in embarrassed circumstances before the half-year's rent becomes payable, the usurer runs at once to the quarter sessions, takes out a decree, and thus anticipates the landlord in demanding payment of his rent. A large number of the decrees which have been issued at the last quarter sessions in the counties of Galway and Clare are of this description.

Becker's account suggests that the banking system functioned as an improvement on the gombeen system and he describes how both responded to the increment of proprietary rights given tenants by the Land Acts:

As the peer, who would never have put his hand into his own pocket to pay for improving his property, suddenly wakes to the value of draining when the government offers a million and a half at 1 per cent, so did the gombeen man, who would never have dreamed of lending more than a pound at a time to a peasant, extend his credit four or five fold when the Land Act of 1870 gave him the first instalment of proprietary right in the land he occupied. The instalment was a very small one, but it was at once discounted by the gombeenman, whose rate of interest enabled him to run extraordinary risks.

As the poor pay dearly for everything, so do they pay an extravagant interest for money. There was once a fashionable West-end usurer who, pretending to know nothing about arithmetic, met his clients on the subject of percentage with 'I don't understand figures, but my terms are a shilling per pound every month. It is easy to reckon up without going into sums on slates.' This poor innocent was charging just 60 percent, but his terms were lavishly liberal as compared with those of the gombeenman. Instead of a shilling per month, the latter charges a shilling a week for every sovereign advanced, and then 'Begorra, it's only the name of a sovereign', which being interpreted signifies that an advance of one pound, less charges, only amounts to 18s. 10d., and that upon this sum a shilling interest must be well and duly paid weekly. Any failure entails a fine, and a failure to pay off the original sovereign borrowed within six months is very heavily fined indeed. I am told that the gombeenman actually puts on 100 percent for this failure of redemption; but, on my principle of believing only a percentage of all I hear, and of taking a liberal discount of all I see, I doubt this enormity. Concerning the shilling interest per week on a pound, there is, however, unhappily no room for doubt, and for small unsecured loans 260 percent per annum is still the ruling figure.

This enormous rate of interest, however, is now only exacted on the very smallest loans, for the old-fashioned gombeenman has lost his customers for larger sums. In old times, he was the only means of obtaining such little sums as five and ten pounds on personal security; but since 1870 the banks have entered into competition with him, have undersold him and, in fact, have 'run him out of the market', except for sums under four or five pounds. The unfortunates who are short of a sovereign or two must look up their old friend in the back shop smelling of bacon, tallow, pepper, tea and whisky, just as their social superiors seek the intrepid 60 percent man of St James's, whose snuggery is perfumed by the best Havannahs that other people's money can buy. But when the soul of Mike rises to the sublime conception of a loan of five pounds, he dismisses the old-fashioned usurer, and hies him to one of the branch banks which abound in every petty townlet in western and southern Ireland. When I say 'abound', I mean to be taken literally. What would be thought in England, I wonder, of four banks in a town like Ennis, or of two in pettifogging places like Kilrush or Ennistymon – mere hamlets of some two thousand inhabitants? Yet these three places have eight branch banking establishments among them. It must not, however, be supposed that Mike gets his paltry four or five pounds on his promissory note without further security. Nothing of the kind. Mike must go through as much artful financiering to raise his five pounds as the Hon. Algernon Deuceace to raise his 'monkey'.

His bill must be well backed by his friends, Thady and Tim. Now, Thady's name on the back of a five-pound bill is not good for much. He is but a peasant, like Mike, not a farmer, properly so called, and even as two blacks will not make a white, so will the joint credit of Mike and

102

Thady not rise to the height of five one-pound notes. But they have a potent ally in Tim, who married Thady's wife's cousin. Tim is a prudent man, has worked hard at his farm and, as a rule, has a matter of twenty or thirty pounds on deposit at the bank, receiving for the same interest at the rate of 1 percent per annum. His name at the back of a five-pound bill is therefore a tower of strength, and, in fact, floats the entire speculation. In commercial phrase, he 'stands to be shot at' while his own deposit money, on which he receives 1 percent, supplies the funds for the bank to lend Mike and Thady, at 10 or 20 percent, for there is no pretence made of doing very small bills at anything approaching ordinary rates. In fact, the present cultivator, acquired under the Land Acts now in force a species of proprietory interest in the soil, has a sort of credit which, backed by a friendly and innocent depositor, can be made an engine for raising ready money in a small way. This help from the banks is so far good that it has relieved the decent peasant from his ancient bloodsucker, the gombeenman. Admitting that, with charges and fine for renewal and so forth, the loan ultimately costs Mike 15 or 20 percent, he is vastly better off than he was under the old system. He gets money to buy pigs to fatten for sale, or manure for his bit of arable land, and if the rate appears high, it is wondrously merciful as compared with that to which he was formerly accustomed.[11]

We have seen how the outsiders who travelled in rural Ireland after the Great Famine described the gombeenman's activities. It is useful now perhaps to consider a typical example of the favourable estimation of his role. Donnelly is one of the most strident:

This general diffusion of retail outlets made possible an enormous extension in the volume of credit given to labourers, and especially to farmers, during the difficult years of depression. The whole subject of credit transactions in nineteenth-century Irish rural society demands fuller analysis than it has so far received. Some historians have shown a misleading tendency to equate the credit-granting shopkeeper with the notorious 'gombeen' man. This equation, to be sure, was frequently made by contemporary writers. Shopkeepers were often branded in the public press as 'meanmongers' who sold Indian meal on time at grossly inflated prices, a practice which, where it existed, concealed the charging of heavy interest. It was quite apparent that shopkeepers bulked large among those who secured civil-hill decrees at quarter sessions. But it is highly unlikely that shopkeepers were generally regarded as detestable usurers by their regular clientele. In popular estimation, the true gombeen men were the operators of those loan offices and pawn shops which proliferated in western towns and villages, the small land agents and bailiffs who provided guano or seed at exorbitant rates, and especially well-to-do tenants who made a lucrative business of lending money to their needy neighbours. Well-informed contemporaries appreciated the constructive role which the enlarged body of shopkeepers played in alleviating hunger by their willingness to allow customers to pile up debts far out of proportion to current means. Shopkeepers may well have kept a watchful eye on their debtors' livestock for signs of total collapse, but this was only elementary caution.[12]

In his anxiety to favourably represent the general category of retailers, Donnelly ignores the gombeenman's activities we have been commenting upon as a serious oppression of the peasantry by one from their own ranks:

What seems beyond question is that, without the great increase in both the number of shopkeepers and the availabillity of retail credit, the fears of mass starvation expressed by many of the western clergy and gentry would have been at least partly confirmed.[13]

Lynch and Vaizey justify the gombeenman's activity as part of the general modernisation of the Irish economy understood particularly in the sense of a differentiation of consumption patterns. The differentiation resulting in the purchase of commodities for cash, made possible more and more by emigrant's remittances, was equated with 'improvement':

The poverty of Irish country people after the Great Famine was often attributed to the activities of the 'gombeen man', but it is not clear what these men are alleged to have done with the money they made from their activities. It seems probable, in fact, that in contrast to many of their clients they stayed in their towns and sooner or later spent their money. The general level of prosperity, therefore, was (at the very least) unaffected, though the distribution of income may have been changed in their favour. The 'gombeen man' usually bought a grocery and whiskey shop, so that the two classes of moneylenders coalesced. The factors made advances for cattle and butter. These were still the main source of cash and credit inside Ireland, because the banks lent only at high rates of interest on good security to substantial people. The other sources of cash came from outside Ireland. The Connaught and Ulster farmers went to England every year, 'the money brought back from England in this way exceeds the rental'.

Between 1848 and 1860, there was a rise in money-incomes in rural Ireland. Some of it came from emigrants' remittances. A class of merchants and shopkeepers emerged; the increase in the number of shop assistants was a sign of this. There was a growth in the number of agricultural labourers paid in money. Diet habits changed. Food was considerably more varied. The consumption of porter became widespread. There is evidence of an improvement in the standard of living of the country folk in the reports of the various royal commissions which investigated rural Ireland. The economy now rested on a healthier basis.[14]

It is interesting, too, to see the manner in which the most monstrous usurious activity's side-by-side existence with emerging famine goes without comment in the same authors' anxiety to identify approvingly with Campbell Foster's comment of over a hundred years earlier:

> There was a great growth of credit during the year 1846–47. In Skibbereen, forty thousand pawn-tickets were issued in the three winter months in a town of fewer than five thousand inhabitants. Without the 'gombeen man' – the village money-lender – the effects of the Great Famine might have been worse; much distress might have been avoided if earlier there had been more of his retail trading activities. The evils of the gombeen system have been exaggerated, and its bad reputation was due mainly to the scarcity of retailing facilities in Ireland, which gave the gombeen man a monopoly and so a power of exploitation.[15]

Following the examination of the role of the gombeenman within the model of patronage in economic, political and ideological terms in contemporary Irish political fairs, Kennedy has accused Gibbon and the present writer of contributing to a demonology.[16] His rehabilitation follows the Donnelly lines, with the addition of an invocation of a 'value-free' position that takes existing credit institutions and their precedents as unquestioned rationality.

If economic historians have been apologetic to him, the gombeenman has been singled out by writers right through the nineteenth century to the present, from Carleton to Bonfighlioli, for unrelenting derision.[17] The literary accounts do more than correct the hagiography of credit. They present a number of characteristics that enable us to feel the presence of the gombeenman in the community, and indeed come near to establishment of a type that encapsulates one of the contradictions of rural society.

Carleton, writing in 1817 in *The Black Prophet*, had this to say of the rural usurer:

> There is to be found in Ireland, and, we presume, in all other countries, a class of hardened wretches, who look forward to a period of dearth as to one of great gain and advantage, and who contrive, by exercising the most heartless and diabolical principles, to make the sickness, famine, and general desolation which scourge their fellow-creatures, so many sources of successful extortion and rapacity, and consequently of gain to themselves.
>
> These are country misers, or money-lenders, who are remarkable for keeping meal until the arrival of what is termed a hard year, or a dear summer, when they sell it out at enormous or usurious prices, and who, at all times and under all circumstances, dispose of it only at terms dictated by their own griping spirit, and the crying necessity of the unhappy purchasers.[18]

We owe to Carleton the creation of the character of Darby Skinadre, the country miser. In drawing his character, Carleton was to anticipate the ideological manipulation of the gombeenman. The invocation of religion is revealed in the passage which follows. In the following century, the national flag was to join the crucifix as the presiding symbol in the literary accounts. The banks, always more sophisticated, were to prominently display the portrait of a well-fed Daniel O'Connell. In the passage, we see the easy transition of Darby from considerations of a spiritual kind to those of commerce:

> 'Well, Jemmy Duggan,' proceeded the miser, addressing a newcomer, 'what's the news wid you? They're hard times, Jemmy; we all know that, an' feel it, too, an' yet we live, most of us, as if there wasn't a God to punish us.'
>
> 'At all events,' replied the man, 'we feel that sufferin' is now, God help us! Between hunger and sickness, the country was never in such a state widin the memory of man. What, in the name o' God, will become of the poor people, I know not. The Lord pity them, an' relieve them.'
>
> 'Amen, amen, Jemmy! Well, Jemmy, can I do anything for you? But, Jemmy, in regard of that, the truth is, we have brought all these scourges on us by our sins and our transgressions; thim that sins Jemmy, must suffer.'
>
> 'There's no one denyin' it, Darby; but you're axin' me can you do anything for me, an' my answer to that is, that you can, if you like.'
>
> 'Ah! Jemmy, you wor ever an' always a wild, heedless, heerum-

skeerum rake, that never was likely to do much good; little religion every rested on you, an' now I'm afeared so sign's on it.'

'Well, well, who's widout sin? I'm sure I'm not. What I want is, to know if you'll credit me for a hundred of meal till the times mends a trifle. I have the six o' them at home widout their dinner this day, an' must go widout it, if you refuse me. When the harvest comes round, I'll pay you.'

'Jemmy, you owe three half-years' rent; an' as for the harvest an' what it'll bring, only jist look at the day that's in it. It goes to my heart to refuse you, poor man; but, Jemmy, you see that you have brought this on yourself. If you had been an attentive, industrious man an' minded your religion, you wouldn't be as you are now. Six you have at home, you say?'[19]

If Carleton was to give us Darby Skinadre, it is undoubtedly Ramon Mór Costello who is the gombeenman par excellence of literature.[20] In this character, Liam O'Flaherty sought to achieve a résumé of the character of Máirtin Mór McDonagh and his uncle. Between Carleton's creation and that of O'Flaherty, shopkeeping had become recognised as an activity that brought wealth and mobility. It also brought adulation and 'respect'. We will discuss Ramon Mór in detail, but let us first look at shopkeeping as a prospect for getting on in the world.

O'Flaherty gives us the following discussion among the Derrane family in his story 'Two Lovely Beasts', in which Colm Derrane, having beaten local prophecy for doom by rearing two calves on one cow, describes his next success and rise in the world:

'I have a plan,' Colm said. 'We are going to open a shop.' His wife made the sign of the Cross on her forehead and looked at him in horror.

'Why not?' said Colm. 'It's only shopkeepers that rise in the world.'

'Are you crazy? his wife said. 'Where would we get the money to open a shop?'

'All we need is courage,' Colm said. 'The few pounds we have saved, together with the price of the pigs, will be enough to open it. I'm telling you, woman, that all we need is courage and willingness. If we all work together night and day . . . '

'God Almighty!' his wife interrupted. 'You've gone mad. Those two beasts have gone to your head.'

'No, then,' said Colm. 'That's not true at all. I was never wiser in my life. The war will last for years yet. It's only now the real fury is coming on the fighting nations. Very well, then. While the mad people are fighting and killing each other, let us make money out of them and rise in the world. There is going to be a demand for everything that can by eaten. There will be a price for everything fit to make your mouth water. Food is going to be more precious than gold. So will clothes. In God's name, then, let us open a shop and stock it with goods.

'Let us go around the parish with our horse and cart, buying up everything the people have to sell, eggs and butter and caragean moss and fish and wool and hides and potatoes. We'll buy everything that can be carted away. We can pay them for what we buy with shop goods. Do you see? Then we'll sell what we buy from the people over in the town at a profit. Later on, we can buy sheep as well and . . . '

'Arrah! You're stark crazy,' his wife interrupted angrily. 'Stop talking like that, man alive, in front of the children.'

At this moment, all the children burst into tears, no longer able to contain their disappointment.

'Stop whinging,' Colm shouted, as he leaped to his feet. 'Is it crying you are because there will be nothing for you from the fair? All right, then. I'm telling you now there will be plenty of sweets and dai-dais for you. Do you hear me? Every day in the year will be like fair day for you.'

His uncouth face, worn to the bone by privation and worry, now glowed with the light of ecstasy, as he struggled to wheedle his family into co-operation with his ambition to 'rise in the world'. Such was the power of the idea that possessed him, that the children stopped crying almost at once. They listened with eagerness to his fantastic promises. Their little faces became as radiant as his own. His wife also became affected, as she saw her young husband trying to win over the children by means of smiles and gaiety and honeyed words. 'I wouldn't believe it,' she said, 'only for I see it with my own eyes.' Tears rolled down her cheeks and her upper lip trembled. 'In fifteen years,' she muttered, as she rubbed her eyes with a corner of her apron, 'I never once saw him dance one of the children on his knee. No, faith, I never once saw him shake a rattle in front of a whinging baby. Yet there he is now, all of a sudden, trying to make a showman of himself. God Almighty! Only for I see it with my own two eyes . . .'

'There will be no end to the riches we'll have when we are shop-keepers,' Colm continued. 'We can have bacon for breakfast. Yes, indeed, we can eat great big rashers of it every morning in the year, except Fridays. The people of the village will be coming to smell the lovely food that's frying on our pan. Oh! I'm telling you that we can have bellies on us like tourists. We'll hardly be able to carry ourselves, as we walk the road, on account of our fat. We'll have ribbons as well and velvet and a mirror in every room.'[21]

Not only the literary accounts give us evidence of the influence of shop-keepers. The Royal Commission on Labour of 1893 contains reference to payment of shop debts by labour, hay and cash from America.[22] The ledger accounts examined show regular estimations by the shopkeeper of the cred-it-worthiness of families.

However, the habit of living on credit had a more serious effect in pol-itical terms. The evidence of Father Flatley, who had served in nine parishes from Spiddal to Achill and hence had an exeptionally extensive acquaintance with the conditions of the people all through that district, is particularly important.[23] It represents a thread of continuity with the old forms of gom-been activity and the newer retail activity. Most importantly, it shatters the myth of the novelty of contemporary Irish brokerage offered by Chubb, Bax, Sacks et al:

52311 In addition to the want of employment and the scarcity of land and the bad quality of the land, there is another cause of poverty to which I wish to call the very serious attention of the Commission, and I believe that it is worse than all other causes of poverty in the congest-ed districts, and that is the habit which the people have acquired of liv-ing on credit and of paying exorbitant prices for the goods that are sup-plied to them. The consequences are not merely economic conse-quences, which are very bad, but there are also terrible consequences of another kind to the man who is his actual slave. Practically he must elect the shopkeeper or his nominee to the District Council or to the County Council, and every other position that is going, with the most frightful results to the district. Another very bad thing in Connemara, and one which is injurious, is that they have to a very large extent got a very low class of magistrates, who are not the right kind of men to appoint. There are about ten or twelve magistrates who are provision dealers. You have most of the District Councillors and County Councillors provision dealers. Without talking of the disadvantage of that to the general com-munity who deal with them, it is decidedly unfair to the provision deal-ers who are not magistrates or members of the Council, and causes a preference to be given to the men who are on the Council or who are magistrates; because the magistrates utilise their position on the bench for the purpose of promoting their business. It is quite a common thing to see magistrates back out their own customers in the face of evidence. They do not look upon it as a thing to be ashamed of, although it is a most flagrant injustice, but as an advertisement for their business.

That is a very well-recognised thing all over Connemara, and on account of this there is tremendous rivalry among shopkeepers and intriguing and canvassing going on for years and years to try to get on the bench as a means of promoting their trade by the way in which they act unfairly in support of their own customers. And not only is this so, but it is a well-known fact that magistrates go to the length of coaching witnesses as to the evidence they will give before the court, and an awful curse in this district, at all events before we got this present doctor, was to use influence with drunken doctors to give such evidence as would either bear heavily upon or tend to make light the charge against people in assault cases. So that it is not only economically but socially a large number of magistrates in the district are the greatest curse in it. I say that deliberately from a knowledge of the facts, and I am not alone in my opinion on that subject; and wonder is that the country is not peaceable considering the injustice that is done very often in the courts. When people could not get justice in the courts, they took justice into their own hands, and there is a great deal of that prevails in that part of the country. I have often been struck with what [Henry] Hallam says in his *History of the Middle Ages*, that most of these disturbances arose from the fact that it was impossible to get justice in the courts.

52373 What you want to impress on the Commission is that one of the causes of poverty and one of the causes of perpetuating congestion and keeping the people from rising is an inflated and exaggerated credit system – is not that what it all comes to? – Yes.

52374 Is there anything in the nature of truck in the business of shopkeeper and people? – Yes, very extensive The shopkeeper gets their cattle and their pigs and sometimes gets holdings of land. Within the last month I saw a specially endorsed writ issued for shop goods against a tenant so that his holding might be seized.

52375 If a customer wants to buy tea, we will say, and to sell eggs, they are exchanged? – Yes. The eggs are sent to the shop and he gets tea and sugar in exchange for the eggs. And when a man is in debt to the shopkeeper, the shopkeeper will watch his cattle at the fair, and he will buy the cattle, and you may be perfectly certain that the shopkeeper will not pay too much for them. Here is another way in which it works out. The origin of a good many shops in Connemara, Achill and County Mayo is that a man got a contract for a bridge or a road or some public

110

work for the government. Immediately he got the contract he started a shop just beside the work, and paid the people, not in cash, but altogether in truck. That is a very common thing through the place. Several shops commenced in that way, and men who were very poor when they got their first contract are very well-off today, and they are the graziers and the grabbers of the country.[24]

It is quite astonishing what political explanations uprooted from history will produce. Chubb, in 1963, located an explanation for brokerage in the psyche of the Irish people:

In the past, oligarchic rule, underemployment and poverty all led most Irish people to view government, even though it was alien, as a potential source of help, jobs or favours, provided one knew how to tap it. By most people, public authorities were thought to be best approached via some intermediary or notable. Forty years' independence notwithstanding, authority is to some extent still thought of in these terms, a potential source of benefits or grants (though no longer to any great extent of jobs), still to be viewed with some suspicion, and still needing the intervention or good offices of a man 'in the know' or a person of affairs.[25]

Bax, taking for granted completely the family system described by Arensberg and Kimball, locates his explanation within the organisation of the family. Indeed, politics becomes a residual activity:

Why then do farmers, shopkeepers, publicans, and the others mentioned command much time for political purposes? At first glance this factor is not evident for them. There is nothing inherent to their occupations which allows them much spare time. However, if we look at the organisational structure of their economic units, which has been amply described by Arensberg and Kimball, much will become clearer. In Ireland, shopkeepers and publicans leave much of the work to the housewife, some resident niece or aunt, or to a grown-up daughter or son, and many of them have a servant for the busy hours of the day. The same is true for the farmers. Partly due to the inheritance system, the children stay long at home, and they can do the work, together with some farm hands, the housewife or an unmarried relative resident in the household. Apparently, then, farmers, small businessmen, publicans and shopkeepers do not have to invest all their time in the management of their enterprises. They can leave much of the work to others while maintaining only the direction. Thus, if they wish, they can invest the surplus time in political activities.[26]

The most alarming error is that of Sacks, who ignores the gombeenman and his emerging political influence altogether:

Political patrons are a relatively novel feature of Donegal society. As noted . . . Irish rural society had no traditional group of patrons like those in many Mediterranean societies. The large Protestant landowners may have had a group of Protestant clients, but Catholics, who were the majority of the country's population, were largely disenfranchised. The influence of such leaders as existed within Catholic society (priests and, later, nationalist leaders) was traditionally restricted to narrow confines. Only with the enfranchisement of Roman Catholics and their later entry into power were the institutions of authority permeable to Catholic influence. Thus the traditional rural patron, whose influence arose from his position, namely as the owner of land or of a large business, was more the exception than the rule in Ireland. Today this situation is changing. Party politicians now fill this role of patron. In fact, a large proportion of the politically influential are those with positions in political parties.[27]

Historically located explanations wear better We have seen how some political and economic issues are raised, by an examination of the gombeenman's activities and the consequences thereby. If the literary evidence exposes an apologetic economic history and a historical political analysis, the sociological models of Irish society accepted uncritically, with the outstanding exception of Gibbon, also show weaknesses.[28] The formal literary criticism which has developed around Anglo-Irish literature has, to its cost, ignored the social circumstances, the social background, and the patronage structure of literature itself. What is very clear is that the gombeenman's activities were well-known to the principals of the Anglo-Irish Literary Revival. Æ (George Russell) could be quoted in the *Galway Express* of 7 September 1910 as describing the power of the gombeenman in the following terms:

All the local appointments are in their gift, and hence you get drunken doctors, drunken rate collectors, drunken JPs, drunken inspectors – in fact, round the gombeen system reels the whole drunken congested world, and underneath this revelry and jobbery the unfortunate peasant labours and gets no return for his labour. Another enters and takes his cattle, his eggs, his oats, his potatoes, his pigs, and gives what he will for them, and the peasant toils on from year to year, being doled out Indian meal, flour, tea and sugar, enough to keep him alive. He is a slave almost

112

as much as if he were an indentured native and had been sold in the slave markets.[29]

Synge knew very well what the gombeenman represented in the Irish countryside. He could write to a friend:

> There are many sides of all that western eye, the groggy – patriot – publican – general shopman who is married to the priest's half-sister and is second cousin once removed of the dispensory doctor, that are horrible and awful. This is the type that is running the present United Irish League anti-grazier campaign, while they're swindling the people themselves in a dozen ways and then buying out their holdings and packing off whole families to America. The subject is too big to go into here, but at best it's beastly. All that side of the matter of course I left untouched in my stuff. I sometimes wish to God I hadn't a soul, and then I could give myself up to putting those lads on the stage. God, wouldn't they hop! In a way it is all heart-rending; in one place the people are starving but wonderfully attractive and charming, and in another place where things are going well, one has a rampant, double-chinned vulgarity I haven't seen the like of. As you know, I have the wildest admiration for the Irish peasants, and for Irish men and women of known or unknown genius – do you know? – but between the two there's an ungodly ruck of fat-faced, sweaty-headed swine.[30]

The loss for literary criticism has been that not only Synge, but those whose task it more explicitly might be if a serious criticism of Anglo-Irish literature were to be attempted, have ignored the unsavoury features of Irish rural life and their mediator the gombeenman. Patrick Sheeran is an exception.[31] His study of O'Flaherty's novels presents us with the social complexities from which the writer worked. He stops short of an explanation in social or literary terms of the gap between O'Flaherty's material for *The House of Gold*, for example, and the text itself.

Our concluding section deals with the historical figure of Máirtin Mór McDonagh and the character based largely on Máirtin Mór in O'Flaherty's novel *The House of Gold*.[32]

It has been said earlier that retail and commercial innovators were treated pejoratively in literature in the last and present century. This could not be said of the newspapers that had been established by the commercial classes in the new Irish state. It was noted earlier that economic history had been apologetic and that literature had stood in contrast. No contrast could be greater than the newspaper tributes to Máirtin Mór McDonagh and the literary depiction of Ramon Mór Costello. O'Flaherty introduced us to Ramon in his drawing room in the following terms:

> Ramon Mór stood on a black rug in front on the empty fireplace with his hands behind his back. With the hair of the rug around his boots, he had the appearance of a large animal standing on a grassy place. He was wearing his hat. His head was thrust forward. His baggy throat, pressed upwards by the collar of his starched shirt front, surged about his jaw in folds. His underlip protruded. His little eyes, fixed on the doctor, looked sinister. The row of hair sticking up behind the rim of his hat on the back of his skull resembled the raised mane of an animal. Enormous, shapeless, with protruding massive shoulders, he looked terrifying.
>
> Before him, the doctor stood quivering like a reed. 'Well?' said Ramon, after they had stared at one another without salutation for several seconds.
>
> The doctor came forward and put his bag on the table. Ramon did not salute him or ask him to be seated. The doctor dropped his bag and then, not knowing how to begin, looked around the room, while he took out his handkerchief and wiped his hands.
>
> The drawing room was very large. It was cluttered with furniture. The furniture did not suit it. Everything lay about pell-mell. Colours contrasted violently. There were too many photographs on the mantelpiece. The walls were covered with pictures that are sold by the dozen in furnishing shops. Over the mantelpiece there hung an enormous portrait of His Holiness the Pope of Rome. The Pope had his hand raised, as if he was blessing Ramon beneath him on the hearth-rug. As this was the room where Ramon received his guests, the parlour of the house, all the heirlooms of the family were therein gathered, including a spinning wheel and the blackthorn stick brought from Dublin by Ramon's father, as a souvenir of Daniel O'Connell's Birth Celebration. The head of O'Connell was carved on the knob of the stick.[33]

Of his economic activities, we get an impression from the conversation between the co-operative-minded curate, Father Fogarty, and the tired, bullied and sullied Father Considine, who lies within Ramon's power:

> 'I know you hold strong personal opinions on this matter,' continued Father Fogarty suavely. 'I know you are an admirer of Ramon Mór. So are we all, to a certain extent. A strong personality, a genius if you will, commands admiration. But the system is wrong, Michael. And it must

114

be abolished. It's really extraordinary that it could be found at the present day in any country in the world, this astounding form of usury. Within a radius of twenty miles of Barra, on all sides, he has the people within his power. All the little shops in the country are his property, so that, if the people don't come directly to him, they have to go to his agents. He can charge whatever price he likes, and as the people are always in his debt, he pays what he likes for their produce, as they have to sell to him, since, as I said before, they are in his debt.

'It is to his advantage to keep them in a state of poverty and to encourage thriftlessness, for his system is only possible among a population degraded by poverty. It's a slavery worse than any practised under the worst feudal system, because there is no elegance. He spends nothing. I believe he doesn't even invest abroad. He just hoards. I have been told that it has become a mania with him, at times, to stuff money into all his pockets and to go about for days with large quantities of it on his person.'

'You've been told lies.'

'That may be. It doesn't concern me. But look at what is happening. The people are flying to America. Unless something is done, we are soon going to have no congregation. Something must be done. He can only be beaten by means of the co-operative system. Public opinion must step in and defend, in the event of his opposition to my scheme, the non-payment or even the repudiation of debts. The case is desperate. And then, in the matter of amusements . . . '

He clenched his fists, raised his elbows, and then struck his elbows against his sides.

'We must rouse the people from their apathy,' he said with great energy.[34]

O'Flaherty's creation is the most powerful presentation in literature of the gombeenman. Yet it is interesting that the principles of destruction postulated are located in the personalities of the plot rather than in the social dynamics being unleashed. The present writer has made this point about Hugh Brody's *Inishkillane*, where separate cameos of the acquisitive and the suffering are presented as if the greed of the one were not accomplishing the destruction of the life-world of the other.[35] The influence of his patron on O'Flaherty has been neglected. There can be no doubt that the separateness of art theory held by Edward Garnett influenced O'Flaherty, who wrote in one of his autobiographical volumes, *Shame the Devil*:

I returned once more to the reality of my position, under the wise guidance of Edward Garnett, whom I met a few days later at my publisher's office. This great man has helped and influenced most of the important writers of his generation. To me his personality and friendship were of incalculable importance. There I was, like the innocent Huron of Voltaire, afloat in a crazy coracle on the sea of London literary life, surrounded by deadly rocks and yet without a thought for the dangers that surrounded me. Like a father he took me under his protection, handling me with the delicacy with which one handles a high-strung young colt, which the least mistake might make unfit for racing. It was the first time I had come in close contact with a cultured English gentleman. The calmness of his judgment, the subtlety of his intellect and the extraordinary nobility of his character were a glorious revelation to me, who had for years mingled almost entirely with rude and brutal types.

So that I was only too willing that he should fashion the development of my literary talent in whatever way he pleased. Artistic beauty being the only thing of real importance in life to him, I became a fervent disciple of that religion.[36]

O'Flaherty's portrayal presents the striking personality rather than the source of economic power. His wife can admire him as 'a strong man', a typification that is common in the literature of the region. It sells short the full social ingress of his activities. Ramon's wife may say how she came to love him once:

'Yes,' she said with a sigh. 'Although I loathe him, I must admit that when I saw him I felt something like love for him. He was so different from all the smelly, unhealthy, ridiculous, shabby people I had been among for years. You know the way people get excited in the city about anything new. They talked about this picturesque figure, the dour business genius, the ruthless type that was going to put the country on its feet after the revolution.[37]

One of the victims of the innovating Ramon can say:

'Devil take his flour and his tea,' said the big man. 'Look at me. I wasn't reared on flour and tea. I was reared on oaten bread, milk, fish, potatoes and butter. Same as everybody was in my young days. And not an ounce or a drop of that food and drink but was come by within a few miles of my father's door, without having to cross the threshold of a shop for it. But all that is changed now, and it's the doing of that skunk from the island of Inismuineach out there.'[38]

116

It is in the management of the linkages, if they be managed, that the literary theory, if there be one, is revealed.

The newspapers have been kind to the gombeenman, it was noted earlier. It is apposite to deal now with the presentation to the public of the achievements of the model for the character of Ramon Mór.

On the first day of December 1934, the *Connacht Tribune* reported the death of Martin McDonagh in the following terms:

> Gloom has been cast over Galway, and indeed over the west, whose sloping hills and green valleys he loved so well, by the death on Saturday at his home Belmore, Salthill of Mr Martin McDonagh, TD, FG. 'Mairtin Mhor', as he was universally known in the County, was one of the greatest men of the West, as his wonderful business record goes far to prove . . .
>
> He was son of Mr Thomas and Mrs McDonagh, Lettermullen and was educated at Tullybeg College, Offaly. Passing on to a great career, he became senior partner in the McDonogh Milling and Trading Company, McDonogh Chemical Works, and the Sawmills of Thomas McDonogh and Sons. He was chairman and principal shareholder in almost all the local industries, including the reopened Galway Woollen Mills and the Galway Foundry and Engineering Company. For a number of years he was chairman of the Galway Urban Council and Harbour Commissioners and a member of the Galway County Council. He was also on the Governing Body of University College, Galway and president of the Galway Chamber of Commerce.[39]

Of his loss in social terms, they wrote:

> We shall miss him sadly in these days when men like him are needed to rebuild the Country that he loved so well according to his lights. Aside from his great public services, in which he never wavered once, he had made up his mind to the right, he was a King among industrialists – in an Alpine village perhaps, but none the less a King. If he had not Midas's gift of making gold, he was endowed with talents and perspicacity that stood him in good stead throughout a business career of half a century. He brought employment to many doors, and the good cheer of a bountiful and good-natured heart when there was none. For beneath a seemingly brusque exterior was a nature that was kindliness itself, when a good deed has to be done without ostentation. These are the traditions that Martin McDonogh has left and surely to leave such noble memories and to live in the hearts of those who are left behind is not to die.[40]

After the thirties the 'gombeenman' was to become defined in terms of services as much as debt-bondage. Yet we have seen a continuous thread that runs from the exploitation of famine to the exploitation of state bureaucratic complexity. In passing, a case emerges for a historically integrated political science, sociology and literary criticism. In the end, of course, the integration which is required is not only that of different intellectual traditions, but of the reflection and action that will free us from the acquisitiveness and its consequences, that has been hidden from us with such tragic success for bourgeois scholarship on Irish affairs.

From Études Irlandaises, Décembre 1985, No. 10, Nouvelle Série, Lille University, Villeneuve, France. A version of this paper was first delivered to the Dublin History Workshop on 11 March 1978.

BUILDING THE BLACK AND GREEN ALLIANCE

It was sometime in the sixties, I recall, that I wrote my first letter to a newspaper. It was to the London *Evening Standard*. I was not aware then, as I am now, of long, consistent anti-Irish prejudice of that supposed organ of opinion. I wrote in reply to an article more or less suggesting the inferior status of the Irish as a race and the great burden thereby visited on Britain by their arrival there in large numbers. The manager of the hotel in Alfriston, Sussex, was more than a little anxious that, if the correspondence developed in the paper, I would avoid giving the address of the Star Inn, where I was working as a waiter.

A few years later, at Manchester University, I was often asked very kindly, of course, if I would read a paper on what we were really like, the Irish. It was the innocent inquiry of those familiar with the practice of investigating what they perceived to be strange and exotic tribes or peoples. English anthropologists were not as welcome as before in Africa, India and the Middle East.

In the intervening years, I have listened with interest to those who profess a commitment to improving Anglo-Irish understanding. The line of argument, it seems to me, becomes a little lopsided. For example, Dr Conor Cruise O'Brien, a thoughtful and provocative writer, regularly invites us Irish to examine our attitudes and assumptions about our neighbours on the slightly larger island. We are, the line goes, in possession of a set of dangerous myths, which, if it could only be discarded, would make us less ferocious people with whom to deal.

Self-reflection can be a good thing. But I cannot recall Conor extending himself with the other side of the argument – British self-reflection on what images they have held over the centuries of the Irish.

This is exactly what I was doing in Haringey last weekend, where I was participating in a weekend discussion aimed at developing a Black and Green Alliance against racism. The Race Equality section of Haringey Council sponsored the event, which led to some very straight talking and, at the end, to the formation of a Working Group from both communities to examine issues of racial intolerance and the possibilities for inter-community alliances.

Haringey is a council that the harridan of 10 Downing Street would like to see go down the tubes. Its fifty-six councillors break down to thirty-eight

Labour and eighteen Tory. It is near the top of the league in terms of ethnic mix, which makes it a most interesting and potentially enriching cultural space. The council has provided a West Indian Cultural Centre, an Irish Cultural Centre, an Indian Cultural Centre, a Chinese Cultural Centre and so forth. The basic idea is that ethnic roots and culture are part of a person's and a community's identity – something to be shared, not obliterated.

Haringey lived within its budget but has been singled out for particular savagery in the way it has been poll-capped. No such special treatment exists for Tory councils. The result will be that ratepayers in Haringey and other areas that tried to address the challenge of living in multicultural and multiracial mutual respect will be under pressure to close such centres as the ones I spoke of. The issue is being tested in court, and elections are being conducted in an unusual atmosphere of tension.

The idea for the weekend came from Bernie Grant, the MP for Tottenham and a member of the Black Section of the Labour Party. Opening with a discussion on 'Colonialism, the Irish and the Caribbean in the Seventeenth and Eighteenth Centuries' on Friday, the discussion addressed the issue as to whether racism is primarily based as a justification for colonisation, exploitation or privilege.

On Saturday, the two papers which led off our discussions were one by Dorothy Kuya, on 'Racial Stereotypes of Blacks in Britain', and one by myself on 'Racial Stereotypes of the Irish in Britain'. The function of a stereotype is to reassure the individual who uses it to reinforce their superiority and on the other hand to rationalise the alleged inferiority of the group against whom one wishes to discriminate.

Liz Curtis's 'Nothing But the Same Old Story: The Roots of Anti-Irish Racism', first published in 1984, is a very valuable and reasonably priced introduction to this topic from the thirteenth century to the 1980s. I felt it was interesting to go back to some of these old images of the Irish.

Gerald of Wales (1146–1223) provided a vitriolic picture of the Irish to justify the Norman conquest in his infamous *Expugnatio Hibernica*. In fairness, however, he had written a similar diatribe on the English, whom he referred to as 'the most worthless of all peoples under heaven . . . in their own land the English are slaves to the Normans, the most abject slaves'.

David Beers Quinn's *The Elizabethans and the Irish*, however, was my starting point. It is in his work that one encounters the debate as to whether or not the Irish could ever be adequately anglicised. As he put it, writing of Francis Bacon and others: 'Most of them wanted to know about Irishmen in order to learn how to turn them into Englishmen.'

120

It is in this period that the Irish provided the standard definition, or measure, for savage. Turberville drew a comparison between the Irish and the Russians: '[The] wild Irish are as civil as the Russians in their kind. Hard choice which is the best of both, each bloody, rude and blind.' There were also frequent descriptions of the other peoples, such as the North American Indians, being colonised.

Already there was an obsession with dress and particularly forms of trousers. The Irish and others were regarded as similar in their scant regard for English 'modesty', which was equated, of course, with human decency.

Songs, bards, eating habits, personal hygiene, norms of marriage, child-bearing practices, housing, above all the alleged backwardness of pastoralism in comparison with cultivation, provided the package for the stereotype of the Irish and other savages. The project was one of the cultural extinction of everything native and the superimposition on it of what was assumed to be a God-ordained superiority that the coloniser or the empire possessed.

Means of communication were singled out as a conduct of culture. African drums were forbidden, as was the speaking of Irish.

Stereotypes were also invented in a similar way *within* England. The Vagrancy Act of 1598 was the start of a long set of Poor Laws that led to the recently dispossessed being branded as a lower species of humanity. The prisons that came into existence as a response to poverty would provide another caste in their turn.

From such stereotypes came the justification of horrific cruelties. The theory was that such subhuman populations needed the most terrifying punishments to deter them. Slaves were cut to pieces. Gilbert of Ireland placed outside his tent rows of heads through which those making their submissions of surrender had to pass.

Migrants have always been at risk for stereotyping. They are seen as marginal people, reluctant to forget what they were, unwilling to be just like the home population.

Frances Finnegan in her book *Poverty and Prejudice* charts the attitude of newspapers such as the *Gazette* of York, which wrote in November 1845:

> The Englishman is patient and forbearing, but he will not endure oppression, he is tractable only so long as he is well used. . . . England's people will ensure no oppression, no injustice, every man is always striving up the ladder for the step above him. The Irishman, on the other hand, though not yet regarded as violent and depraved, cuts by contrast a poor figure. He is contented as he is satisfied with shelter and a turf fire and potatoes and water to live on.

And again in its editorial of 10 July 1847:

Famine and pestilence have, we trust, taught wisdom, and English benevolence conquered in some degree the prejudices of the Celt. The Irish people are not so stolid as not to perceive that the acts of the Saxons give the lie to the ravings of the lay and clerical agitators, and that in the hour of need, when tens of thousands were falling victim to famine, the exciters of turbulence, even if they were willing, were powerless to check its ravages until Saxon energy and Christian philanthropy stepped between the living and the dead.

A Glasgow newspaper gives the image that was commonly held. It was of:

The ape-faced, small-headed Irishman who showed 'the unmistakable width of the mouth, immense expense of chin' and 'forehead villainous low, so characteristic of the lowest Irish'.

The nineteenth century marked the transition of the savage Celt to primitive ape in English images of the Irish. It was a good title Perry Curtis chose for his analysis of cartoons of the period: *Apes and Angels*. For before Victorian insecurities as to whether they were descended from apes or angels, we encountered the simianising of 'Paddy'. Class, religion, race, poverty, Catholicism and Celtic origins put Paddy in the image of an orangutan. The ignorance involved was also unfair to what we now know of orangutans.

The image of Parnell in *Punch* used such images. There also was his depiction as a Frankenstein. Regular images too were of an imperious Anglo-Saxon advising Hibernia as to how she might be saved from a fate worse than death at the paws of a simian Irish peasant.

The image crossed the Atlantic. A *Harpers* cartoon showed a set of scales with a black from the South on one side and our apelike Irish figure on the other, with John Bull and Uncle Sam conferring in the corner as to whether democracy could survive either or both. Perry Curtis summarised it as follows:

The simianising of Paddy in the 1850s thus emanated from the convergency of deep, powerful emotions about the nature of man, the security of property, and the preservation of privilege. Since the very integrity of English civilisation seemed to be menaced by Darwinism, democracy, republicanism, socialism and Fenianism, one convenient way of epitomising those fears was to shift the burden of proximity onto the burly shoulders of those Irish agitators who wanted nothing better than to strike terror into the hearts of their oppressors.

Today, these stereotypes still exist. The so-called Irish jobs, the cartoons of Jak and others, the London *Evening Standard*, John Junor, all plough them out.

In our times, the stereotype of all Irish as ultimately prone to terrorism and violence is used to justify the abuse of justice towards the Guildford Four, the Birmingham Six, the Manchester Three and others. It is used to justify the Prevention of Terrorism Act abuses. It facilitates discrimination in employment, housing, social welfare and health.

As we held our discussions, common experiences led to a possible common agenda for the Black and Green Alliance. A history of mutual suspicion and even racism has to be transcended. But it is worth it if we are ever to celebrate our common humanity; if we are to press for its realisation in political and economic terms, and to give racism its proper attention, to get on to what perhaps now is a forbidden word in some circles in Ireland – socialist society.

So, if we are to have historical revisionism, let's all, on both sides of the Irish Sea, revise our images of each other. Douglas Hurd, British foreign secretary, for example, might like to revise the image he has of Ireland in his novel. It is of Ireland as an old hag crooning by the fireplace and rearing her children on a diet of hate. Yes! Let's start at the top.

Hot Press, 11 April 1990

THE THREAT TO THE ENVIRONMENT'S

MARVELLOUS SYMMETRY

Writers on the environment, on contemporary industrialisation, on what might be loosely termed contemporary social change, are writing in an increasingly melancholy vein of our inability to protect ourselves from the worst excesses of our actions, structures, assumptions and institutions.

The passion with which Gregory Bateson writes of the pain of having placed trust where we should not, of having not placed trust where it might surely have been placed, is typical.[1] An unquestioned reliance on science and technology was viewed as the certain route to a progress that has never been qualitatively assessed. The marvellous symmetry of the patterns of simple arrangements has been destroyed with abandon. Few could quibble with what he has listed as the basic assumptions which govern our relationships with the larger ecosystem of our fellow Earth-inhabitants:

> The ideas which dominate our civilisation at the present time date, in their most virulent form, from the Industrial Revolution. They may be summarised as:
>
> (a)   It's us *against* the environment.
> (b)   It's us *against* other men.
> (c)   It's the *individual* (or the individual, the company, or the individual nation) that matters.
> (d)   We *can* have unilateral control over the environment and must strive for that control.
> (e)   We live within an *infinitely* expanding 'frontier'.
> (f)   Economic determinism is common sense.
> (g)   Technology will do it for us.
>
> We submit that these ideas are simply proved *false* by the great but ultimately destructive achievements of our technology in the last 150 years. Likewise, they appear to be false under modern ecological theory. The creature that wins against its environment destroys itself.

The interest in Bateson's work is widespread, but to this writer at least such interest smacks of a new dishonesty. Certainly it was never the intention of Bateson that his work would salve the consciences of those who transfer to the mode of their existence the guilt of their rationally calculated actions.

Such latter, of course, have a more palatable message from Alvin Toffler, who, having neatly ignored the historical location of the contemporary ecological crisis, goes so far as to suggest that a counter-administrative structure aimed at our salvation should be embarked upon with enthusiasm. Indeed, while the smug would regard it as optimistic, the quotation which follows reveals in a most interesting manner the arrogance of those who, having refused to reflect on the possibility that they may be in error, go further and assert instead that salvation through further excess is but a matter of time.

It is clear that there is a new interest in the environment and on technological effects. But this springs less from any new feelings of responsibility for life in all its forms than from the simple realisation that contemporary vulgarisation can no longer be masked. The concern of those with economic power is how to acquire an environmentally aware image on the cheap – an ecologically acceptable face.

The economic barons rest assured with certain assumptions. Our present values need not be changed. Advertising can continue to create artificial need. Over-consumption in the so-called developed world can create famine in the Third World. Our city centres can die. Our suburbs can sprawl indefinitely. A continent can be defoliated in the name of a war insisted upon by the corrupt or the unscrupulous. The economy must achieve growth at the expense of welfare. Decisions must become more centralised. Our children must learn to abandon fantasy and imagination in schools where repetition will serve them well. It may represent perhaps their first shaky steps to distinction as leading citizens, scientists of note, men who eat in the university. The list is endless. The fallacy is complete in its dishonesty, its ethical bankruptcy.

It is against the background of such well-bedded values that the new critiques have appeared. Compassion perhaps indicates that they should be taken seriously.

It is fair to say, however, judged by any terms, that the accounts which have appeared are but a flimsy substitute for any adequate analysis of the nature and effect of technology on our society. The point will be made later that the substitution of science and technology as the scapegoats for dangerous political attitudes is possible for the simple reason that such a substitution absolves one from commitment to any major change in political values. In short, most accounts are written against the background of the depoliticised society in which we live; a society not accidentally depoliticised but one in which the majority are deliberately excluded from power in the interests of the elite.

But there are those who still pin their faith in what Mr Harold Wilson successfully sold on an electoral occasion as 'the white heat of technological revolution'. Mr Wilson was not the only academic carried away by the inevitable link between technology, science and progress. Had not many a distinguished British historian much earlier expressed impatience that the East was simply intractable to the formula which had delivered an obviously superior British achievement. Surely it is obvious that a flurry of words, an interest in the previously unruffled in simple nature by way of fad is an inadequate response. Words indeed there have been in plenty, ranging from appeals for beautification at home to organisational bitchiness from the European Commission, whose contribution to date is to express a preference for the work of agencies to the efforts of the people, however misguided.

It can be reasonably assumed that most serious scholars, honest and dishonest, now see the weaknesses of the technology of the larger industrial nations. Those weaknesses, reflected in environmental despoliation and alienation at home are also more than obvious through their exploitation in Africa.

David Dickson's book *Alternative Technology*, one of the most important to appear on the subject to date, clearly rationalises that a revolutionary transformation in science and technology, themselves signifying a new relationship with nature, for example, while popular, avoids the task which faces us all, which is inescapably political.[2]

The depoliticised analysis of technology, while it may not have been his conscious intention, owes much of its popularity to Herbert Marcuse. One of the effects of Marcuse's writing has been his attempt to elevate the place of technology in the definition of modern industrial 'rationalisation'.

The most impressive critique of Marcuse's particular treatment of 'rationalisation', seen as 'not rationality as such but rather, in the name of rationality, a specific form of political domination', is the essay written for Marcuse's seventieth birthday by Jurgen Habermas.[3] Marcuse and others have written in popular form of the changed character of oppression and exploitation in industrialised countries, yet the move from a manipulated science or technology to the idea of emancipation through a change in the structure or connections of either, is attractive and has been noted by Habermas.

The tacit despair of Dickson's statement, with which this article began, is of course to be viewed with even greater import when one realises the following, particularly among the young, which Marcuse and others have attacted. To my mind, the critique of Habermas of the suggestion that a solution to the contemporary crisis can be found in the admonition that 'instead of treating nature as the object of possible technological control, we can encounter her as an opposing partner in a possible interaction. We can seek out a fraternal rather than an exploited nature', is unassailable.

Having made that point, however, it is of interest to note the general change in the manner in which the traditional concept of technology as the automatic agent of progress has come to be challenged; how science has come to be feared. Dickson's reminder is close to Bateson's reference to the pain of misplaced trust.

In an academic atmosphere where science is neutral, and unquestioned, where utility is rarely debated; in a country where to question the necessity of a consumer manipulation is tantamount to treason; where dogma has long won its victory over the dialectic; where the schizophrenic division of work, poetry and science sustains the social divisions necessary to motivate interaction; to hope for a debate on the true content of technology is a vain hope. Perhaps there may be solace in the Tao: 'You cannot stop the birds of sadness flying over your head, but you can stop them from building nests in your hair.'

Education Times, 16 October 1975

127

A Writer for Our People

That Irish literature in general has been parasitical, i.e. that it has sung *of* the people rather than *for* the people, is not a new suggestion. That modern Irish literature has been descriptive at its worst, has sometimes reached the level of a revelatory explication, but has never been subversive in tracing out the contradictions of the state as structures impinge upon our people, is a thesis that this reviewer holds to be undeniable.

Put more bluntly, that writing which has drawn the most public attention has unfailingly been informed by nostalgia, or, on occasion, its variation, bitter memory. Literature has had its purpose defined. 'Entertainment is the spice of life.' To jog the sensibilities into a critical self-appraisal has been dangerous at least.

Peadar O'Donnell has adverted to the reality, the necessity of the role literature can play in revealing the systematic degradation involved as state bureaucracy extends further and further into the lives of people.

He has chosen an island setting for his latest novel, *Proud Island*; this choice of setting provides the boundaries of a community bounded most importantly by the sea and the complex arrangements necessary for survival.

There has been, of course, quite a number of accounts of life on islands: the Blaskets, Gola, Aran and others. No work, however, has grappled as thoroughly with 'gombeenism' as it makes its thrust into a small community. Again, too, to date the inexorable linking of peripheral regions into the cash-nexus economy has gone uncharted. In this book, O'Donnell encounters both these major themes.

The book is not a political diatribe, rather it is a sensitive reconstruction of the effects of both the phenomena referred to above. With exquisite literary precision, the contradictions of island life emerge and speak through one character after another. In my view, it is a testimony to the integrity of O'Donnell's view on literature that art and life are inseparable.

A major defect of Hugh Brody's *Innishkillane*, for example, is that, while it redirects Irish sociology in an empathetic direction, it presents studies of the main participants as cameos – separate from each other and, of course, he fails where O'Donnell succeeds.

Cameos, however brilliant, are not an adequate replacement for structure and its effects.

An example may be necessary. We cannot help but note the manner in which Brody fails to link the acquisitive greed of Michael of the petrol pumps, the supermarket and farms with the total collapse of Joseph, who suffered a nervous breakdown.

It is as if the activities of the two were discrete, separate from each other – that the greed of the one did not account for the vanguard ingress into the lifeworld of the other, and to destruction.

O'Donnell, in this novel, makes no such mistake. We are presented with a vision of a community thrown into the throes of a conflict spearheaded by the introduction of the cash-nexus economy.

Minnie McBride gets £500 for her place and the seed is sown. Indeed, the island has begun to experience its major radical change. An islander remarks:

> Bear in mind that this is the first time ever on this island the mainland touched us and now it lets loose the idea of how much money any place is worth. There are people on the island who could get strange notions. There is no talking what will come of all this.

The striking difference also between the work of Liam O'Flaherty, for example, is the manner in which O'Donnell has succeeded in transcending a mere reaction to the events of nature and has managed by such a transcendence to locate such events as the shifting of the herring shoals and the strategies of reaction thereto into the wider arena of the structure of power on the island.

A possible exception in O'Flaherty's work is *The House of Gold*, and there the events are located in a family rather than centrally in a community.

Those who have read the work of Dr Gibbon and myself on patrons, clients and brokers will read with interest of the visits of the TD and his local representative or broker Johnny Anthon. At times the broker's power appears to shift. We have, too, the upright stand of Hughie Duffy, who would be free of patronage. We encounter the largeness of his vision. After all, he was a man of strange ideas. Two examples will suffice:

> When you are bait fishing Susan you throw out scraps of food to draw fish around your hood. That's what this TD of ours does. I suppose that's all the poor fellow is let do to hold votes. He likely sees through Johnny Anthon's tricks; not that they would upset him so long as Johnny Anthon's talk gets him votes.

And again he reminisces:

When we were behind the barbed wire there was a guard who would
sometimes flick a piece of tobacco across to us. When he went home on
holidays he boasted about it.

Hughie goes on to comment on a topic that is avoided assiduously by
politicians today – the dole.

Now the barbed wire is this rule they have against us in Dublin to keep
us trapped in our hardship. The last thing we had in our mind was that
there was any amongst us would make a rule like that. To be sure the
dole is as worthwhile as anything else but it is only scraps through the
wire to keep us quiet.

The introduction of the land to the cash-nexus is accomplished by the
TD, who is also an auctioneer. The inevitable sign 'No Trespass' is placed on
Minnie's land. After an initial rumble through the island, the phrase is
reduced to the level of 'mind the dresser' at local dances.

All along one suspects that Hughie and Susan are dismayed at the inexorable thrust of greed capitalism from the mainland into their community. It
is in their house that the students who visit the island get a hearing. The
power of the broker is well articulated in Susan's phrase:

I'd be afraid of my life you wouldn't get much of a hearing. The island
is mostly said by Johnny Anthon and in his eyes you'll be only children.
But you will have your say. My man will see to that.

This fine, sensitive book deals not only with power but also with intimate
marital relationships on the island. Transitions are accomplished through the
catharsis provided by the death of the strongest man on the island. There is
Mary Jim, who confronts the students with the phrase 'leave the road out
clear for us'. Mary Jim later becomes the greatest source of consolation for
Susan in her agony.

With subtlety, we are invited to the question as to whether it is island life
or a disappointed sexual relationship that is the source of the actions and
words of Mary Jim. At one stage, she can say rather desperately:

What do men know about living? Slave away and hand over the few
shillings you make. Put your cap on your head and walk out. That's a
man for you. Does he see a woman withering or the girl he married turning into a hag?

It is of course the nonappearance of the herring and their threatened return which contributes most to the tension on the island. This latter forces a gamble, with disastrous results. The major human force against patronage is eliminated. A gamble with the sea has had a major consequence.

O'Donnell has managed to bring together in the succeeding chapters not only the new opportunities for exploitation provided for the auctioneer TD but he reveals also a talent which he has developed with the novel form in his two previous works – a tremendous perception of the poignancy of that individual suffering which arises from structural contradictions. There is, for example, the description of the reaction of Susan as her man's boat fails to return:

> I stood there among the neighbours . . . boats came in one by one but no Hughie. I threw myself into the dark to cry, for my heart told me he was not coming. It was the right of other women to be happy when their men came in and not to have to hold themselves in check because of me.

It would be unfair to the reader to comment in close detail on the death of Hughie – the strongest, independent, implacable threat to increased dependency. All the themes already discussed are deepened and widened – particularly the speedy exploitation by the TD of new opportunities. Has the island now moved into modernity? Has it succumbed to forces over which it can never again have control? Can an honest confrontation between husband and wife leading to a happy resolution compensate in some measure for larger events? How forceful is the suggestion 'The mountainy people are faring no better than us'?

Peadar O'Donnell once again has written a novel which rises far above the level of description of nostalgia and places him among the few writers who have written *for* rather than *of* our people.

The reader can form his or her own opinion and can evaluate also the motivation of Susan as she adjusts to widowhood and the islanders' own involvement in the dramatic resolution of her problem. Any one of these themes would have provided the basis of a novel in itself, but Peadar O'Donnell's holistic vision of the world, in which events are seen against the backdrop of major social change, makes this book probably his most tremendous achievement to date.

It is a challenge, perhaps an invitation, to those who, for a range of motives, insist on the unnecessary division of art from life to bravely accept and take advantage, in these ragged literary times, to come into the open and, with a sense of bravery, accept the title of 'parasite' or, on reflection, to engage in a literature of relevance.

This book raises questions that go far deeper than the circumstance of an island facing the throes of change. It should be read widely despite its high price – a factor for which Peadar O'Donnell cannot be held culpable.

Review of Proud Island by Peadar O'Donnell, Sunday Press, 11 January 1976

PART III

THE ARROW OR THE TARGET?

IRELAND AND THE CULTURAL SPACE

THE PUBLIC SPACE UNDER ATTACK

After the election of November 1992, I became minister for Arts, Culture and the Gaeltacht with responsibility for, among other things, broadcasting and film, the natural and built heritage, arts policy and, to an extent, issues of language. During this period as minister, I would also serve as president of the Council of Culture Ministers and the Council of Broadcasting Ministers.

While the composition of the government changed, I held the same ministry in both administrations. The issues that would dominate at home were the decision as to whether or not to renew the ban under Section 31 of the Broadcasting Act, and the decision as to whether or not we should proceed with the establishment of Teilifís na Gaeilge.

I had been interested for a very long time in the arts, and I knew in particular of the courage of those in the film community who, after the unwarranted dismissal of the first Film Board, had kept film-making alive through the barter and exchange of their personal skills and limited resources.

I moved to take a number of decisions together in the general film area – re-funding the Film Board, changing the tax regime into a pre-production instrument, getting a decision on the establishment of Teilifís na Gaeilge, and publication of an excellent report of a Working Group on the future of the film industry.

It was very clear that the atmosphere in Europe was hostile to public-service broadcasting. The debate in Europe on film was also not very favourable. There was a resentment with regard to any suggestion of a European quota for films: I recall the Danish Minister saying 'Quotas are for fish!'

The debate in Europe was not simply one of a choice between left- and right-wing views on culture, but on the extent to which the Right would in effect destroy the public world. The European Community had made scant reference to culture in its founding documents. (There may be many reasons for this: it was regarded as a matter with which the Council of Europe might deal, it had a bad history of abuse in the period of fascism, and many countries regarded it as a matter of exclusive national concern.) Article 128 of the Maastricht Treaty was the only legal basis upon which one might fight for a European Union culture policy.

I reached the conclusion very early on that, among the commissioners, the culture commissioner held very little influence. The degree to which the competition commissioner has been able to allow the emergence of clear monopolies in different forms of the media without comment is quite appalling, and yet at the same time he has consistently harassed public-service broadcasting.

My arguments at the European level were that culture was linked to citizenship. I used the concept of 'the cultural space' to suggest that such a space was wider than the economic space, and that, if the economy deprived you of the opportunity to work, this should not mean that you automatically lost your right to participate in the cultural space. I was thus speaking of cultural rights and the need for a cultural policy for the European Union. All these matters came to a head during the Irish presidency of the EU.

After I had ceased to be a Minister, I was invited to speak about the general issue of the decline in public-service broadcasting, including in New Zealand at a time when a discussion on the licence fee was taking place. At this time, Jenny Shipley's right-wing government was being replaced by the Labour government of Helen Clarke; I had discussions with both the outgoing and incoming Prime Ministers on cultural issues in the particular context of New Zealand's various cultures. Quite separately, some representatives of the Maori community would come to study the establishment of TnaG.

What follows is a selection of some of the pieces I wrote at this time, on these issues.

THE TYRANNY OF IMAGES

LITERATURE, ETHNOGRAPHY AND POLITICAL COMMENTARY

ON THE WEST OF IRELAND

The Report of the International Commission for the Study of Communication Problems, published in 1980, has at the end of the foreword the brave statement that 'with the coming at a new world communication order, each people must be able to learn from the others, while at the same time conveying to them its own understanding of its own condition and its own view of world affairs. Mankind will then have made a decisive step forward on the path to freedom, democracy and fellowship.'

It makes a number of recommendations towards this end, including:

§ The encouragement of tolerance and understanding.

§ The reduction of dependence on the part of developing countries.

§ The recognition of communication as a basic human right and its democratisation.

§ The development of comprehensive national communication policies.

§ Social participation at all levels.

The report calls for new attitudes for overcoming stereotyped thinking and the need to promote more understanding of diversity and plurality, with full respect for the dignity and equality of peoples living in different conditions and acting in different ways.

The report goes on to make eighty-two specific recommendations, all of them an excellent basis for discussion of a national broadcasting policy. I can endorse them all and state my own unequivocal commitment to public-service broadcasting. These aims will require international conventions and domestic legislation, fought for in international and national arenas, but we will be required too to work through these implications for our taken-for-granted world-views and practices.

I work as a politician in a political system that has shown an extraordinary lack of interest to these crucial areas of policy. The current fashion of confusing ignorance for pragmatism in political discourse reinforces my despair at ever hearing a comprehensive debate on the future of information systems. Yet it must come, and the urgency of its coming must be stated.

I do not propose to follow this theme here. Neither do I intend to dwell on the question of the interconnections between science, technology and society – the debate as to whether technology is neutral, deterministic or instrumental. This classic argument in political philosophy and history, contributed to by such figures as Mauss, Rousseau, Ellul and a whole host of modern writers, among whom Jonathan Bentham shines, will not be my concern. Yet the arguments about the delivery of science and technology, in form and consequence, stand at the back of the discussion of the impact of the media.

Let me state my own position simply and then move on. I believe that technology is instrumental but that behind its development, application and control lie a series of political decisions that are themselves reflective of the structure of power in a society. There is no need to assert a straight connection between economic interests and the media, for example. There is a new body of neo-Marxist writing that addresses itself to the role of ideology – a body of literature both valuable and useful – that sees this reflection as complex and mediated.

I prefer instead to move on and to draw on some of my own experiences as a socialist politician living and working in the west of Ireland. I will reflect too on my experience as an academic who left this region for training in sociology and social anthropology in the United States and Britain, who returned to apply a positivism in my work that I have come to reject as alienating, who has had to remove with some pain the ideological glasses I had been given in these countries for seeing my own people. It was not that I reacted by taking refuge in the thickets of history; it was that I cannot find any meaning in ahistorical social science.

The literary accounts of the west of Inland have been a systematic distortion in general, an impediment indeed to understanding the experience of the inhabitants of the west of Ireland. This literary view had as a major error that it shared with the ethnographic accounts the myth of the sealed community, a community often represented as acting out the last rituals of a previous order. Let me take for example the literary image of the inhabitants of the west of Ireland in the late nineteenth century. What was developed by Revivalists was an artificial literary construct of the Gaels which stressed the noble origins of the peasantry, that appealed to God and men to work for the restoration of our castles and our grandeur. It may be understandable as a reaction to the British racialist stereotype, but it omitted the structurally based exploitation through rents and usury which oppressed the people.

Alf MacLochlainn has described it aptly as misguided antiquarianism. It was something that went further than rejection of colonial superiority. It went on to assert a superiority of its own for Gaelic society towards which Irish men and women should aspire.

Pearse's speech at the graveside of O'Donovan Rossa is quoted by MacLochlainn as an example:

> And here we have the secret of Rossa's magic, of Rossa's power. He came out of the Gaelic tradition. He was of the Gael. He thought in a Gaelic way; he spoke in Gaelic accents. He was the spiritual and intellectual descendant of Colm Cille and Sean an Diomais . . . To him the Gael and the Gaelic ways were splendid and holy, worthy of all homage and all service; for the English he had a hatred that was tinctured with contempt. He looked upon them as an inferior race, morally and intellectually.

This aristocratic invention of course was to be popularised as an image of not only the west but of Ireland, by Yeats and others. Standing as context to it was a land teeming with people in the nineteenth century, with tiny holdings, fractionalised further and further by subdivision, a population that had paid a calamitous price for its dependence on the potato as a basic diet. Then too this population was not homogeneous. It was multi-stranded. The agricultural labourers, for example, had taken the brunt of the Famine and the succeeding migration. They were annihilated. Those who survived them were to lay the basis of the cattle economy of the region. After the disappearance of the landlords, a new breed of native predators – the graziers, or gombeenmen turned graziers, were to provoke a confrontation between their greed and the life prospects of the landless peasants. If church and nationalism could be used against the landlords, it was less successful against a predator who would call himself an Irishman, who could send a son to the national seminary or an unattractive daughter to a convent. On the greed, the destruction, the miserliness, the new great literature was silent. Carleton's Darby Skinadre preceded the great literary revival.

Of course, in the rural areas there was song and dance; there were entertainment practices and an oral tradition in storytelling. There was music too.

It was of the people. It was to be regarded as coarse and not sufficiently uplifting by the self-appointed revivalists. It was sad and often angry, and rang of the experience of poverty. It had to give way to the melodious reconstruction of the Gaelic past. Even into the twentieth century, those who communicated works in Irish to the revivalist centre were conscious that the prevailing revivalist view was that it were better that language would die than bawdy recollections be printed in it. Revival then involved a form of *control*, even a death of the participatory culture; certainly the turning of a blind eye to the verses and songs that mocked gombeenmen and their victims. Importantly too, the myth of the homogeneous peasantry glossed over the structure of economic and social reactions of the nineteenth century in the west of Ireland. Today that loose structure is being recovered by a new generation of historians who have even prepared television documentaries on specific themes of landholding, migration and family life. Some questions must be posed – why were the facts of that century hidden from us? Why is it safe to recover them now? If they were hidden then from our ancestors, are we being cut off from analysis of our contemporary structure in the same way? The gatekeepers of television and film feel that yesterday is safely within the perimeter of the allowable. Today's structures are without nostalgia as a convention prevails. Realism is the realism of the past.

Of course, the Irish of the west of Ireland in the nineteenth and twentieth centuries were not a sealed community. In pre-Famine times, up to sixty thousand seasonal migrants worked the harvest in England, very many from County Mayo, for example. They were displaced by changes in the agricultural economy of Britain, by the technological innovation of the McCormick mowing machine. They were of two economies and were of three worlds: of their home parish, of the migrating group, and of the community of destination. Had they no culture? They certainly had no place in the revivalist high culture. This was opposed to their low culture. Of course they had their own songs and dances, tales of hardship and poverty. They were obliterated as a class, and the class of peasant proprietors took their potato patches, lived to debate Home Rule, and founded the cattle economy. But in the present century, I would argue that the usual form of migration is circulatory – people moving from one setting to another and back again. The migrant is the norm in coastal parishes. The deviant is the person who does not move. Yet literature, film and ethnography cling to the orthodoxy of an individual and a community staying in one place.

The racist discrimination against Irish migrants heightened in the late nineteenth century and represents an unbroken thread to the London *Evening Standard* of today. Of these people, the forgotten people, as far as literature of the revival was concerned, *Frasers Magazine* could write:

> The English people are nationally industrious – they prefer a life of honest labour to one of idleness. They are a persevering as well as an energetic race, who for the most part comprehend their own interests perfectly, and assiduously pursue them. Now of all the Celtic tribes, famous everywhere for their indolence and fickleness, as the Celts everywhere are, the Irish are admitted to be the most idle and the most fickle. They will not work if they can exist without it. Even here in London, though ignorant disclaimers assert the reverse, the Irish labourers are the least satisfactory people in the world to deal with.

And in the same year, when, apart from a few brave exceptions such as the Tukes of York, Irish people were abandoned to die, their plight ignored, the same magazine could write:

> Born in a cabin and reared to look with complacency on the bundle of rags which covers his person, and the mess of potatoes which fills his belly, the young Irish peasant never acquired a taste for higher things, and cannot therefore understand even here in England – where by the way his associations continue to be Irish still – that his interests and those of his employer are identical.

And *Blackwoods Magazine* in the previous year:

> the real truth is . . . that though there is more squalid filth and raggedness in Ireland (for those are national tastes), there is much less real misery or distress in the country than exists in England.

What we have just heard is the prejudice of the coloniser as an image of our migrating proletariat. Equally, much later we have the re-colonisation of their culture by a censorious revivalist movement which within its own form produced major literary figures. Brian Ó Cuiv, writing in *Eigse* in 1966, gives us an example in regard to the Irish language. In 1893, Hyde had published his *Love Songs of Connacht* and in 1895 Father Peter O'Leary could write of Padraig Ó Laoghaire and An Seabhach that it was a great pity

> . . . that they don't take care not to print impure things. Padraig gave a lecture in Cork the other day and, upon my word, he made me ashamed. I wasn't there and it's a good thing that I wasn't. I would never have

allowed it if I had been. He was dealing with love songs – girls and boys and illegitimate children and things like that, in front of the audience. Shouldn't we be able to get enough fine, pure, neat Irish without putting decadent things like that before the people. These love songs are doing great harm to Irish . . . No doubt he didn't think of any harm, but if the lecture is read to anyone in English, he will be told, as An Craoibhín was in my presence. If that is the sort of thing we are to get in Irish, the sooner it is dead the better . . . I told him to print no word in Irish which would not be fully suitable to print in English.

In revivalism, we encounter a control that involves suppression of the body, of love, of experience. The corpse of the colonised can be exhumed in the form approved by the gatekeeper for the dominant culture, reflecting faithfully the literary and aesthetic norms of the coloniser.

If I might give a small example from literary production of the novel: in the twentieth century, we have been given in the character of Ramon Mór in O'Flaherty's *House of Gold* one of the great gombeenmen of fiction. Yet that now leaves untouched the consequences of Ramon's greed across a whole region. The ending is managed melodramatically by the destruction of the individual personalities involved. If we look at the correspondence between Edward Garnett and Liam O'Flaherty, we get an idea how the author had had conveyed to him what Garnett felt the appropriate novel form was. We see too, for at least the period during which O'Flaherty was influenced by it, how a view from the literary centre could deflect a writer from the destruction all around him and from the realist rather than the melodramatic portrayal of it.

In April 1924, O'Flaherty wrote to Garnett: 'I go around and get all kinds of copy here but I never hear anything of what is happening in the civilised world – which is of course across the Channel.' More important is his May letter of the same year:

> One writes as one sees or else one is a mountebank. You yourself were principally the cause of my becoming a puritan in art, instead of becoming an artist who is subtle enough to accept what the best people think proper and artistically required in his own age. I will write in the future for the satisfaction of my own soul since that too is the most important thing in the world or in the next either.

The west has been the place to where, in a short story of Seán O'Faoláin, the protagonists flee from the domesticity of Dublin for a dirty weekend in Salthill, travelling via Lough Derg. The west's mountains and lakes wrote a script for *Ryan's Daughter*, where the human relationships are but an extension of the physical terrain.

(As an aside, let me say that it as arguable that the distortion of the west has now become less serious than the parallel distortion of the urban experience, to which moralists, Catholic intellectuals and hypocritical politicians had contrasted it. We are at the moment in the midst of a virulent anti-urbanism reminiscent of Josiah Strong, who could write that God created men in a garden, and that the city was the result of the Fall.)

While it is true that involuntary migration drove millions from the west of Ireland, many have left the constricted, stifling world of the countryside by choice. Others have left it too late to leave, as for example Patrick Kavanagh's Maguire: at once a victim of fear and obligation; somebody for whom what the romanticist would extol as a spirit of place had become the ambience of a daily prison. Kavanagh writes:

> Maguire was faithful to death:
> He stayed with his mother till she died
> At the age of ninety-one.
> She stayed too long,
> Wife and mother in one.
> When she died
> The knuckle-bones were cutting the skin of her son's backside
> And he was sixty-five.

The distortion of the west in literature is easy to prove. By distortion I mean the conscious construction of a world-view that contradicts and ignores economic and social realities. The distortion too of the experience of the city would be easy to prove.

This double distortion, with its moralistic anti-urbanism, has robbed us of the reality of the periphery and the city. Can it be denied that broadcasting in its assumptions has avoided this distortion? I believe it has not. Have we not had a diet of mean streets and ample valleys?

It is important, of course, to draw a distinction between the work of ethnographically sensitive writers like Synge and the revivalists. Scholars of Anglo-Irish literature have failed, as have the literary, film, and media critics, to expose and confront the ideological sources of this false literary world-view.

The obduracy of the myth of the homogeneous peasantry of the west is difficult to understand, when it was so clear to Synge, for example. He was able to record a first-class ethnography of the life of the women on Aran. He was able to construct a literary work in *The Playboy of the Western World* which subverted all the bogus values of Revivalism, and he, like Æ, saw the destructive impact of the gombeenman on the life-world of the community:

> There are sides of all that Western life, the groggy patriot-publican general shop man who is married to the priest's half-sister and is second cousin once-removed of the dispensary doctor, that are horrible and awful. This is the type that is running the present United Irish League anti-grazier campaign . . . I sometimes wish to God I hadn't a soul and then I could give myself up to putting these lads on the stage. God wouldn't they hop.

Synge, drawing from a careful ethnography, acknowledging at once its limitations and importance, could transcend it. His influence on the literary image of the periphery, as I said, struck at the heart of Revivalism.

The moral vision of the west has then too been a rich source for the rhetoric of politicians and the sermons of priests, both removed from the hardships of life within the region at its worst. Canon Sheehan, after all, wrote for all of them:

> Across the light of sea sleep the three islands that link us with the past, and whose traditions, were we otherwise, would shame us. They are Aran-na-Naomh, Arran of the Saints . . . a place for the hermit and the saint; and, mark you . . . the hermit and the saint must again resume their rightful places in the economy of new orders and systems! You cannot do without them. They symbolise . . . comfort without wealth, perfect physical health without passion, love without desire . . . clean bodies, keen minds, pure hearts – what better world can the philosopher construct, or poet dream of?

Within the sociological tradition we can denote three clear phases. First, there is the classical anthropologist study *The Irish Countryman* of Arensberg and Kimball, and the studies that followed its basic functionalist paradigm. It presents an image of an ordered world of role allocation between the sexes, of inheritance and marriage, of intergenerational authority, of co-operation.

Second, from the end of the nineteen sixties through the seventies, there has been a native empiricism reflecting the training, mostly abroad, of the first wave of post-clericalist sociologists, who have acquired their sociological training in the positivistic tradition of American sociology. They have approached the west and its problems from the perspective of modernisation theory. The current Taoiseach, Dr Garret FitzGerald, an economist, is a loose affiliate of this school. His proposals for so-called western development – a massive injection of capital and the institutional framework through which it would flow – remind me of a television advertisement for an all-round worm drench.

Finally, and most recently, there have been the demoralisation studies represented by Brody and Scheper-Hughes in particular. They depict the west of Ireland as a community in decline. Tradition-bound, relatively isolated communities are depicted as caving in owing to the collapse of their own integrative mechanisms and the external changes of moderation.

In the early nineteen thirties, Conrad Arensberg and Solon Kimball found a harmonious, integrated, homogeneous, stable society, where there was 'an absolute coincidence of "social" and "economic" features.' The inhabitants were depicted as 'relatively undisturbed by short- or even long-term trends in the market. The farmer was indisputably in control of his farm and his household; it was not the market or any external force which shaped his economic and agronomic practices, but simply 'tradition' and the obligations it specified to relatives, neighbours and the community in general. Among the people, long years of intimate association in acts and events of a common life have built up very complete adaptations and very close emotional bonds. Within the community, virtually no status or class differentiation is depicted. Only 'deeper' bonds separate its members – father and son are the only designations of status among them. The entire system is underwritten by mutual aid.

In 1973, Hugh Brody published an account of a parish he calls Innishkillane, not far from Luogh. He finds that only demoralised, contracted vestiges are left of the integrated, working system described by Arensberg and Kimball. He depicts a reconstituted family life, with such features as the isolation of each home, the increasing loneliness of many people, the decline of community. He sets out to describe the new role of *money*, which is usurping many traditional activities and founding new kinds of social relations. He sees the change in the countryside in terms of a battle with capitalist society and the consciousness it creates. The traditional farming society, the community and its life, so tenderly described by the Gaeltacht authors of Kerry and Donegal, Muiris Ó Suilleabháin, Tomas Ó Criomhtháin, Peig Sayers, the

145

culture admired and explored by Yeats and Synge, is transformed. 'Consciousness has been re-structured and life has been re-evaluated.' Brody feels that the demoralisation of those who remain in Inishkillane is something like anomie, as schematised by Robert Merton. The people feel that their society does not function for them, that it *could* not function for them. To be demoralised is, for them, to lose belief in the social advantage or moral worth of their own small society. Brody thinks that all evidence points to a critical turning point some thirty years ago:

> When two families worked together at the bog – or the sowing or the harvest – it was customary for the receiving family to entertain the helpers after work – poteen and tea would be provided, stories and songs exchanged, dances tried out in the kitchen. At a number of points of the year ceilidhes were mixed with work. The older people had a tradition called *bothántaíocht* or night-walking; all who had anything to discuss went to a certain house chosen for the night, while the younger people sang and danced outside. Amusements untainted with economic interest were the province of the young at crossroads dances or of the couples dodging detection along country lanes after dark.
>
> The winter however was the time for merry-making par excellence. There was little to be done on the land after the harvest until about St Brigid's day, when the land was prepared for the new year's crops. . . . The people gave themselves up to the celebration of Christmas, and the numerous weddings which took place at this time. Winter was the natural time for giving in to a marriage. The heir to a farm by his wedding marked his assumption of responsibility for a cycle of work lasting for the most part of a year. Also the bride's dowry had to be settled by her father, and he was best able to calculate it after seeing the year's produce, and most ready to enter long and exacting negotiations when they had time on his hands.

In his present-day study of Inishkillane, Brody finds a complete reversal and impoverishment of this seasonal cycle of work and festivity. One symptom of this disintegration is the behaviour of the inhabitants in the bars and pubs. I quote:

> Tourists to the villages of the western seaboard are likely to be struck by a quite remorseless consumption of porter and whiskey. . . . But the tourist will also observe that this volume of drink is taken with great enjoyment, and the drunkenness it precipitates is full of laughter. . . . The form assumed by drunkenness yields insight. Drunken behaviour

varies with the time of year. The drunkenness in which the tourist participates occurs during the brief summer holiday season. It is a drunkenness of elation and extroversion. In the winter months, however, this elation gives way to its opposite. Then men in the bars during the summer talk fast and loud. In winter the same men talk – when they talk at all – slowly and quietly. As they drink in the winter months they appear depressed and withdrawn. They appear to join closely in evident despair. This despair is not expressed in discussion among the drinkers. Rather, they exchange silence as if it were words.

It is only after the beginning of July that a number of tourists begin to arrive in the remoter seaboard villages. Very few remain after mid-September. Only with the presence of the tourists for a few months is the prolonged withdrawal and quiet of the Irish countryside much interrupted. What the tourists bring each year . . . is reassurance.

The tourists affirm their esteem for the rural milieu and its ways. By travelling to a remote parish the tourists indicate approval of it. The presence of these outsiders, these representatives of the social and cultural forms which the country people so frequently unquestioningly assume to be superior to their own thus gives a renewed confidence to their own society and culture. The quality of life in rural Ireland today is indicated by the atrophy (for most of the year) of the social quality which formerly imbued almost every part of the year's activity. There has evolved a radical opposition between the short tourist season and the principal mood of the rest of the year.

In the 'old days' there were two major festive periods in the calendar – family rites of passage were celebrated and the harvest season, when parties, dances and night-walking marked the rituals of the payment and acknowledgement of peasant mutual aid. The present stunted and degenerate character of festivities stands as a symbol for the passing of this entire system. Traditional forms of peasant co-operation have collapsed, and their attendant recreational activities have became transformed into a degrading search for reassurance that 'community' is still a real entity.

Brody also describes a new phenomenon, one of which there is no mention in Arensberg's and Kimball's work – the gombeenman – a man whose claim to authority is based on his entrepreneurial skills and nothing else. Arensberg and Kimball describe shopkeepers in towns, but mostly confine themselves to an account of their trading practices and methods of training assistants. To them, he was simply a purveyor of food and goods. Brody's example is that of Michael Ryan, who owns a shop, 'Michael's':

> The family centre their activity on the shop, which has an enormous stock. Most of the parishioners make most of their purchases there. It is not the only shop in the parish, but it is the only general store.
>
> Michael's shop is also a guesthouse accommodating about fourteen visitors. This number is locally quite remarkable. They pay for help during the tourist time, which makes them unique among the local guesthouses.
>
> Michael also operates the local taxi service. He owns two cars and a mini-bus. The journeys he makes vary from a few miles across the parish to over a hundred miles to cities, with railway stations and airports. The mini-bus is mainly used for taking the local youth to and from all the dances in the district. The taxi service is kept busy, and the fares are high. As a local man, Michael inherited the family farm. To it he added three other large pieces of land. He owns over two hundred acres and has grazing rights on as much again. The entire farm is for fattening cattle. He buys calves, ranges them . . . and markets them as bullocks and heifers. He farms exclusively for the market. In owning two small boats he is apparently implicated in another traditional activity. The boats are used for inshore lobster fishing. He gives use of the boats to a fisherman–farmer in return for a share of profit of the catch.
>
> Michael's economic life is underpinned by a distinctive consciousness. There is in air of officiousness about his dealings in the shop, which evokes even if it does not presuppose a sense of superiority. Like many busy men, he seems authoritative. As a locally important businessman, he has established and justified in the eyes of outsiders, many Inishkillane parishioners, and probably himself, a basis for authority . . .

For Brody, the gombeenman is a symptom of the newly established dominance of the cash economy. He detects the invasion of the cash nexus and its transformation of 'human social relations into purely economic ones.' The gombeenman has no natural sympathy with his clients, nor does he recognise or respect their 'way of life'. His only contribution to the community is his manifold exploitation of it. He is the representative in its midst of the forces working for its destruction (ubiquitous 'urbanism') and in the process he is the only person who profits by it.

To what does Brody attribute these drastic changes in the fabric of a social life? His explanation is roughly as follows: since the nineteen thirties and, more particularly, since the fifties, the infrastructure of Irish society has to a degree become 'modernised'. Rural electrification has occurred and the cinema, radio and television have by turns made an appearance in the community. Together with the British press, they have acted as the bearers of metropolitan values, and to a great extent have served to provide sources of alternative norms with which to assess local society. This arbitrary external change has had the effect of inducing increasing relative deprivation amongst the rural population as a whole and young people in particular. This in turn has had the twin effect of demoralising the population and stimulating emigration amongst youth. The metropolitan culture becomes the preferred choice.

This has its own repercussions, principally an increase in the flow of emigrants' remittances into the community. These sources of retail, together with the generic demoralisation in consequence of the devaluation of present life, induced the farmers to contract their farming operations. This in turn leads to a decline in their solidarity and allows the rise to pre-eminence of the shopkeeper over the now-atomised rural society.

None of this is sustainable against historical evidence. Cash had been around for a hundred years before, Brody says, gombeenmen had been involved in usury, and so on.

Of course, what should not have been taken for granted was that Arensberg and Kimball's account was an adequate picture of moral society. Its functionalism had blocked it from seeing many of the conflicts of the thirties in rural Ireland – conflict about land, about politics, about a campaigning Church which was seeking to achieve a comprehensive hegemony in sexual and social behaviour, which would require censorship, control of entertainment and licencing hours, end the crossroads dancing and mount sporadic attacks on fiddle music.

Brody can but present us with cameos, so very like the media and film response, unlinked together. We are not allowed to see that it is the greed of Michael that accomplishes the destruction of the life-world of his neighbours. We are not allowed to see these connections which represent the local form of the development of capitalism in agriculture.

Nancy Scheper-Hughes is a favourite guest on TV shows in the United States where the Irish are discussed. She has became an authority on the 'mad Irish' of Ballybran, a remote seaboard parish in County Kerry. She utilised a model that she describes as a cultural diagnosis of those pathogenic stresses which surround the coming of age in rural Ireland today. Her ethnography has been faulted on grounds of representativeness. She spoke, for example, to mostly middle-class women, and in so far as smallholder schizophrenics predominate in the parish, there are problems about generalisability. I prefer to ignore the academic norm of leaving it with such a dismissal. Her work is still valuable and tells us much about what we want to avoid, about savagery and fear. It may be a significant step towards a critical realism, about the harshness of child-rearing practices, about marriage, about coldness. She may have been insightful and disturbing. Let me give you some examples.

An assistant psychiatrist in the county hospital speaks of the old:

> Many of the old people are weak and delusional from hunger and lone-liness. If they seem 'paranoid' in their accusations against kin and neigh-bours, their accusations are often well founded. For every single old farmer, there are a host of greedy neighbours waiting to pounce on his land and possessions.

Living with the old people:

> The worst part of living with the old people that first year was their watching me to see if I were pregnant. The old couple feared the worst and kept asking friends of mine if I were pregnant yet – it was humili-ating.

Of pregnancy:

> My troubles really began when I became pregnant. I think the old woman was jealous of me for it. She never helped me at my chores and there were days I would be carrying four buckets of milk on my own and she would just let me struggle. If I complained and said I was tired and wanted to sleep a bit during the day, she wouldn't say anything to me, but I would overhear her telling a neighbour that I thought I was a 'pet', where no O'Donahue woman had needed to rest when they were preg-nant. So I kept on working even though my feet and legs were swollen and my blood pressure was high. I had to speak out to see the doctor because the old people thought a woman was 'soft' who went to the doc-tor just for pregnancy.

Of child-rearing:

> It was so very wrong, but no woman in my generation ever knew the pleasure and warmth of cuddling a baby. We never thought we had time for that. Most women were needed on the farm, and me, I was needed by the whole community. There were times when I would be called out

for a birth and Michael would have to drive me. I'd sprinkle the babies' with holy water and leave them in the care of the Sacred Heart.

Of love:

Sarah first saw me at Castlefair. I went over selling a calf. We took a liking to each other and after I came home I asked my father would she suit. He said he knew the girl and that her 'history' was good. So, come Shrovetide, our hands were clasped (i.e. the match was made) and the next day we had a fine Irish wedding. We killed two sheep and drank four barrels of porter. The match was a good one, and it 'took'.

Of 'talking distant':

Well, I wouldn't will it on a person – the hell I lived through . . . no one ever knew the pain I suffered. I came in, a shy, nervous, frightened bride, into a house filled with silent strangers. At first I thought they were queer-like because any of them didn't talk. They would sit around the fire and read.

Sometimes a whole night would pass without a single word spoken. As 'the woman coming in' I was the last to speak, and the first one to serve on the old people. I sat in a corner and I had to think about them all the time. I married into the whole lot of them! And with all the attention given the old woman, I forgot about my husband. Himself and I weren't given any privacy – we couldn't even whisper to each other in our room at night for fear they might hear us. We began on the wrong foot – we had to talk distant to each other in front of the old people and the habit grew on us, even until after they died we spoke to each other in the same way.

Michael was a hackney driver for the village and the times I dreaded most were when I had to go along with him to pick up a customer in Tralee. We'd get in the car together and it was like we'd be strangers, trying hard to think of what in the world to say to each other. Finally, I would give up and turn on the radio, and we'd both be relieved.

Of the inability to communicate and its heartbreak:

Jack and Nora were married for over thirty years and had five children. 'Not once in his whole life did that man, may he rest in peace, call me by my Christian name,' said Nora of her recently deceased husband. 'He couldn't bring himself to it. He would come in from work, and yell up the stairs 'Hey you, I'm home', and I'd be there, gritting my teeth, saying, 'Nora, Nora, did you ever tell him how you felt?' I asked, and Nora replied: 'I did, yes, finally. It was on his death bed and I held him, cradled in my arms, and for the first time in my life I said, 'Jack, I love you. You were an honest, upright, good-living man, but like all the Nelligans before you, you were a cold man, Jack, and I wish it could have been different between us.'

She examines the mental illness in western Ireland in the context of the social stresses caused by cultural disintegration, economic decline, de-population and social isolation. It is valuable and insightful, but without a context. Ballybran has no economic connections with the outer world, no real ideological location, no history.

Damian Hannan's work in the nineteen seventies on role division among young couples contradicts much of this on the basis of a sample survey. I still insist that Scheper-Hughes's work on older women in a remote area is a step towards the real. In general, however, the ethnography of Ireland is distorted rather than revelatory of Irish rural society. We have then literary and ethnographic models that are presentations of a structureless society.

We know that the nineteen thirties was a period of conflict over land and politics. We know that the smaller farms continued to dwindle in number. We know that cooring had quickly been abandoned for a horse or, better, a mowing machine of one's own. We know most importantly that the gombeenman had flourished from the previous century and that a government report in 1906 had found dependency and demoralisation in the west. Brody et al have, like the literary figures who needed the castles of our ancestors, fantasised a mythical community from which they could measure demoralisation and decay.

Exploitation and domination in the west has a longer history than Brody and Scheper-Hughes comprehend. Yet too have film-makers and broadcasters not revelled in this image of the traditional community giving way under a modernism that has no author? It surely was not necessary for them to become marooned within the literary and ethnographic distortions.

I finally turn to the treatment of the political in Irish broadcasting. I saw it as operating within rules of a consensus that has incorporated many of the features of the ethnographic and literary distortions. Countrywide programmes open with shots of bleak landscapes that introduce stories about ewes that have had their third set of triplets. Bog cotton blows in the breeze as we fade out, and we close our eyes with an image of a brilliant blaze of furze bush-es. We owe to RTÉ a debt of considerable magnitude for collecting folk material that would have disappeared. But that said, it has shown a flair for the exotic not matched by investigation of the contemporary.

The discussion of matters political on RTÉ can best be described as a celebration of consensus and of the political culture. Minority political view-points find themselves being treated, at best, paternistically and, more usual-ly, in a dismissive way. There are some minority voices, of course, that can-not be presented at all. My experience over ten years living as a socialist in the periphery is one of being presented as a political deviant. Programmes are structured around the government: announcements of the day, and main opposition comments on them, even though these may not differ in sub-stance from the government statements. The running order of the pro-gramme dictates that the interviewer comes to the lunatic leftie last. The mode of the usual interviewer is to put himself, or herself, in the shoes of the ordinary man or woman in the street. John Westergaard has written: 'The voice of dissent, when it is heard as more than an indecipherable crackle of background noise, is still heard on the defensive: trapped in a pre-set frame of discourse with little or no opportunity to substitute another of its own.'

This exactly fits my own experience based on appearing for ten years on television and radio in discussions with RTÉ broadcasters about politics, except occasionally where the programmes have been in the Irish language.

Irish politics is not divided on ideological grounds, for many historical and indeed tragic reasons. The political culture is, as I have described it, in other writings clientelist and populist. Politicians can sink faster from aspects of their personality than from policy. As in literature, we have in politics extolled gatekeepers and strong men rather than social movements. It is clear that this set of attitudes is destructive to the illusion of a democratic, partic-ipatory basis for the legitimacy of the state. Yet it finds a place within broad-casting where 'grass roots' feeling is extolled and a great stress is placed on loyalty and unity. Cracks, not politics, dominate the newsrooms. As to the consequences, again John Westgaard puts it well:

> The framework of perception which people bring to their viewing, lis-tening and reading – the codes with which they decode media messages – come from somewhere, are formed at some time, and are liable to be re-formed over time. The problem defies solution by empirical measure-ment. But is it hardly conceivable that long-term exposure to the media themselves has no significant part to play among the sources for those

predispositions by which people make sense both of the world and, in turn, of the particular interpretations of the world on offer from the media. For another, those predispositions do not typically take the shape of neat patterns of coherent and mutually consistent ideas in individual minds: they are often internally contradictory, ambivalent, comprised of elements which point that way as well as this. It is that, above all, I suggest, on which the social significance of the slant of press and broadcasting presentation hangs.

It has been common in recent characterisations of the British manual working-class culture and consciousness to highlight features whose effect is to encourage socio-political accommodation and popular acquiescence in the present structure of class relations. Radical critique is then explicitly or by implication denied significant indigenous roots in the Weltanschaung of wage earners.

RTÉ's current-affairs output has in general supported the consensus that there are no classes in Irish life, only arguments about changing political personalities. Again, I stress, I speak of the usual. There are exceptions, and brave ones. In the field of women's issues, programmers have made programmes under the gaze of a chairman of an Authority that bans discussion on amending our Constitution on the basis that, as he feels abortion to be murder, we should not debate it on our most popular discussion and entertainment show. I have concentrated on what was proximate to my experience. These issues I have touched on I see as hidden sources of control. Of course the great battle will be between public-service broadcasting and commercial interests. I have stressed in detail some upsets of what I call hidden control drawn from ideology, because I feel we have to go further than winning the major confrontation, go deeper into our own cultural assumptions. I believe with Stuart Hall, for example, that the world tends to be classified out and ordered through structures which most directly express the power, the position, the hegemony of the powerful interests in the society. And I agree with him that there will be more than one tendency at work within the dominant ideas of a society. Groups or classes which do not stand at the apex of power nevertheless find ways of expressing and realising in their culture their subordinate position and experiences. This is internalised colonisation. Would that literature, ethnography, film and broadcasting subverted this distortion, rather than feeding it.

At the worst, then, we can have the use of technology as a means of feeding distorted imagery, at best the use of technology in a way that will allow the forging of a new democratic order that is freer, more equal, less repressed. Defensively asserted, it can protect us from the abuse and degradation of powerful international corporations. Without control, we become the victims of the same technology, not its masters.

But what form should control take? Here the answers are less certain. I am in favour, unreservedly, as I have stated, of the concept of public-service broadcasting, but so far this has not meant democratic control of the media; it has meant centralised, government-influenced control as an alternative to commercial abuse. Its classic expression has been through a form of consensus management. Practitioners have derived their professional ethos within this, in my country at least. It has been near-impossible to express alternatives other than as a deviant. Programme-makers unhappy within this constricting consensus give the impression at times of poor Mrs Gaskell, who, having lost her baby, was to go on to write realistically and movingly of child labour and child poverty. In mourning for the dead child of their radicalism they make programmes about dead and dying radicals and movements long gone, rather than the messy and dangerous present. Film-makers take as natural settings for elemental conflicts, landscapes, to which are added peasants, without histories or present structural locations.

Yet there are the brave exceptions. *The Ballroom of Romance* and *Poitín* are sufficiently close to the bone to subvert the fallacious imagery and add much to our understanding of ourselves. I believe that the contribution *Missing* made to the public awareness of what was the regular oppression in Chile was immense, and did more than a hundred speeches. There are hundreds more in film and television: artists with courage.

Control, then, is about power. Behind it lies political choices that should and must be discussed. These choices affect the future of ourselves and our children. Our right to know and touch the world, to incorporate its hurt, to celebrate its struggle, to offer solidarity, to love.

Public-service broadcasting has to be restated then in new principles rather than rejected. It should not be left go by default. We need to look at how we have been colonised and how we can incorporate our experience of colonisation to turn the tables on the coloniser, even if it means marriage to the coloniser's daughter, with the particular historical resonance that has in Irish history. We do need to ask what has been done in the name of objectivity, neutrality, impartiality and balance. We need to ask whose consensus these values have served. We need to defend the freedom of art to subvert the existing repressions.

155

However, the worst fate of the colonised is when they take to themselves the version the colonisers have of them. Film-makers and broadcaster must not receive the distorted imagery of the periphery as their fate. They must destroy it that we may breathe. The argument is not any longer between elitism and commercialism. It is more complex: it is about the possibility of democracy, peace and a world community committed to a better version of ourselves. Broadcasters and film-makers, many of them, are crossing the road to that struggle. Many are taking the first steps that will make it possible.

One version of control that I would find attractive would be the dissemination of technological capacity through the educational system, the demythologising of technique, the establishment of a creative chaos which would develop a disdain for the bland and the packaged. At the end of the day, access is not about the drawing-room recitation learned from one's elders; it is the right to tell one's story, to hear the story of every other man and woman, to respond to one's environment and to put one's imprint with respect on it. To live in the whole world.

Let us above all else live in the present, then, with enough courage not only to reject an escape into the past but to unmask the facts of exploitation and domination, to celebrate the body as well as the mind, so that there may be options of justice and freedom, of love and sensuality, in the future. The devil take reconstitution of the peasantry. On to the new community. Let our liberation be one not only of the mind but of the heart.

From the Crane Bag, Vol. 8, No. 2, 1984; based on a paper read to the Fourth Festival of Celtic Film-makers and Broadcasters in Edinburgh, 1983

CULTURE, DEMOCRACY AND PARTICIPATION

When I agreed to give this lecture I was coming to the end of almost twenty-five years of lecturing in a university. It was an experience for which I will always remain grateful. I feel privileged to have been able to approach the complexity of issues, and later the incomparable challenge and satisfaction of offering an elucidation of what might be tentative explanations to students, interested or uninterested.

Now, at only a short distance from such experience, I find myself with responsibilities for arts, culture, the Gaeltacht, heritage and broadcasting. I have had to migrate, as it were, between the rhetoric of academic discourse, political language, administrative communication and what was for me a recovered pursuit of authenticity through poetry. In writing this lecture out of the flux of what is now my life, I felt as if I was on a train passing stations where I once disembarked with a different suitcase.

As a sociologist, I began my consideration of culture in terms of its functions. Sir Edward Tylor wrote that culture was 'that complex whole which includes knowledge, belief, art, morals, law, custom and any other capabilities and habits acquired by man as a member of society.' While Tylor's definition has survived into that of others, there are so many issues that have now emerged since his work fed into the dominating paradigm of the social sciences, structural functionalism. Culture was envisaged in such a theoretical approach as an integrated set of ideas, values, attitudes and norms of life which possessed a certain stability in a given society. Yet our society is characterised so much more by change than by stability.

The earlier writers too stressed the learned nature of culture. The concept of socialisation was developed; crudely put, it showed how society entered the individual and the individual entered society.

Yet Tylor's legacy was valuable. It stressed the shared nature of beliefs and the norms, values and attitudes that were connected with such beliefs. These three interconnected phenomena were communicated through signals, and the specifically human achievement was to establish an enormously complicated communication system based on a symbolic-order.

In 1969, George Steiner wrote in an article in *Encounter*, under the title 'The Language Animal':

At a time when it is the fashion to describe man as a 'naked ape' or a biological species whose main motives of conduct are territorial in the animal sense . . . we are, as Hesiod or Xenophon may have been among the first to say, 'an animal, a life form that speaks'. Or, as Herder put it, 'a language creature' (man) alone speaks language and, as Chomsky formulates it, does not select a signal from a finite behaviourial repertoire, innate or learned.

Man's capacity to articulate a future tense – in itself a metaphysical and logical scandal – his ability and need to dream forward, to hope, make him unique. Such capacity is inseparable from grammar, from the conventional power of language to exist in advance of that which it designates.

How well Beckett understood this. Contained in the quotation is a recognition that culture contains at its roots a paradox. To feel secure, we may wish to concede to culture a deterministic force. Yet our human impulse to be free breaks away and rejects such determinism. We encounter culture as a process, a tool for redefinition. Even language, the finest tool in the communicative order that is part of culture, continually reinvents itself. We conclude with Berger that we are neither wholly determined nor wholly free. We wrestle with the ghosts of language for the blueprint of the prison of determinism from which we would escape.

Culture has been utilised in most cultures as a resource to handle the dilemma that we are at once finite in our physical existence as animals and infinite in our imagination, at once both animal and god-like. It is not accidental that any serious comparative work on culture shows a vast array of strategies that are provoked by death, where the finitude of physical form and the infinity of imagination are posed with stark reality.

Of course, some scholars, such as Peter Worsley, have raised questions as to whether 'culture' has conceptual utility at all. I do not share his view. He was, I believe, responding to a situation in the social sciences of the seventies and eighties where 'culture' had become a residual category of explanation from a badly structured period of empiricism in that field. He did, however, sound a timely warning as to the danger of imprecision in definition.

Culture is processual. It is predicated on the symbolic. It need not be deterministic. Language is its greatest tool but is not a neutral one. Within an adequate construction of culture, time and space have to be transcended. Dream is as important as object. There may be cultural constants, but we have learned that there are few cultural certainties.

The response to such a set of assertions has been in the last hundred years influenced by the social setting, and indeed social class, from which the response has come. F. R. Leavis and T. S. Eliot, while brilliant exponents of a personal view of high culture based on order, are not accidental contributors to such a theory. A definition of a 'high' or 'hegemonic' culture based on order is a product of the structure of power, influence and authority in the social setting.

Where such a view has obtained a hegemony, it has often been at the cost of suppressing stories, dreams, rationalisations of the self and others, of those excluded from power and participation. The evidence of the suppression of the cultural expressions of women in patriarchal society is overwhelming, as it is of the traditions and stories of workers and all those dominated, exploited or excluded. The relationship between the coloniser and the colonised, so brilliantly elucidated by Franz Fanon, but above all in my view by Albert Memmi, has been invaluable. The project of colonisation, wherever it occurred, had a particular profile of cultural assertions.

One culture does not simply replace another. The cultures of the dominating and the dominated intermix to create something that is not simply reducible to one or the other. Both may have a dual rhetorical structure, one formal, the other informal, as James C. Scott in his recent *Domination and the Arts of Resistance: Hidden Transcripts* has shown.

I find interesting, however, the scholarly neglect of a middle period between the hegemony of the dominating power and the hegemony of those who have won freedom. When such a situation arises, it is not possible simply to go back to a moment before domination and re-institute it as the present or the desirable future. One may do so at a rhetorical level, but it is at the cost of a complex reality which is ignored at the price of tolerance. The distortion of the coloniser is challenged by another distortion, the pre-colonial reality, asserted with a dubious content and described as a blueprint for the future in conditions of freedom.

We have to learn on this island that tolerance requires more than the recognition of different versions of ourselves, of how we have come to be the way we are. It requires a recognition of what we have taken into ourselves from each other. We cannot live, except neurotically, if we deny parts of our inherited present complexity. Yet if we accomplish this task of recognizing the complex tapestry that is our identity, we will have pushed ourselves not only towards tolerance but through a process of healing.

Culture can be an abyss. It can also be a space of healing. Even more so, it can be a space of celebration. It can be this latter, however, only if it is not reduced and restricted to being an adjunct of the economic. The cultural space should be one defined by celebratory citizenship, as available to the unemployed as to the employed, and not scarred by patriarchy, exploitation, domination, ageism or racial prejudice.

The existence of cultural objects is important; the integrity of the cultural space is much more so. This raises the question as to what requirements are made of such a space in conditions of democracy, and what is to be the character of participation within such a cultural space in a democracy.

It is necessary for me to stress the complexity of the issue of culture if policy initiatives are to be justified with precision, but also, much more importantly, in an open, transparent and accountable way. Otherwise, language means anything you wish it to mean. I have taken my stand unequivocally on a social definition of creativity. Personal genius I acknowledge, respect and salute, but I ask how much creativity has been sacrificed, at what enormous cost, where the social definition of creativity and the centrality of the cultural space in policy-making has not been recognised. In the European Community, such recognition is coming, and is welcome, but it has been late.

The chairman of An Chomhairle Ealaíon/The Arts Council, Dr Colm Ó hEocha, in a recent address at Louvain, perceptively pointed out, among many other things, the Irish contribution historically to the rich supra-national tapestry that is the European cultural inheritance. Most importantly, he stressed how the Maastricht Treaty fills a lacuna in the Treaty of Rome in its statement that:

> The Community shall contribute to the development of quality education by encouraging co-operation between Member States and, if necessary, by supporting and supplementing their action, while fully respecting the responsibility of the Member States for the control of teaching and the organisation of education systems and their cultural and linguistic diversity.

The European Community has neglected, and neglects, the cultural space at its peril. At a time of rising anti-immigrant feeling, and indeed racism, in so many parts of Europe, the tolerance that respect for every story carries is now more crucial than ever. It would be little less than a disgrace, too, if the principle of subsidiarity was abused to impede new transnational cultural initiatives.

I am convinced that we will end this century and begin the new one with

THE ARROW OR THE TARGET?

the debate on cultural pluralism being at the centre of things. If the shift in international politics has been from a polarisation of East and West towards a North–South divide, and if the issues of debt, trade and aid are now crucial, so also is the issue of cultural pluralism. Wars are born of fear based on ignorance and stereotypes. Peace is equally sown in the mind, as the founder of UNESCO recognised. That organisation, however, has been seriously damaged by opposition to the concept of a free pluralist communicative order, as envisaged in the McBride Report on the New World Communication Order.

That agenda has to be restored. If we at home are to benefit from our cultural resources, arts education will have to be made central in the curriculum. It is not sufficient to lurk behind voluntary child-improvement sessions purchased on the market outside of the school day.

We will have to release ourselves from many myths, including the one that artists flourish below the poverty line. We will have to recognise that institutional provision for the arts is as important to our infrastructure as a people as roads, roundabouts or bypasses are. We will have to recognise that true access means more than the possibility of entering public places of culture: it requires having access to the creativity of the self in interaction with others.

There is of course an economic case to be made for arts expenditure. It is not, I emphasise, the crucial justification for such expenditure – I see that as a right. Yet it is true that jobs cost less, are more enduring, are more suitable in many cases, and achieve excellence in the arts. This is demonstrably so in film, video, publishing, music and dance.

We have to recognise too that, by enriching the capacity for community arts, we are liberating our citizenry from the determinism of a narrow economic consumerism. I have, as minister for broadcasting, for example, to indicate where I stand on the choice of constituting my fellow citizens as market segments or as citizens with rights within a communicative order.

I have chosen consciously to follow the latter path, agreeing with the late Raymond Williams that, even in the era of satellite broadcasting, we have the right to be, as he put it, 'the arrow, not the target'.

That is why I attach importance to Teilifís na Gaeilge. I want the means of the modern communicative order to be available to those who wish to use the Irish language and rear their children in its ambience.

I want, in conclusion, to take up a contemporary debate to which the French writer Alain Touraine, among others, has contributed: the role of culture and participation in what he describes as 'post-industrial society'. Touraine is concerned with 'social passivity' in the face of the mass commercialisation of leisure. While I do not agree with his conclusions, he has rightly identified the crucial distinction between active participation in cultural activity and passive consumption of cultural products or, much worse, alienated withdrawal from the social world.

Standing behind the dilemma which Touraine addresses is the question of freedom. Is freedom to be defined by a consumer choice of an ever-widening array of televisual products? Is it to stop short of social participation or of live performance directed at an audience? Which cultural model is in the ascendent: one of passive consumption or one of active participation? The answer in Europe might be so depressing as to bury the question.

These are questions upon which we must have debate, have policies and reach conclusions. How we answer these questions will depend upon the assumptions from which we depart. If one begins with a radical individualism, as has prevailed for over a decade and a half, and which now, in my view, is, thankfully, on the decline, there are implications for every form of cultural activity: film, drama, dance and publishing. We should never forget that nadir of contemporary civilisation reflected in Mrs Thatcher's phrase: 'There is no such thing as society.' It reflects a radical, self-obsessed, consumerist view of life. It is as immiserating as it is dangerous. With it came both the need and the proliferation in supply, public and private, of mechanisms of security: the atomisation of life. It contaminated every cultural institution, from education to the opera.

Standing against this contamination was the irrepressible humanity of communities and groups, carriers of and heirs to old and ancient solidarities, and an artistic community that by and large refused to be subverted by it. Now, however, in so many places we are having to re-make the social solidarities. Neither will it be sufficient for us to reach for 'tradition', as some nostalgic better place and more secure time. We have to make our own. When we celebrate together, we release something quite beyond ourselves.

This century will end and the new one begin with all the issues as to our future being faced not only in the political and economic sphere but in the cultural sphere also. I go so far as to say that it is there that the shape of the future will be forged. Will we learn from feminism? Will we accept ecological responsibility? Will we, above all, stop crucifying the undeveloped world through the relationships of old: trade and debt? Will we make international capital accountable? Will we extend democracy? Will we put an end to war and feed the children of the planet? Will we immunise them and create a space for them?

All these issues are about how we look at each other and either avert our gaze or celebrate our interdependency. It has been a privilege to speak to you and particularly to honour Robert Adams, surgeon, scholar, fine judge of horses, and your President in 1840, 1860/61 and 1867/68. I am not sure what that noted anatomist would have made of my dissection of culture, but I hope his spirit is not displeased.

The 22nd Robert Adams Lecture, delivered to the Royal College of Surgeons in Ireland, in University College Galway, on 23 April 1993

ACTIVE CITIZENS OR PASSIVE CONSUMERS?

CULTURE, DEMOCRACY AND PUBLIC-SERVICE BROADCASTING

IN THE ERA OF AN UNACCOUNTABLE MARKET

The times through which we are now living are for many people who gave, and give their energies to the public world, times of considerable pessimism. It is as if what is happening constitutes an imperceptible drift away from policy, from ideas, from philosophies. It is a condition that writers such as Charles Taylor, in his work *The Ethics of Authenticity*, describe as a drift to unfreedom.

I believe the manner in which we are uncritically accepting unaccountable markets as a substitute for accountable public policy represents one of the most serious aspects of this drift away from democracy. Indeed, I believe we are now living through the early stages of a deep enslavement. It is a historical moment of the greatest importance: we are faced with a choice between a retreat from the public world, or the substitution of existence as consumers for an active life as citizens.

The loss of the public world is being experienced through the subjugation of the cultural space to a set of economic policies derived historically from a very narrow ideological furrow: the adherents of Van Hayek and the New Right.

It is a time of the greatest pessimism for even such distinguished historians of, and contributors to, public-service broadcasting as Michael Tracey, whose seminal work *The Decline and Fall of Public Service Broadcasting* charts the story of broadcasting right up to its present time of crisis. And a crisis it is. Broadcasting now stands to be judged as a production space for commodified entertainment product rather than as a public space where citizens listen and view, to be informed, educated and entertained.

Broadcasting has always been inescapably cultural. There have been debates about the meaning of culture; I am using the term here in the sense it is used by UNESCO in the report 'Our Creative Diversity', or by the Council of Europe in its document 'In From the Margins' – i.e. in an anthropological sense, as the full way of life of the people.

We spend a great deal of our conscious life watching and listening to what is broadcast. The late, great Raymond Williams gave as the title to his last paper 'Be the Arrow Not the Target'. When, as broadcasting minister, I was publishing a Green Paper on the future of broadcasting in Ireland, I had this title in mind when I entitled the Green Paper: 'Broadcasting in the Future Tense: Active or Passive?' From when I read his work for the first time in the late 1950s or early 1960s, I was moved by Williams's commitment to public education and to the role of the media in the deepening, widening and enriching of the life of the public. Indeed, Michael Tracey's book, to which I have referred, quotes a phrase of Williams in which he describes the BBC's early view of itself in the world as 'an authoritarian system with a conscience'. Many may disagree with the Arnoldian elitism or the excessive reliance on tradition, but the notion that broadcasting had to engage with what was debated as the public good was unquestioned.

That public world, in which there is a connection between philosophy and politics, between ethics and economics, between culture and public-service broadcasting, is under severe threat, as its tradition of public space and service is allowed to slip away. I want to suggest that the losers will be not only broadcasters and their audiences but also the wider fabric of society, across a long spectrum of time, and that society may not be able to recover the values it is now, almost unconsciously, losing.

In the course of a recent discussion on the BBC, Tracey makes reference to a document published in the 1980s by the Broadcasting Research Unit in London, which set out eight principles of public-service broadcasting:

1   Universality of availability.

2   Universality of appeal.

3   Provision for minorities, especially those disadvantaged by physical or social circumstance.

4   Service the public sphere – the nation speaking to itself.

5   A commitment to the education of the public.

6   Public broadcasting should be distanced from all vested interests.

7   Broadcasting should be so structured as to encourage competition in good programming rather than competition for numbers.

8   The rules of broadcasting should liberate rather than restrict the programme-maker.

It is easy to see how such principles fit within a model of active participatory and democratic citizenship. It is equally clear that they do not constitute an agenda which would be accepted readily by those who are providing product for the commercial audio-visual market at the present time.

The issue of the licence fee as a source of funding was closely linked to the notion of community and what citizens held in common. Public-service broadcasting was not merely symbolic; it was taken for granted that it was on the public service channels that one expected coverage of the great events and personages of one's time. There was a sense in which the licence fee funded the public service broadcasting system, a system that contributed to cohesion, integration and a sense of identity.

Ireland has had both the challenge and the benefit of being a next-door neighbour to the BBC. It is not surprising then that there has always been a pursuit of high standards in Irish broadcasting. Indeed there are times when one can detect the ghost of Lord Reith in some of the statements of those who have been given charge of Irish broadcasting. In more recent times, I recall the chairman of RTÉ of the day describing RTÉ to me as a business with so many thousand employees. I always refer to it as the national broad-caster. This shift from national broadcaster to large commercial unit with thousands of employees had started in Britain and completely changed the character of British broadcasting. The ethos forced on public-service broad-casting in Britain was born in an anti–state enterprise environment.

Reflecting on this now, I have come to the conclusion that the only sure rock upon which the future of public-service broadcasting might be built is one that puts the programme-makers at the centre of things and is suspicious of alleged technical managerial expertise. If the absence of public under-standing is losing some support for public-service broadcasting is resulting in some support for public-service broadcasting being lost, I also have the feel-ing that the subjugation of broadcasting values to organisational ones is part of the loss of confidence that is now so clear in so many places in contem-porary society.

In recent years, of course, there has been a fundamental and rapid change in technology. This has represented a particular kind of seduction. Many politicians seem lost in awe at the mention of the digital superhighway. It is as if it were all too exciting, too promising as a competitive tool in the market to be made amenable to regulation.

If the technology has arrived with great rapidity, the issue as to how it should be applied has, by contrast, generated a deadly silence. Yet how this matter is handled will decide whether we deepen and widen communications or open up a new fissure in society between the information-rich and the information-poor. The European Union is a good example of how those who are anxious to make profits from 'new services' have, with the assistance of the European Commission, steamrollered those who are interested in securing the future of public-service broadcasting and in ensuring accountability to the public from those who have constructed new monopolies. Put bluntly, the Commission has worked very hard at deregulating public-service broadcasting but, despite pressure from the European Parliament again and again, has refused to bring in a directive on concentration of ownership – something which is increasing every day. Those who support public-service broadcasting are sometimes pilloried as backward traditionalists, old regulationists standing in the way of the shining future, with its new services. It was one of the achievements of the Irish presidency of the European Union that we managed to put a special protocol in the Amsterdam Treaty that protected public-service broadcasting to a certain degree. Let us be clear, however: the pressure for commercial services delivered on market principles is even more likely to succeed in a new European Parliament that is right of centre.

In Europe today, nearly every country is preparing or drafting broadcasting legislation that will attempt to strike a balance with the marketplace. In almost every member state, the hard technology of communications is seeking to establish a hegemony over what is perceived to be the softer cultural target of broadcasting within culture. This issue arises regularly when such issues as whether or not there should be a different regulator for content and mode of delivery are considered. These are not just issues as to political turf. Behind them is a huge body of investment whose short-term profit may require the public interest to be forgotten.

The main tendencies in communications at the present time include convergence of technology, concentration of ownership in a number of international conglomerates, and fragmentation of audiences. These tendencies occur at a time when the prevailing ideology guiding economic-policy decisions places an emphasis on unrestricted market adjustments.

The circumstances of these transitions are different from those of other historical shifts that have occurred in the industrial era. It is very different to question, indeed identify, the assumptions upon which these recent transitions are based. We are drifting into, rather than choosing, this new condition of our unfreedom – our existence as consumers rather than citizens.

Citizenship, the public space, the shared moment, the common history, the shared community of the imagination, are perceived as tired old phrases; *interests* are what have to be addressed. A private world of consumer choice and its advertisements has replaced an older but still necessary debate about adequate provision in the public space. With these shifts in private consumption, it is arguable whether there is any real meaning to our use of the word 'culture' at all. When a lifestyle is something to which we aspire, cultural product has a meaning quite different, a mode of production quite different, from any previous concept of shared meaning.

It is when we are alone, consuming privately, consumed in our consumption, that we experience a peculiarly new form of alienation and loneliness. We seek relief in the television. We are open to be entertained. We are willing to be subscribed to be entertained. Indeed, the smart box on the television may take the thinking out of it for us altogether. Lots of purchased fantasy in front of the television – that is what generates profits from the less than twenty large conglomerates that monopolise close to 80 percent of all the 'entertainment product' sold on the planet. It will reassure us no doubt as well that the same people are caring for our children with an equivalent monopoly in video games – except of course that in this case the number of companies is closer to one dozen.

There are rare exceptions to this – moments when the public world is rediscovered. I was moved by the account in Michael Tracey's *The Decline and Fall of Public Service Broadcasting* of the forty-eight hours around the death of President John F. Kennedy, when advertisements disappeared and a vast, diverse community shared a moment of grief. It was a public moment to which immense personal emotion was brought by so many – and became part of the collective memory.

Watching the near-total eclipse in Ireland recently was also interesting in its own way, in so far as people left their private space to share the experience. They gathered in little groups at corners, and in public places, occasionally sharing glasses – refugees from the almost-lost world of the public and the communal.

At the bases of the choices we will make in the next few years are some fundamental value choices involving such questions as:

§ What value do we put on the public world?

§ What value do we put on issues beyond the immediate, beyond a single life-span?

§ How do we wish to remember and be remembered?

§ What do we wish to be free to imagine?

Such value choices raise questions about the cultural space, its relationship to the economic space, and how the cultural space is to be defined: is it to be open or closed, democratic or autocratic, fixed by tradition or flexible to the contemporary and the as-yet-unremembered?

For example, if the cultural space was defined in some Arnoldian way, stressing an elitist version of the inherited tradition of the powerful, and if the focus of the beautiful, the true and the good was defined by a particular class, most would find this to be oppressive or conservative, or both. We would find it easier again to reject a statistical definition. In a curious way, there has always been public support for a definition of culture that would have critical capacity at its centre, emphasising, I suppose, that to live reflexively in one's world is both one of the most basic and one of the most difficult instincts we share in our common humanity.

There was always, then, a debate as to what constituted cultural value. Those who made programmes knew that sometimes their work would strike a strange resonance with the past; sometimes it would be anticipatory in its innovation. Nothing was really predictable but the standard had to have, at its root, respect for freedom and creativity.

What we now face is an uncritical acceptance of the provisions of the market. A market segment has to be filled. A programme has to be provided. It can be made expensively at home or can be purchased cheaply from those who are dumping product from abroad. These are not choices without consequence. It is not only the programme-maker who does not get to make his or her programme; it is that a story in the public world is being suppressed. It is that another group of consumers is being given a formula-produced, homogenised product.

Let me emphasise the distinction between making a programme, with its high, fixed costs, and providing a programme, with its low, variable costs. Making a programme in the full consciousness that it will resonate with a public of which the maker is a part is qualitatively different from filling an entertainment slot with a product from a pool of homogenised programmes purchased from the west coast of the United States for a market located anywhere at any time.

Perhaps the most serious debate on television production in recent times in Ireland was that which is described in Jack Dowling, Lelia Doolan and Bob Quinn's *Sit Down and Be Counted: The Cultural Evolution of a Television Station*. Published in 1969, with an introduction by Raymond Williams, it is an extraordinary book in its attempt to marry issues of organisation, authority, philosophy, science, culture and human behaviour among a complex group of talented and often difficult people. The book represents a remarkable moment in Irish television history – the moment prior to surrender of the intellectual and aesthetic to a more short-term organisational and accountancy-based ethos.

I thought of this book often during the period in which two major decisions had to be taken concerning television production. The first of these was the prohibition on interviews with members of listed proscribed organisations – the infamous Section 31 of Irish broadcasting law. The second was in the period of my taking a decision over proposals for the establishment of an Irish-language television station – Teilefís na Gaeilge.

In relation to the first of these, I could discern opinion being quite divided among broadcasting practitioners. While the majority appeared to hold an anti-censorship view, I was in no doubt about the existence of a group that was happy to live with the organisational neatness of a prohibition. Not having to exercise discretion always helps the dedicated organisational person. On the second issue, Teilefís na Gaeilge, I must be brief. However, let me say that the issue was primarily one of economics versus culture. The new service was established with valuable assistance from the most senior levels within RTÉ, and grave reservations from others. It must be remembered that this station, created to serve the Irish-language community, was established as an extension to public-service broadcasting at the very time a blizzard of commercialism was blowing across the broadcasting world. Today, with its young staff, it is, as a publisher broadcaster, successful, and in a good position to make the shift to a new technological environment. What I want to place on record, however, is the sheer vitriol that informed some of the opposition. Modern consumers were going to be exercising their choices, their freedom with a zapper. The campaign was personalised and bitter, and guided by the leading newspaper group, which has been adjudicated to have a dominant or near-monopoly position in Irish newspapers: the Irish Independent Group.

It is one of the inescapable facts of our existence that we live by images. The issue, however, is which images, drawn for which purposes, will proliferate. The decision in such matters is personal, insofar as a final personal choice is made; however, it is also inescapably contextual and cultural. Some choices rather than others are facilitated. There is a curious parallel for me in the destruction of the public spaces in Europe, sometimes in the name of urban renewal, and the commodification of the media. It is as if we might make a parallel between the spatial order of the city under pressure for different land uses and spectrum, which, until recent technological advances, was scarce. As the mark of possession on the spatial order, or on the spectrum, becomes more prominent, it assumes the status of a brand in a retail sense, producing a set of seamless fantasies for a seamless collection of consumers.

In a paper to which I will refer later, Professor Farrel Corcoran wrote of the voyeurism as to the criminal which can be exploited as a substitute for news or current affairs. He describes three major network evening news programmes in 1995, broadcasting a total of 2,574 crime stories:

> A fascination with crime dominates both news and entertainment genres. . . . Local news, too, is dominated by a nightly extravaganza of mayhem: fires, personal tragedies, train wrecks, highway disasters, interspersed with the terminal inanity of cloned information that passes for party-political debate. Television schedules flirt with soft porn, celebrate gross consumption, glorify guns, and demonise all the wretched of the earth. The relentless earnings pressure of commercial broadcasting makes programming just another corporate operation, driven by the same demands of the financial market as steel making, banking or fast-food merchandising.

Professor Corcoran saw as one of the sources of the reduction in standards the fact that 'too few people make decisions about what the population needs to know, resulting in a one-dimensional, smooth-edged cultural flow that colonises the national symbolic environment.'

I am not arguing for a return to a world that was simple in its class divisions, resolute in its Arnoldian assumptions. I am simply saying that if the public space – and public-service broadcasting is an important part of this space – is lessened, there will be an immense social loss at the level of integration, cohesion and sense of community.

If there is a loss of discourse through public-service broadcasting, and if it is accompanied by low turn-out in elections, low political participation and the emergence of, as it were, an etiquette of being apolitical, then the confrontation between the beneficiaries and the losers of the markets will, in the decades to come, be unmedited by institutions such as trade unions and political parties. Such confrontations, without a mediating discourse, will carry a far greater risk of violence.

Public-service broadcasting is important, then. It is important that it continues to enjoy widespread public support. Indeed, many of those who are opposed to the concept of the public-service broadcaster are willing to retain the concept of public-service broadcasting itself.

The definition of public-service broadcasting and of the public-service broadcaster is a matter of some importance. There is always a tendency for those who offer – usually under some form of licensing regulation – news, current affairs or weather to say that this constitutes their public-service contribution.

In Ireland, commercial radio interests have made a case in recent years for the licence fee to be shared on such a basis. To me, the structure of the public space across the programming schedules is what is important. The broadcaster has to be assessed by the totality and the philosophy of content. The issue is not one of having a sprinkling of one of the eight values we mentioned at the outset. It is how all these are achieved continuously for a significant proportion of the public in a universal way.

One of the important benefits of having a vibrant public-service-broadcasting arrangement is that, in addition to inviting citizens to experience the timeless, the universal, the unimagined, it is also a rich source of creativity – a creativity that is not confined to the broadcasting station or to one activity.

We have arrived at a situation in which it is perfectly clear that public-service broadcasting will exist in future in a mixed model of broadcasting. If it is the strong partner in such a mixed model, if it itself values creativity and programme-making as its principal definition of itself, it will have a positive effect as to standards on its partners within the mixed model. If it is the weaker partner, it will seek to compete with what surrounds it and will embark, perhaps imperceptibly, on a process of self-commercialisation, with the downgrading of programme-making and an obsessive, market-led concentration on programme acquisition and provision.

Time does not allow me to develop the institutional and organisational implications of all this. I believe, for example, that when independent commissioning is facilitated by a national broadcaster, this can be of benefit to both the commissioning authority and the independent producer involved. It does, however, require an ethics of production, delivery and administration.

On 26 September 1996, Professor Farrel Corcoran delivered a paper entitled 'The Future of Public Service Broadcasting in the Single Audio-visual Market' to an informal meeting of ministers of the European Union with responsibility for culture and audio-visual matters. Among the topics he dealt with was the issue of the European Broadcasting Union, which had served to provide the widest possible provision of free-to-air broadcasting for its members by having an ability-to-pay clause:

> The Commission Decision of June 1993 ruled that the effect of the
> EBU provisions governing the joint acquisition of television rights to

172

sport events was to strengthen the market position of its members to the disadvantage of private, commercial competitors, contrary to Article 85 (1) of the Treaty of Rome. Nevertheless, the Decision granted the EBU an exemption for a five-year period under certain conditions, within the meaning of Article 85 (3) ('... allowing consumers a fair share of the resulting benefit ... '). However, a subsequent action taken against this Decision by a number of private broadcasters resulted in a rejection in July 1996 by the Court of First Instance of the European Communities of the Commission's use of the concept of 'particular public mission' in granting the exemption until 1998, in relation to the EBU's argument that was derived from Article 85 (3). In effect, the Court has annulled the Commission's 1993 Decision.

Whatever the legal outcome of the appeal in this case, the question for policy-makers should be a citizen-centred one. Are the social benefits delivered to viewers by public-service broadcasters' action co-operatively in the EBU insufficient when balanced against the supposed harm inflicted on private broadcasters by barriers to entry constituted by public-service broadcasters' joint acquisition of programming rights?

Professor Corcoran went on to list a number of challenges to licence fee as income to public-service broadcasters:

1   Private broadcasters from France, Spain and Portugal have lodged complaints alleging that consumer levies, direct subsidies or periodic capital injections confer unfair advantages on public-service broadcasters. A decision against the use of licence fees would, of course, strike at the very heart of public-service broadcasting. In response to the complaint, DGIV has commissioned a consultant's report, which has been distributed to Member States for comment, and will undertake a similar study of the licence situation in new Member States and EFTA States. Only then will it 'encourage a debate on the way forward'.

In the past, the Commission has approved 'aid' to broadcasters as long as the aid is shown to be necessary for the promotion and/or preservation of European culture and is proportional to these goals. But arguing that licence fees are a form of 'state aid' is fraught with dangers from a public-service-broadcasting point of view, if it means that cultural policy must always, ultimately, be subservient to competition policy and be 'shoehorned' only by way of exception to market rules. A more helpful approach is contained in the legal opinion tabled by ARD and ZDF in May 1996, prepared by Professor Thomas Opperman of Tubingen University, on how German broadcasters' receipt of licence-fee income can be reconciled with European law on state aid. He argues that (a) licence fees cannot be regarded as preferential treatment, rather they represent appropriate remuneration for provision of basic service; (b) licence fees are not a form of state aid because they are not granted freely by the state, since they are unavoidable constitutional requirement in Germany; (c) they are not allocated out of public coffers, but are a charge on the citizen not directly borne by the state budget within the meaning of Article 92; (d) public-service broadcasting is, in fact, in an unfavourable competitive situation compared to its private rivals, since it must allocate its resources in accordance with its remit, and this means that it cannot stake everything on audience ratings.

2   The European Radio Association has filed a complaint against public service radio having unfair advantage because of its 'priority access to frequencies, larger number of transmitters and double funding'.

3   Toy Manufacturers Europe, the toy-industries lobby group, has lodged complaints against the Greek ban on toy advertising in daytime television and also against Sweden and Belgium, and promises to do the same against Ireland this autumn. In the Irish case, RTÉ argues that its public-service remit obliges it to take seriously research findings indicating that pre-school children do not understand the persuasive intent of advertising (the 'caveat emptor' factor in selling) and therefore access to them by advertisers should be restricted.

Decisions on cases like these will determine whether the emergence of a single market will benefit producers alone, or whether the benefits will actually move from the level of corporate enterprise to that of the viewer. It is sometimes observed by academic researchers that there is a palpable bias against public-service broadcasting, and the EBU in particular, perceptible in the very organisational culture of the Commission, where the everyday discourse of even junior officers in some Directorates tends to assume that the very notion of public-service broadcasting is an anachronism in today's media landscape. This bias is evident even in areas that are not directly concerned with broadcasting. In the ongoing debate in the Bangemann Forum on the Information Society, for instance, Mr Bangemann has dissociated himself from the conclusions of Working Group V (the Cultural Dimension and Future of Media) regarding the importance of a modern public broadcasting service for the development of an information society accessible to all.

I believe that public-service broadcasting, unambiguously funded by the licence fee – an important practical and emblematic bond with the citizen – can be a powerful space of creativity. The importance of creativity is enhanced rather than lessened in a model of mixed production. There is an interaction of standards that is most important for the overall quality of the broadcasting that emerges. It is from an atmosphere like this that many learn what they will later use for a source of innovation in the cultural industries. In this space, it becomes clear that, rather than it being the case that we must wait for the surpluses of the economic space to allow cultural events to happen, and cultural products to emerge, economics can be made human again by being made creative.

There was a time when the arts were not a specialist, separate activity but the possession of every man and woman who partook of a culture – its stories, poems, carpentry, pots, utensils and so on. When the anthropologist Margaret Mead began her study of the Balinese, she attempted to explain to them the Western view of art as a 'heightened' representation of life. At first they could not understand, for they had no frames to put around their pictures. Eventually they followed her explanation – and, as soon as they did, told her: 'We have no art. We just do everything as well as we can.' That world is now lost, but one of the aims of a comprehensive arts policy might be to combat the growing compartmentalisation of the modern economic systems and to restore expressive freedom to the individual, so that every man and woman can again be in some sense an artist. The arts administrator, like any true professional, moves to that ideal, if impossible, situation where his or her skills would no longer be necessary, because the arts would have returned to the wider practices of a fulfilled life. But how do we combat the detachment of the arts from the disciplines of economics, politics and philosophy? And how, in doing so, might we reconnect the conduct of economic policy to the ethical vision?

In Ireland, as commercialism in radio, and more recently in TV, asserted itself, one could see the ethos changing along a line of self-commercialisation. Many, for example, are unhappy at the existence of advertising for children but, nevertheless, they are anxious to retain the advertising income from this source. The incredibly difficult task of satisfying advertisers with ratings, while retaining a commitment to programming quality, is getting more difficult all the time. Sporting rights, of course, have become a matter of such fierce competition by satellite purchasers that the general access of citizens to significant sporting events cannot any longer be taken for granted. A minority of events may be protected, but the reality is that something even as basically social as sport may be changed fundamentally as it becomes a television commodity. The case has been made, of course, and needs to be made again and again, about the importance of media education in generating a critical capacity which all citizens need in a world in which consumption of the media is becoming more central to their lives.

Professor Benjamin R. Barber in his book *Jihad vs. McWorld*, published in 1995, provides a description of the alternative to a diverse world which he calls 'McWorld':

> McWorld is a product of popular culture driven by expansionist commerce. Its template is American, its form style. Its goods are as much images as material, an aesthetic as well as a product line. It is about culture as commodity, apparel as ideology. Its symbols are Harley-Davidson motorcycles and Cadillac motor cars hoisted from the roadways, where they once represented a mode of transportation, to the marquees of global market cafés like Harley-Davidson's and the Hard Rock Cafés, where they became the icons of a lifestyle. You don't drive them, you feel their vibes and rock to the images they conjure up from old movies and new celebrities. Music, video, theatre, books and theme parks – the new churches of commercial civilisation, in which malls are public squares and suburbs the neighbourless neighbourhoods – all are constructed as image exports creating a common world taste around common logos, advertising slogans, stars, songs, brand names, jingles and trademarks.

If I might return for a moment to the possible connection between culture and violence, I note what Professor Barber has to say of the conversion of the impulse for identity from innocence to hatred of the stranger:

> What ends as Jihad may begin as a simple search for a local identity, some set of common personal attributes to hold out against the numbing and neutering uniformities of industrial modernisation and the colonising culture of McWorld.

We live in a Europe that at the time of the ascendancy of the Right championed deregulation and, in an extremely ideological way, announced that the hidden trend of the market would guide us. In his book, Barber described the character of such a period:

> . . . the absence of common will and that conscious and collective human control under the guidance of law we call democracy . . . both make war on the sovereign nation-state and thus undermine the nation-state's democratic institutions. Each eschews civil society and belittles democratic citizenship, neither seeks alternative democratic institutions.

Their common thread is indifference to civil liberty. Jihad forges communities of blood rooted in exclusion and hatred, communities that slight democracy in favour of tyrannical paternalism or consensual tribalism. McWorld forges global markets rooted in consumption and profit, leaving to an untrustworthy, if not altogether fictitious, invisible hand issues of public interest and common goods that once might have been nurtured by democratic citizenries and their watchful governments. Such governments, intimidated by market ideology, are actually pulling back at the very moment they ought to be aggressively intervening. What was once understood as protecting the public interest is now excoriated as heavy-handed regulatory browbeating . . . . Today . . . we seem intent on re-creating a world in which our only choices are the secular universalism of the cosmopolitan market and the everyday particularism of the fractious tribe.

Professor Barber's analysis may be somewhat apocalyptic, but it does stress the important issues of identity and diversity.

With digitalisation comes an entirely new set of policy decisions which policy-makers cannot avoid. For example, there will be competition between political providers as to mode of delivery. It will be important to insist that content is even more important than capacity. The debate cannot afford to be exclusively technical, except at a huge democratic cost. Blurring the values content of the new revolution suits the conglomerates, which benefit from a concentration of ownership as the shared space comes under threat. We should remember the injunction of one great writer on broadcasting: 'We humanise what is going on in the world and within ourselves only by speaking of it, and in the course of speaking about it we learn to be human.' We live by stories, and the principles by which stories are selected, the skill with which they are told, and their resonance or otherwise in our own culture is a fundamental democratic concern.

In a recent 'Report to the Joint Committee on Heritage and the Irish Language of the Irish Parliament', I set out the issues that had to be decided as I saw them. These included:

§ Universal access – which means would best approximate it?

§ The contextualisation, or separating out, of entertainment as an aspect of broadcasting.

§ The distribution of spare spectrum.

§ The timing of analogue switch-off.

§ The nature of electronic programme guides.

§ Content – the issue of appropriate regulation.

§ The number of channels to be allocated.

§ The position of existing licence-holders for cable and satellite.

§ The European context, particularly in relation to Télévision Sans Frontières, the European Union commitment to storing and exchanging broadcasting space without the hindrance of national borders or legislation restricting such.

§ Tiered subscriptions, which I saw as creating a new circumstance for the public-service broadcaster should it continue to be the sole beneficiary of the broadcasting licence.

§ The nature of the 'must carry' obligation.

§ Local television.

§ Interactive services.

§ Digital radio.

In August 1999, my successor announced that the government had approved the drafting of legislation in relation to broadcasting, including a decision to allow the speedy and effective introduction of digital terrestrial television in Ireland.

We have to some extent debated the legislation but I believe that there will be a consensus that the issues are too important to leave to the market. This is an attitude that I believe is shared by most thoughtful authors on the subject. For example, Andrew Graham and Gavyn Davies in their *Broadcasting Society and Policy in the Multimedia Age* suggest that:

What public policy, therefore, requires is a positive force that would:

§ act as a counterweight to the private concentration of ownership;

§ deliver national coverage so as to counteract fragmentation of audiences;

§ provide a 'centre of excellence' which both makes and broadcasts programmes;

§ be large enough to influence the market and so act as the guarantor of quality; and

§ widen choice both now and in the future by complementing the market through pursuit of public-service purposes.

The best way to provide this positive pressure is via public-service broadcasting (not as a substitute to the commercial sector but as a complement to it). The conclusion of this part of the argument is that, while a public-service broadcaster, such as the BBC, has no right to exist, there are purposes for its existence. Moreover, contrary to the conventional wisdom, the new technology increases, rather than deceases, the need for such a broadcaster.

In the end, we are left with the conclusion that we should use the new convergence in technology to give a leadership role to public-service broadcasting in a mixed model. We should do that, and fund it through the licence fee; and, rejecting populist arguments to the contrary, we should issue an invitation to the alternative to populism – an active citizenship that will enable us to feel at home in our world.

Delivered as part of the symposium 'Counting the Cultural Beat',
held in Wellington, New Zealand, 31 August 1999

In the event, the Irish government abandoned its proposals for transfer to digital broadcasting. Time was lost, the broadcasting space was lost to outside interests, and now further commercialisation is likely to be facilitated as a sole option.

MDH, 2006

The Migrant's Return

A Personal Reflection on the

Importance of Raymond Williams

As a student in University College Galway, I read a paper on how Raymond Williams was bridging the gap between literary criticism and sociological theory, but the first real introduction I had to his work was when I read *The Country and the City* in the 1970s. I still recall the sense of excitement, over twenty years ago, that I felt when I read it. I saw it as a work of integration. It gave a sense of wholeness, of complexity respected and easy generalisation rejected. The literary evidence united not only different disciplines but also analysis and craft.

Here was a scholar moving between literature, history and sociology at a time when practitioners were shrinking their interests into ever-narrower areas, when the areas where different disciplines met were being abandoned in the name of specialisation. Here was a scholar who rendered the arid polarity between tradition and modernity redundant. I was at that time surrounded by scholars working on the concept of the contrast between the small community and the urban metropolis. At best – or maybe, with arrogant licence – they were constructing models of transition from underdevelopment to development. Raymond Williams's sense of history, including its conflicts, restored the integrity of time, space and community for me. He textured the analysis of change with the detail of truly human experience.

I wanted to know Raymond Williams but I never was to meet him. Therefore, what I have to say now does not constitute any attempt at making evaluations or judgments, at ransacking the work for its fit with the demands of any paradigm or method. It is merely a description of an encounter, at a distance, of a migrant, with just some facets of the extraordinary contribution of an intellectual giant who himself migrated across so many dimensions of human experience and reflection.

Reading more of Williams's work, I began in the seventies to construct my image of him. Beyond the integration and the genuine dialectic of his

180

method, I welcomed his commitment to a politics that opposed economic exploitation, cultural domination and personal repression in the practical democratic work of extension education. I was myself at this time a teacher in a university extra-mural programme. Driving at night on the roads in the west of Ireland, I asked myself how the works could keep appearing when at the same time the author was finding the time to deliver such an enormous commitment to literacy. A fashionable word at the time was 'praxis'. It contained the suggestion that theoretical analysis could be combined with action. Raymond Williams was already doing it.

I was then a young academic in Manchester, the only member of my family to have attended a university. (Half my family finished second level.) I stayed for a while with my sister and my brother-in-law, who drove a machine on a building site. I was a migrant. Born in a city, reared on a small farm in County Clare, getting to university by accident, working summers in England, my earlier life was characterised by a concentration on escape through education. I was a migrant on the way, as I saw it then, to a better future.

I sensed the strangeness of the city that the migrant feels. But I was hungry too for the warmth of the crowded space, for the speed of novelty, for anonymity. I had read Walt Whitman, that exceptional poet of the city, of daytime steel and evening promiscuity. I mention this to emphasise that it was as a peasant, in transition without knowing it to further insecurity, that I read, and then seized on, Williams's work for its ring of truth and humanity. For me, Williams was making a narrative drawing from, and revealing, a lost wholeness from buried stories of the ordinary; and he could accommodate the sense intimacies of rural life with the wonder of the migrant in the city.

I was at that time going to postgraduate seminars in Dover Street, where I was updating Arensberg and Kimball's study of *Family and Community in Ireland*, a structural functionalist study of Irish society in the 1930s by two Harvard scholars. The absence of conflict in that work struck me forcefully, but I was not in a great position to ask questions. I was a migrant carrying a peasant experience, shopping with many others, Africans in particular, for a theoretical model in which to enclose the experience of my people. I became interested in Williams's life, and in particular his migration from Wales to Cambridge. I was not then in a position to evaluate the arguments about him – arguments which were not materialist enough for certain sections of English Marxism and not speculative enough for certain strains of post-1968 French Marxism. Like any newly arrived migrant, I listened carefully and in silence to the syntax and the accent of academic discourse.

Before Manchester, I had been to the United States. Young Irish academics at this time were frequently educated at postgraduate level in the United States through a generous system of fellowships, as I was. We were, as Orlando Fals Borda put it, given ideological glasses through which we were asked to interpret our own society. We were then, and remain, indebted for what was an introduction to method but, when the method became an empiricism closely lodged within a structural functionalist prison, the burden became apparent: we were victims of a quiet Western intellectual colonisation.

From the end of the sixties to the eighties, Irish social studies wore the spancel of the Princeton Studies of Gabriel Almond, Sidney Verba and others. The modernisation model, which saw a transition from rural traditional society to industrial urban society, was in the ascendant. I was in revolt at this, hence my feeling for Williams's work. I was interested in migration and in particular the figure of the migrant in literature. I had come to the conclusion that the essence of the migratory experience was in the literary accounts in a way that was systematically missed in overdetermined models in the social sciences. The literature, such as the novels of Patrick McGill, caught the flux of the migratory experience.

The accessibility of Williams's books offered a warmth too, and a generosity that contrasted with the affected distance of some members of the academic community, who seemed to see inaccessibility of conceptual structures as a mark of excellence. In a political sense, too, the inclusive invitation to reflection in Williams's work shone like a beacon. There was an invitation to integrate biography and history in a patient way – something that stood in contrast to the unwelcoming coldness of certain sections of the then-fashionable materialist Left.

I often asked myself why generosity did not inform those circles that analysed and aimed to organise, to build solidarity. Would an inclusiveness not give strength? Would it not appeal to the heart as well as the head? Even today, I ask if this cerebral excess and heady indulgence, this essential intolerance, was not a precursor to the failure of nerve that came later in so many places on the Left? But that Left had courage, and it was taking part in an engaged intellectual work. The longing I had, I recall, was that it also be inclusive, be warm in its invitation for all the biographies that could build its version of the future. Why did so many who lacked theoretical sophistication but who possessed a rage against inequality, and a thirst for a better system, have to be excluded, through either indifference or intolerance?

182

Thinking like this, in conditions of insecurity of the life and the intellect – a migrant's condition – imagine the the force with which a passage like the following from *The Country and the City* struck me:

> Thus at once, for me, before the argument starts, country life has many meanings. It is the elms, the way, the white horse, in the field beyond the window where I am writing. It is the men in the November evening, walking back from farming with their hands in their pockets, in the pockets of their khaki coats; and the women in headscarves, outside their cottages, waiting for the blue bus that will take them, inside school hours, to work in the harvest. It is the tractor on the road, leaving its tracks of serrated pressed mud; the light in the small hours, in the pig-farm across the road, in the crisis of a litter; the slow brown van met at the difficult corner, with the crowded sheep jammed to its slatted sides; the heavy smell, on still evenings, of the silage ricks fed with molasses. It is also the sour land, on the thick boulder day, not far up the road, that is selling for housing, for a speculative development, at twelve thousand pounds an acre.

The eye for revelatory and resonant image is here. All the senses are informing both the heart and the head. In such a passage, we sense the intellect integrated with the heart, the heart generous, enabling all the senses to store and reconstruct those intimacies and sensations that are the very essence of human life. But this rural recollection is not a blindfold of nostalgia or pseudo-pastoralism. When the balance requires it, Williams could also write of the city:

> The lights of the City. I go out in the dark before bed, and look at the glow in the sky; a look at the city while remembering Hardy's Jude who stood and looked at the distant, attainable, and unattainable Christminster.

It is not that the city is less than the country. It is that the abuses of either constitute the structures for analysis. Generosity of mind enabled Williams to use the senses to inform the intellectual analysis of not only the early experience but also of the ever-succeeding new steps on the escalator of experience, to wonder, to reject, to analyse. I used his masterly exposition of the pseudo-pastoral in my teaching to expose an abuse of the concept of community that was reactionary. I was brash enough then to suggest its replacement altogether with the concept of reciprocity. I saw so little of genuine solidarity in the alleged bonds of parish and place. I knew from personal experience the difference between the loan, which would have allowed the purchase of a cow, and the gift of potatoes when a family was finished after the death of a cow. I was reacting to the myth of the homogeneous peasantry, the exclusion of conflict in the studies of rural societies. The reactionary view, later to resurface again and again, was that, to march from the present into the past, back from urban to rural, from industrial life to agricultural life, would restore a golden age.

I feel now that a substitution of reciprocity for community might have reflected, on my part, an impatient materialism, an urge to locate an economic analysis in place of a reductive nostalgia. Now, in times when freedom is abused in definition to imply some type of unlimited consumer choice, when all the solidarities of decency have been undermined, when intellectuals have abandoned the public sphere, I would instead seek to redefine, indeed reforge, community as a concept rather than abandoning it. Williams's reassertion of the concepts of culture and community in the conditions of the miners' strikes in the eighties roots these conflicts in a historical continuity of struggle. He returned to the key concepts of community and culture because he heard them being vindicated from the mouths of those involved in a struggle for survival.

Williams made it home to Wales, and to the roots of his key concepts. He was a returned migrant with a particular experience that constituted a set of tools sharpened on the migrant journey, enabling him to integrate – the life and the history, the place of transience, the place of origin, the analytical and the literary.

He reflects, I suggest, a migrant's experience in the manner in which he continually widens his gaze and extends his concern in an atmosphere of change. He is open to the new, which he analyses and incorporates. At the heart of the migrant experience, I have suggested, is transience. Literature has caught this element of transience so much better than the over-determining social sciences, which have largely seen the migrant as being acted upon, drawn between formative influences at the point of origin and the negotiated influences at the point of destination. They have missed entirely the complexity of the transitional experience. The world of 'in between' is a world of suitcases, of visits to train stations, of images caught in family photos and strange workplaces. I recall being very powerfully moved when I read for the first time John Berger's *A Seventh Man*, which illustrates this point so powerfully.

This transience carries an insecurity with it, but also an openness to the renegotiation of experience. Circular migration was a reality long before its recognition in work such as that of J. Clyde Mitchell and Valdo Pons. It was a powerful insight that helped refine the model of cause and effect in migration studies. Instead of being victim to two determining systems, the migrant is continually drawing and reinventing his or her own world. It is a version that is of both origin and destination, and that transcends both.

The country and the city are reconstructed by the migrant. The migrant invents and reflects much more than the causal models allowed. Crucially in the act of migration, systems for the handling of experience are constructed that are not reducible to those of place of origin or destination. In Williams's work, the powerful insights of the returned migrant are reflected in the renewed strength of the idea of being both Welsh and European which is at the heart of his later writing.

The analysis developed in metropolitan space and brought home is reinvigorated by the opening of the suitcase, the vindication of the integrity of memory. The analysis is richer for having been away. It is richer by its transcending all stereotypes of the sedentary isolated. The analysis is not about the integrity of the archaic or of the ghetto. It is about similar struggles, on common values, in pursuit of cultural diversity as a tool of democracy. It binds in the same sheaf the remembered experience of childhood and place with the accumulated experience of transience in migration. This would not be possible if transience was experienced as a negative impulse to amnesia. The unremitting invitation to the migrant is to such amnesia, to an eschewing not just of a childhood sense memory, but also to an avoidance of any radical analysis of the social base of experience, of its mode of production.

The requirements of a socially pleasing present mobility require a forgetting of the earlier life. This of course can be projected on to the past of one's people. It constitutes a violence against the integrity of memory. I believe that reconstruction of the migrant experience, requiring a continual reforging of consciousness as it does, is an invaluable tool well beyond the physical experience of migration itself. Space is but one dimension to migration, as the work of James Joyce attests in the experience of a single day in the life of the famous migrant Leopold Bloom.

Returning to my analogy, may I suggest that the requirement to be of one place is a lesser burden than the requirement to be of one version of one analysis for all time and in all circumstances. The returned migrant is in a unique position within the society to which he or she has returned. The migrant is a carrier of cultural influences, mediated through memory of community of origin, the community of transience and the community of destination that has been abandoned for the return home. That return has been an ideal that will have changed as circumstances change in the space of transience. Often rehearsed, eventually achieved, for the migrant it is a new state, not an old state recovered.

The dominant loyalty may be to one of these sets of cultural influences, in a form of capitulation. But the compromise also contains a capacity to reconstruct an identity older than that originally left, more processual than that originally experienced, and more idealistic, perhaps, than that held by those in the space of home encountered on the return home.

We might see this as an analogy for political vision. The settled ideas made in travel and reforged are often, on revaluation directed towards reconstruction. Values are deepened on the journey, even though the circumstances and experience will suggest and demand a more complex articulation of them.

In September 1969, Williams wrote a preface for the most important book on Irish communications, *Sit Down and Be Counted*, by Jack Dowling, Lelia Doolan and Bob Quinn. The book came after principled discussion, culminating in resignation, on the role of creativity in the organisation of the national broadcaster, RTÉ. Williams wrote – after a passage on the failure of colleagues and intellectuals to support those brave people who constituted the Prague Spring (and whose efforts he believed were not wasted) – 'some of the changes they spoke for are beginning to come through!':

> This will be the case, also, I believe, in the recent difficulties in Dublin, from which this present book springs. In a crowded few days there, this spring, I saw the unmistakable signs of an extraordinary creative vitality – of the kind we can properly expect from an Irish Culture – and, less happily, some of the signs of that familiar tension between producers and an intermediate authority. I do not know the events from within but I am sure of this; that the voices I heard there, speaking of their own land and of its renewal, are at once Irish and international, in the most authentic senses. Deeply responsible to their own people, rather than to an Irish sector of the international market, painfully aware of the pressures and conflicts of real growth and change, they spoke in Irish accents of Irish problems which were to me, from across the sea, structurally very close to the problems of culture and society, the internal but general problems of communications throughout Europe and North America.

186

We are all indebted to Alan O'Connor for his brilliant annotated biblio-graphical summary of Williams's work. In that review, we can see how the books and articles came tumbling out, including *Television, Technology and Cultural Form.* The preface to *Sit Down and Be Counted*, reflecting on the impact of the coming conflict on technology through the media structures, ended with the assertion:

> There is good reason to believe that many people will resist this worst of developments, but as the size of effective decision-taking communi-ties gets so much larger, and as the scale and complexity of interlocking agencies makes identification, let alone struggle, more difficult, it is not enough to rely on unaided virtues. Within the next few years, decisions will be taken, or fail to be taken, which will to a large extent determine which of these possible roads we are likely to take for the remainder of this century. But if action is necessary now, its first conditions are infor-mation, analysis, education, discussion, to which this book is offered as a small contribution and, it is hoped, an incentive.

That passage was typical, revealing as it did the integration of culture and communications which was at the centre of Williams's work. There was an integration too of analysis and the demands of solidarity. There was in it a generous recognition of similar concerns in a diversity of cultural settings.

Five years later, in *Television, Technology and Cultural Form*, Williams wrote:

> Legislation on foreign agencies, in the whole field of communications, is then a necessary and urgent objective. What is already a serious situa-tion will have become virtually irretrievable by the 1980s, unless very strong action is taken. In another dimension, there must be continual pressure for proper international agreements on satellite television, in particular refusing all control bodies with weighted voting, since these in practice would mean control by the superpowers. Smaller nations may seem to have little to bargain with, but while they retain control over ground-stations and over foreign or foreign-hired broadcasting or cable distribution systems, they are in fact in a strong position. The positive position in these negotiations can then be the institution of internation-al and transnational television systems under democratic international agencies.
>
> All this will take time and prolonged effort. The struggle will reach into every corner of society. But that is precisely what is at stake: a new universal accessibility. Over a wide range, from general television through commercial advertising to centralised information and data-

processing systems, the technology that is now or is becoming available can be used to affect, to alter, and in some cases to control our whole social process.

And it is ironic that the uses offer such extreme social choices. We could have inexpensive, locally based yet internationally extended television systems, making possible communication and information-sharing on a scale that not long ago would have seemed utopian. These are the contemporary tools of the long revolution towards an educated and participatory democracy, and of the recovery of effective communication in complex urban and industrial societies. But they are also the tools of what would be, in context, a short and successful counter-revolution, in which, under the cover of talk about choice and competition, a few para-national corporations, with their attendant states and agencies, could reach farther into our lives, at every level from news to psychodrama, until individual and collective response to many different kinds of experience and problem became almost limited to choice between their programmed possibilities.

How prophetic that passage now seems, and how depressing the changes that have taken place since it was written. Twenty-two years later, we are witnessing the last great colonisation – the colonisation of the imagination. It is being brought about not with force of arms or naked power, but through a quiet acquiescence in unfreedom, spreading like a virus, changing categories of citizenship to ones of consumer fetish. Passivity expands as activity becomes more difficult in the cultural and communicative space. Convergence of technology, concentration of ownership, and the powerlessness of elected governments in the face of unelected transnational conglomerates have created an environment where the world's people are the target not the arrow, as Williams put it.

It is hard to avoid a feeling of despair as the requirements of the international entertainment market are substituted for the building of cultural diversity. New services are constituted as consumable commodities rather than tools of communication. Citizenship within a democratic society, active and free to communicate, is one possibility. Standing against it is the concept of consumerism, insatiable, private and free to buy, buy, buy; passive in a world of advertising images. The latter version is in the ascendant. Society itself is questioned as an idea.

The forms of communication are adjusting to the new reality. News and current affairs are changing to manage what is felt to be the changed interests of the mass audience. There is a comprehensive decontextualisation of

188

time and space. Viewers and listeners are assumed to want an instant voyeuristic relationship with events, devoid of any context in history or social space. Broadcasting is seen as a corporate part of the entertainment business rather than as a tool of communication within a democratic society. Broadcasting, film, music are defined as commodities for exchange, to be regulated within competition rules for an international trade rather than as expressions of cultural diversity. Worse, the gap between the speed of technological application and any accountable discourse has widened and is widening every day. We cannot afford to exclude ourselves from any forum of that necessary discourse. One of the spaces of the discourse is the European Union.

I have sought in the European Council to develop the concept of 'the cultural space'. I see this as being wider than the economic space, and involving more of the life of European citizens. It is diverse – a mosaic, as it were – with many tones, shades and threads, always carrying the possibility of deeper layers of discovery. It has an opposite tendency to the homogenising tendency of a economic market. Why should that cultural space be dependent on concessions from the economic space? Spending money on cultural objects or temples is very different from making provision for a democratic, accessible, active cultural space. If the economy excludes the unemployed, the under-employed and the poor, why should they suffer a double exclusion, from the cultural space too? Would not tolerance be assisted by an inclusive cultural space of diversity, and would not broadcasting as a tool of communication be a crucial part of that cultural space?

During the Irish presidency of the European Union, and indeed for the last few years, I have sought to focus attention on the importance of culture. However limited the context of the European institutions are, it is an easier option not to engage, to assert an oppositional purity. There is a price, let no one ignore it, for choosing to go to the centre of the machine. Yet the decision is not one between brave opposition and capitulation. It is tactical and even requires great moral courage.

I have not time to dwell on why the founding treaties made no reference to culture. It is only in the Maastricht Treaty, particularly in Article 128, that we get explicit reference to it. Recently, I spoke to the European Parliament on the importance of taking this small instrument and using it to build the cultural space. I spoke as follows:

> I do not need to draw the attention of this Assembly to the inclusion of Article 128 in the Maastricht Treaty. Until this time, the affairs of the

Union have essentially been dominated by the four freedoms that constitute the basis of the Single Market – free movement of goods, persons, services and capital. As you are all aware, the Article, which is tempered by subsidiarity consideration, can be considered really in two parts: there are the actions that can be taken under paragraph 2, which can be aimed at encouraging cooperation between Member States and, if necessary, supporting and supplementing their action in a number of specified areas, and there is the vital provision in paragraph 4, which places a legal responsibility on the Community to take cultural aspects into account in its action under other provisions of the Treaty. It is therefore a priority of the Irish presidency to seek to give meaningful effect to this legal provision.

I am passionately convinced that culture can contribute to the objectives of the Community through enhancement of citizenship, personal and human development, greater economic and social cohesion, improvement of employment opportunities, elimination of exclusion, and enrichment of the quality of life of our citizens.

As I said in the course of the seminar I organised in Galway last September, involving my European ministerial colleagues with responsibility for cultural matters, I am seriously concerned that, as we approach the end of this century and the new millennium, there is a real danger that we may be reaching a crisis in relation to the concept of European civilisation and that our citizens are being gradually turned into passive consumers, without compassion and care for one another in an ever more aggressive, deregulated and competitive society. I am afraid that we are being dehumanised and I am convinced that the Community has an obligation to take this situation into account and to address it as a priority. On the other hand, I am optimistic that, if we are prepared to take the legal opportunity presented by Article 128 (4) of the Maastricht Treaty to place the cultural dimension more centre stage in the policy-making deliberations of the Union, we can pull back from the brink.

I am happy to inform you that my colleagues agreed that there was an urgent need for a practical approach in the Community to enhance the role of culture within the parameters of the Maastricht Treaty.

You will, I am sure, be aware of the First Report by the Commission on the Consideration of Cultural Aspects in European Community Action. This report represents a valuable first step in determining the areas in which other provisions of the Treaty, and actions arising from them, have an impact on and benefit the cultural sector. I am endeavouring to promote a resolution for adoption by Council relating to the integration of cultural aspects into community actions, based on this report.

This resolution, if adopted, will set for the Council the task of establishing effective and coherent procedures by which the impact of other Community policies in the field of culture can be monitored and adjusted as necessary.

It will also invite the Commission, inter alia, to establish enhanced and effective procedures to ensure better coordination of its actions in accordance with cultural objectives and to develop appropriate procedures for assessing at the outset of the development of policies under other provisions of the Treaty what proposals are likely to have an impact on culture and to identify these in its annual work programme. I readily admit that the task we have set ourselves in this area is a difficult one, given the requirement for unanimity, but I am confident that the momentum of the Irish presidency in this matter will not be lost next year.

The questions that I had posed in Galway to the culture ministers were:

§ Do we accept that the role of culture should be enhanced within the parameters of the Maastricht Treaty?

§ Do we accept that the citizens of Europe have an inalienable right to access to culture and to affirm and express their cultural identity?

§ As culture is now an activity that has a legal basis under the Treaty, do we accept that it forms an integral part of Community action and as such must be accorded parity of treatment with other actions under the treaty?

§ Do we accept that culture can contribute to the objectives of the Community through enhancement of citizenship, personal and human development, greater economic and social cohesion, improvement of employment opportunities, elimination of exclusion, and enrichment of the quality of life of her citizens?

To the ministers for the audio-visual, I posed the following questions:

§ Do we see ourselves as having any responsibility to prevent the emergence of an information-rich and an information-poor division in the society of the future or are we simply going to pay lip service to the concerns in a market-led policy which serves only the interests of service providers or infrastructure operators?

§ How do we ensure that the legal provision of Article 128 (4) of the Maastricht Treaty is fully implemented in the development of Europe audio-visual policy?

191

§   Is television licence fee funding to be regarded as a state aid or appropriate payment for universal service, even in the context of dual funding?

§   Do we accept that we must defend the concept of public-service broadcasting as opposed to the concept of attempting to categorise public-service programming on all channels, be they commercial or public?

§   Can we accept that co-operation between public-service broadcasters, particularly the concept of the collective acquisition of broadcasting rights, sports events and other forms of popular programming that have always featured in the schedules of public-service broadcasters, is fundamentally in the public interest?

These are the questions that I brought to the European Council when I was minister, and particularly during the Irish presidency in 1996. When I began, I was very much in a minority, but I have seen how colleagues have come to see the consequences of deregulation, the fragmentation of audiences, and the privatisation of experience. They are reflecting on the values at the heart of public-service broadcasting. A better attitude in the Council of Ministers, a parallel interest in the European Parliament – these are good developments. They are, however, only part of the necessary response.

I am acutely aware that whatever happens in the European Union will be seen as an event at the administrative level. It may be perceived as an administrative event from the top which serves as a force for homogenisation, an obstacle to the liberation that is needed in the face of transnational conglomerate power. That is why cultural diversity as a key aim is so important. Even more important is that, if such a recognition came to be and prevailed, it has to be delivered within a model of citizenship.

If this does not happen, if the multi-stranded discourse needed does not emerge, we will have failed. The European initiative is part of what is needed, but it is necessarily a part linked to other components of the discourse. Those other linked parts include an integrated, engaged scholarship which is generous and accessible as a resource for discussion. A new ethos of discussion that is open and exploratory must replace the denunciatory and the eclectic.

A public debate is essential on the issues at stake: the future role of culture and the audio-visual. This will require innovation if it is to get beneath the layers of unfreedom assimilated by people whose comfort in the world is as consumers, who in television terms are content with a choice between what is available rather than a choice as to what television might do. The debate about Teilifís na Gaeilge was very illustrative of this. It was

essentially an argument about the expenditure of money for a cultural purpose. It had two polar expressions. On one side was the consumer abso-
lutism: Who will watch it? Who will pay for it? This argument was presented
as being modern, and suggested that the cultural thinking behind the decision
to establish the new service was built on a definition of culture that was
archaic, irredentist and 'traditional'.

On the other side was an argument that had considerable force. In its
original version, it asserted the right of those who lived in the Gaeltacht to
have the means of communication – television – available to them as a right.
Later, the decision being to have a national service, those who wished to have
Irish-language programmes, wherever they lived, joined in. They made the
language argument. I linked my arguments always to cultural policy and
broadcasting policy. The new service is crucial for the language but is also a
key element in implementing and facilitating cultural diversity and in reassert-
ing the philosophy of public-service broadcasting.

Now that the new service is established, the sense that the right thing has
been done is palpable. There is a sense that it was important not to lose the
last opportunity – and it *was* the last opportunity. The sense is one of quiet
relief too, of having come down on the cultural side of the argument. Then
also the youth of the staff – average age twenty-four – seems to affirm a
combination of an important component of identity, national self-respect,
with the new technology.

The debate was valuable but did not engage many of the tiers of the
society from whom we would have expected a response. It was perceived as
political and therefore in some way as a grubby issue. Unless, I repeat, there
is an easy movement between those engaged in intellectual work – and indeed
in any type of work, because all work raises issues of culture – we will not
make a new departure.

In a recent work entitled *Critical Regionalism and Cultural Studies*, Cheryl
Temple Herr compared Ireland and the Midwest of the United States. The
book makes a valuable contribution to a methodology of connecting similar
experiences and strategies between regions in different locations throughout
the world. The work is illustrative too of the widening gap between the social
issues and the discourse, as it invents and utilises what seems to be a necessary new language for some parts of cultural studies. The forces that benefit
from the parts of the discourse not coming together will be the transnational economic conglomerates. As tabloidisation extends from print right
through the visual media, a fragmented politics can be mocked by the media

for an alienated public made insatiable for voyeuristic detail. How long will it be before a senior media mogul will publicly announce: 'There is no such thing as politics'?

At the moment, the fragmentation is growing. The politics of disintegration is a first step in the disintegration of politics. The next century could see a regeneration of involvement, engagement and inclusion, assisted by the wonderful capacities of technology. We could come to know diverse stories from all over the planet. We could come to care and construct mechanisms of communication that could liberate. We could live lives of authenticity at a personal and social level.

If, alternatively, we sink into the mire of the purely private consumed experience, broken off from each other, we will see security as having to be purchased by the included waged consumers to protect themselves from the excluded they have chosen not to see. In such a scenario, where solidarities have evaporated, the political institutions have been weakened, and the practice of politics has been made unacceptable, there would be no institutional vehicle for the delivery of the anger and the fear on each side of the divide.

Many contradictions sit side by side in the area in which I live. I recently watched some young people reacting to a Teilifís na Gaeilge programme. I was pleased to see how easily they identified with it. But I noted too how they were dressed. Baseball caps on their heads, jeans and runners emblazoned with the logos of US multinationals on their feet – sartorially colonised from head to toe, they were watching a programme, with new technology providing state-of-the-art graphics, in a language thousands of years old. Many parts of the world have these contradictions in common. Common to them too is the resource of irony, the greatest defensive tool for the colonised everywhere. Irony has always delivered a discourse of defence and subversion, as Declan Kiberd writes in his treatment of Oscar Wilde in *Inventing Ireland*.

We have then common situations in multiple spaces, and common causes in diverse cultural settings strung out between the traditional and the modern, and more usually in a flux between the layers of these elements. It is a rich resource. We have common tools capable of more than the force of the avant garde, which itself was a strategy of the periphery. We should share and utilise them.

The questions I raised earlier have implications for the public, for the political parties, for intellectuals, for the media. What would create a counter-tide? The multifaceted response I have described fits with the spirit of what Raymond Williams suggested: 'analysis, education, discussion'. The gap is so great between the social manifestation of the forces of convergence, concentration and decontextualisation, and the necessary discourse. There is a dearth of intellectual engagement. Passivity grows with isolated individual consumerism. Activism declines; solidarities wither. Policies fit into decontextualised tabloid versions of the media rather than being the best way of challenging these tendencies. Politics itself is mocked: indeed, the crossover between intellectual work and politics has never been at a lower ebb in nearly every country in Europe. Not only is there an absence of integration, there is a comprehensive moral cowardice.

I reflect on such things from experience. I speak now from the centre of the machine. To some, I am contaminated already. I have moved from the moral innocence of analytic neutrality in academic life, or in principled opposition, to a position in the Cabinet. To draw on my opening metaphor: it is as if I have moved from the certainties of my rural life to the threatening, promiscuous City. I am fallen. If Josiah Strong could write in the nineteenth century, 'God created Man in a Garden. The City is the result of the Fall', there are those who would say I was created for opposition and that to be in government is a fallen, sinful state.

Yet if the Country and the City have to be embraced in the single life of the migrant, so too must moments be considered when opportunities arise to have an impact on circumstances that are urgent and will not wait. Even to such sinners, Raymond Williams's work resonates. I quoted him in my Green Paper on the future of Irish broadcasting, 'Broadcasting in the Future Tense: Active or Passive?' I believe Williams would have liked our new broadcaster. It is young, decentralised, bright and hopeful, and it is established as a public-service broadcaster, a publisher broadcaster, within a policy of active culture – culture defined inclusively – aimed at enhancing democracy, and extending it. These small efforts will come to fruition if a thousand other initiatives all over Europe emerge among citizens, and come home to the best versions of their structures of feeling. It requires the discourse I have mentioned. Discordant it may be, but it is also necessary. The questions must be asked consciously: Who are we? How may we communicate?

It will require a change of attitude too. If we are compelled to go on in a disengaged, broken discourse, mocking each other's efforts as insufficient and hopeless, excluding rather than including our potential allies, then the darkness closes in. My migrant journey continues, and on that journey I have valued, and continue to value, the migratory and partial stories of others.

The Left, revealing its solidarities of origin, can, I believe, from its migrant encounters integrate for its supporters not just biography and history, as the best of Western rational thought would suggest, but also the biographical, the historical, the mythic, and the imagined future through the construction of theory drawing on feminism, social ecology and an engaged psychoanalysis, as well as its other resources. It can, like so many returned migrants, construct a praxis of integrated life and dream. The journey through a dark period is not a defeat: it is a transient experience on the way home to the values that will reinvigorate, for a new journey, a wider circular, extended migration, punctuated with return.

We are migrants in the space of discourse, in the space of organisation and agitation; in the choice between a remembered politics of integration and an emerging politics of disintegration, brought about, I repeat, by a quiet acquiescence to an ideology of fragmentation in broadcasting, privatisation of consumption, and alienation from social values. We are dislocated migrants in transition. Our migrants' return is clear. It is back with our battered suitcases of experience to the point of origin where, by instinct or learning, we developed a humanist instinct for decency, and for solidarity in the struggle for that decency. That demand will require, I repeat again, an inclusive discussion, a committed intellectual engagement, a definition of politics which is as innovative as it is inclusive.

We do not have to eschew tradition to mould modernity. Those of us who are on the periphery have much more than the irony I mentioned as a tool of survival. We have our very distance from the paradigms in decay. We have an opportunity to construct all the alternative values of generosity, of tolerance, of openness, of courage, that the times demand.

In that task, the work and life of Raymond Williams is a source of inspiration. It has been a privilege to give this lecture in honour of a great Welsh giant of the intellect and the heart, whose indomitable commitment to Wales and Europe, to socialism, to culture and to community, will never be forgotten. That is as it should be.

Delivered at BBC Radio, Cardiff, Wales, on 15 November 1996

PART IV

IRELAND AND THE GLOBAL COMMUNITY

On the Irreformable Neo-liberal Model and the Challenge to the Universality of Human Rights

In 1983, John Waters interviewed me for *Hot Press,* and shortly afterwards Niall Stokes, the editor of that magazine, asked me to contribute a fortnightly column. I recall getting some back issues and some copies of *NME,* taking them to Cork, where I was speaking, and laying them out on the floor so as to get an idea of how a column might be shaped for a rock paper.

The rough guidelines were that the column could be anything from eight hundred and two thousand words in length and that I 'be as direct as you can'. I wrote the column for ten years, with no censorship whatsoever. Sometimes a longer piece was flagged as needing to be shortened, or I might be asked to write two longer pieces on a particular column.

The process of getting the column into print moved through the whole gamut of technology and communications. I recall sending the manuscript in handwritten form with the waiter on the train from Galway to Dublin. I have telephoned it in from abroad and, most often, faxed it in. (I am convinced that the fax is the most useful invention of my lifetime!) With the arrival of email, my column was coming to an end, and as I had become Minister for Arts, Culture and the Gaeltacht, I felt that I should not continue to write the column. Now, I am not so sure that my decision was the correct one.

At any event, in that ten years from 1983 to 1992, I wrote approximately two hundred columns. For me, writing the columns served as a kind of intellectual diary on events that were happening at home – including divisive referenda, issues of civil rights, and the relationship between church and state.

This decade was also one of upheaval abroad. In El Salvador, the revolt of the colonels replaced a dictatorship with an authoritarian regime. In Nicaragua, the Sandinistas overthrew the dictatorship of the Somoza family. Central and South America were beginning the end of military authoritarian rule. In Chile, Augusto Pinochet was attempting to remain in office for life, but the 'Marche de la Alegría' of the people put paid to that, and, as I write, he is likely to end his days in prison for fraud and complicity in the drug trade. In Turkey, General Evren ruled with a militaristic authoritarianism that trampled on human rights and leaned with particular ferocity on the Kurdish people, their culture, their way of life and their language.

By the end of the 1980s, the Gulf war would come, but that decade was just another added to the misery of yet another generation of Palestinians, for whom refugee life, occupation and injustice were to continue. That they were to continue alongside international lack of interest about breaches of international law made it all the more immoral.

I wrote of these events in *Hot Press*. I also wrote of the emerging Thatcherite/Reaganite ideology, which would dominate the decade, and its consequences. While a full assessment of where the 1980s fits into twentieth-century history must wait, what follows are some of the pieces as they were written in *Hot Press* or elsewhere at the time.

THE CASE FOR AN OIREACHTAS
FOREIGN-POLICY COMMITTEE

As we near the end of 1987, the prospect of a Foreign Affairs Committee of the Oireachtas being established seems bleak. Persistent questions on the Order of Business by myself and others have drawn the response from the Taoiseach that such a suggestion was 'under consideration', 'under deep consideration' and, most recently, in response to my wry observation that it might be in fermentation, 'under considered consideration'.

Indeed the possibility, previously existing, of discussion on Overseas Development Aid has been ended with the failure of the government to re-establish the Joint Committee on Development Co-operation. This failure has been condemned by all the development agencies, and the Oireachtas members who had preciously served on the Committee for Development Co-operation have taken the unusual step of reconstituting the committee on an ad hoc basis serviced by themselves.

Such a development indicates the interest of the Oireachtas, and indeed of the public, in aid issues and in foreign policy.

On 10 December 1986, Seanad Éireann was the forum in which we last discussed the case for a Joint Committee on Foreign Policy. On that day I moved the following motion:

1   That it is expedient, in view of the importance of allowing the maximum public participation in, and political accountability on, such issues, for example, as the need to reaffirm the principle of the neutrality of Ireland in international affairs and to declare that Ireland's foreign and defence policies continue to be based on this principle, demilitarisation and development strategy, and providing an opportunity for debate in the foreign affairs of the state that a joint committee (which shall be called the Joint Committee on Foreign Policy) consisting of seven members of Seanad Éireann and eight members of Dail Éireann be appointed to review, examine and report to each House with its recommendations on all aspects of foreign policy of the state.

2   That the joint committee shall have power to appoint sub-committees and to refer to such sub-committees any matters comprehended by paragraph (1) of this resolution.

3   That provision be made for the appointment of substitutes to act for members of the joint committee or each sub-committee who are unable to attend particular meetings.

4   That the Joint Committee and each sub-committee, previous to the commencement of business, shall elect one of its members to be chairman, who shall have only one vote.

5   That all questions in the joint committee and in each sub-committee shall be determined by a majority of votes of the members present and voting, and in the event of there being an equality of votes the question shall be decided in the negative.

6   That the joint committee and each sub-committee shall have power to send for persons, papers and records and, subject to the consent of the minister for the public service, to engage the services of persons with specialist or technical knowledge to assist it for the purpose of particular inquiries.

7   That any member of either House may attend and be heard in the proceedings of the joint committee, or in each sub-committee, without having a right to vote, subject to the prior consent of the joint committee or the sub-committees, as the case may be.

8   That the joint committee and each sub-committee shall have power to print and publish from time to time minutes of evidence taken before it, together with such related documents as it thinks fit.

9   That every report of the joint committee shall, on adoption by the joint committee, be laid before both Houses of the Oireachtas forthwith, whereupon the joint committee shall be empowered to print and publish such report, together with such related documents as it thinks fit.

10   That no document relating to matters comprehended by paragraph (1) of this resolution received by the clerk to the joint committee or to each sub-committee shall be withdrawn or altered without the knowledge and approval of the joint committee or the sub-committees, as the case may be.

11   That the quorum of the joint committee shall be four, of whom at least one shall be a member of Seanad Éireann and one shall be a member of Dáil Éireann, and that the quorum of each sub-commitee shall be three at least, one of whom shall be a member of Seanad Éireann and one a member of Dáil Éireann.

My intentions for moving the motion to such a committee were:

(a) To create a forum that would give a greater parliamentary accountability for foreign-policy formulation and practice, but briefly I was seeking to move foreign policy from the realms of quasi-secret and unaccountable diplomacy, as I saw it, to publicly accountable foreign policy established by Parliament.

(b) To create a far greater awareness and public participation in foreign-policy issues. I was influenced at the time by the general public dissatisfaction at the secretive atmosphere in which aspects of European political co-operation had been conducted for some time, and the influence of this on the quality of the debate on the Single European Act in particular.

(c) To create a forum in which such issues as neutrality, disarmament, nuclear proliferation, development and other issues of public concern could be debated. I saw the committee as building a bridge to the public.

(d) To develop a framework within which elected representatives might actually take initiatives in developing awareness in policy where it either did not exist or was in need of articulation.

I was conscious in moving my motion on behalf of the Labour Party that, not only had such a proposal been a long-standing one in that party, but that the idea had support from Fine Gael, and that the University Senators were in favour of such a proposal. Initially, it seemed that the proposal would succeed. The Fianna Fáil group in the Seanad indicated to me that they were in support. The proposal, however, had touched nerves within the diplomatic establishment. The Fianna Fáil group was instructed to withdraw support after the foreign-affairs spokesman had been lobbied. More seriously, the Leader of the Seanad, Professor James Dooge, himself a distinguished and innovative former foreign minister, tabled an amendment on behalf of his party, Fine Gael:

> To delete all words after 'That' and substitute the following: Seanad Éireann is of the opinion that consideration be given to the establishment of a joint committee on foreign affairs in order to promote as wide a consensus as possible on all matters of foreign policy and that informal all-party discussions be initiated to discuss the terms of reference, the structure and the procedures of the proposed committee on foreign affairs.

The effect the amendment would have is clear. It not only removed the teeth of the committee but also threw the entire proposal into the wilderness of a vague parliamentary consensus, yet to be achieved.

The speech by Professor Dooge was undoubtedly the clearest negative critique of what was proposed. He drew principally from a report of a conference of European speakers, held in Copenhagen in June 1984, and whose proceedings had been published by the European Centre for Parliamentary Research and Documentation. The conference had included a session on 'Parliament and Foreign Policy'.

The principal paper had been presented by Dr P. A. J. M. Steenkamp, president of the First Chamber, the Netherlands. It was an extraordinarily conservative paper, weighted in favour of diplomatic 'professional' activity being seen as in conflict with 'emotional' public opinion. Describing the evolution of public interest in the Netherlands, Dr Steenkamp wrote:

> Undeniably, a contrast began to emerge between the emotional approach by part of public opinion (often fed by pacificism and moralism) and the business-like approach of the government, aiming at the feasible.

Dr Steenkamp was concerned that public or parliamentary conviction could be an obstacle to diplomacy: 'For what may happen is that a government is forced by Parliament to assume a certain starting point in negotiations which from the beginning does not stand a chance.'

Professor Dooge was somewhat selective in his use of the conference proceedings referred to. Many of the thirteen countries' representatives took a position in favour of parliamentary sovereignty and involvement. It was the strongest form of committee – the Danish committee – that was singled out as an immovable example, as a hindrance to diplomacy, by Professor Dooge.

Senator Mary Robinson found the case for accountability, participation and openness that the motion provided convincing as much as she thought the amendment vague. She added the valuable comment that it was an appropriate time to establish such a committee, as we had had good experience with our new committees.

I had an inescapable feeling that it was the mandarins of Leinster House and their spokesperson versus the public representatives. The debate ended with twelve votes in favour of the original proposal and twenty-one votes against. Fine Gael voted against; Fianna Fáil abstained. The motion, as amended, was passed. There the parliamentary debate rests.

At the moment, Irish parliamentarians serve in an Oireachtas with very formal structures for the debate of the principles of foreign policy. The fora are shrinking as the public interest grows. Those with orthodox views in foreign policy travel to the Inter Parliamentary Union, so they regard occasional debates, such as at Estimates Time, as sufficient. The frequency with which members of the Oireachtas put down motions on foreign-policy issues in Question Time contradicts such a supercilious view of the role of parliamentarians in this field. The few academics who have written on Irish foreign policy and who criticised parliamentarians in the past for lack of interest showed a marked reluctance to engage the mandarins in debate.

Already this year, parliamentary initiatives have been taken to change Ireland's voting at the UN on the occupancy by Morocco of the territory of the Sahara Arab Democratic Republic, on Esquipulas II, and the Arias proposals for Central American peace. They have found a sympathetic response from the minister for foreign affairs. The present scandal of the destruction of the committee on development co-operation remains.

The parliamentary demand for involvement is fuelled by the pressure of the public, and I have no doubt that in time we will get our joint committee on foreign affairs. Everybody wants it, except those who believe in diplomatic elitism. This influence is waning. It is worth continuing the struggle to make what is said and done, or not said and done, in the wider world, in our name as Irish citizens, accountable. Hasten the day.

Studies, Spring 1988

A Joint Oireachtas Committee was established in 1993. The author is one of its longest-serving members.

MDH, 2006

TURKEY

THE TRIAL

I have been invited to attend a trial of 759 citizens of Fatsa, a small town of 23,000 inhabitants on the Black Sea. Of the 759 who are accused, 263, including the former Mayor of Fatsa, Fikri Sonmez, face the death penalty.

The background to the trial is interesting. In 1979, the tailor Fikri Sonmez won the municipal elections in Fatsa and introduced a remarkable system of autonomous local government in the town. Through eleven district committees, in which a large portion of the town's populations actively participated, all administrative problems were dealt with in accordance with the real needs of the population. The town hall ceased to be a symbol of anonymous central bureaucracy but became the focal point of all these committees.

This lasted for eight months and became known as the 'Fatsa experiment' throughout Turkey. Indeed, it was seen as a model by all progressive forces in the country. However, Fatsa began to be increasingly criticised by the forces of reaction and the military forces. In July 1980, the army marched into Fatsa and arrested four hundred citizens. Their houses were pointed out to the military by masked informers. After the military putsch of September 1980, the repression was greatly stepped up, and more arrests took place. Since then, most of those who participated in any of the committees have been arrested. They, including the mayor, have been held in military prison.

Now, after thirty months, the trial is under way. All seven hundred accused have refused to make a statement. The European Committee for the Defence of Refugees and Immigrants has asked councils and local-government representatives in Europe to express their solidarity by taking an interest in the trial. In January, the Dutch lawyer Mr Koers had observed the opening of the trial with a team from the church television channel, KON.

During April last, on the introduction of Dr Noel Browne, I met representatives of a European Co-operative Union called Longo Mai. They were sponsoring the case of those accused. On 4 May 1983, Galway Corporation agreed a motion from myself expressing our concern about the conditions in which those who had been arrested were being held, and agreed to send a letter to that effect. I was invited to be part of the first international-observers' group to attend the trial. It is ironic that corporations and councils can send delegates to all kinds of meetings abroad but, I was informed, had no power to give me a penny towards my costs. However, the Federated Workers' Union of Ireland, conscious no doubt that many of the 759 are workers and trade-union officials, gave some money towards the costs.

The case for an international observation team is well justified by the results from another trial we know little about, to our shame: the trial of the workers of Yeni Celtek. The town of Yeni Celtek lies in the northern region of Turkey, known as Amasya. Yeralti Maden was a union founded to challenge the connection between an existing union and conservative elements among the employers and undemocratic forces.

The new union was founded by a mining engineer and some of the miners from Yeni Celtek. After strikes in 1976 and 1978, considerable gains were made in social and economic terms for the mine-workers. In April 1980, a third strike was called as a result of a walkout from negotiations by the employers' representatives. From May 1980, the miners occupied, maintained and developed the mine themselves.

The army authorities prepared to move. I have described their July 1980 operation in Fatsa and Suluova. Due to the intervention of a commission, however, their activity was not extended to Yeni Celtek. On 12 September 1980, the army seized power in Turkey. The evening before, tanks had surrounded Yeni Celtek. On the morning of the 12th, the mass arrests began. Farmers, teachers, old people, children and small tradesmen were all arrested. The operation lasted fifty days. Day after day, the arrested were tortured in what has been described as the slaughterhouse. They were held for between 60 and 180 days, depending on their ability to resist interrogation. On 16 September, the legal adviser to the Union Yeralti Moden-Is, Emin Yugar, arrived in Suluova from Ankara to represent the arrested miners. He was himself arrested.

The forms of torture used were particularly vicious. One of the methods most frequently employed was torture by electric shocks. Pseudo-hangings were carried out. Many of the prisoners are today partly paralysed. I quote from the pamphlet 'The Workers of Yeni Celtek':

> The military were particularly severe towards Celtin Uygur, president of Yeralti Maden-Is. He faced prosecution not only in connection with events at Yeni Celtek, but also because he was a member of the progressive trade union DISK, as well as the left-wing organisation Devrinci Yoe. . . . He was held in custody for about a year, his fingers and ribs

were broken and one of his kidneys was seriously damaged. After 180 days, those accused were removed from military prison. Those who went on trial were made up of 510 mine workers, 105 farmers, forty-three small tradesmen, eighteen teachers, nine students, three engineers,and one lawyer. Four hundred and twenty-seven of them were aged under thirty-six, and the eldest was sixty-two.

On 15 April, the trial opened before a military tribunal in the army barracks at Amasya. The hearing was adjourned until 25 June. The 689 accused were represented by around thirty lawyers. On 23 June, the hearing was again adjourned. Such trials can last up to two years.

A news bulletin from the European Committee for the Defence of Refugees and Immigrants has this to say:

> The importance of such international observer groups attending trials can be seen in the reaction of the military junta to foreign protests against the mass-trial of miners from Yeni Celtek. Since this trial has become known in Europe, and above all among miners and their unions, the military authorities felt obliged to provisionally release the majority of the accused.

Hot Press, Vol. 7, No. 13, 8 July 1983

I have just returned from Amasya in northern Turkey, where I have been observing the Fatsa trial. Arriving in Istanbul on the way to Ankara, the most vivid impression I had was of the heavy military atmosphere. I hope that a closet capitalist in Leitrim who finds my column redolent with paranoid socialism will believe me when I write that guns are guns and tanks are tanks: both were in abundance. I admit that, when I was asked to travel in a military jeep from one terminal to another, I was somewhat apprehensive. It was paranoia, of course; my luggage had simply been mislaid.

Ankara is a crowded city – a city of contrasts, with tree-lined suburbs that include an embassy district and hills that hold houses precariously perched on plateaus overlooking one another. There are many blocks of flats on the outskirts, and a glittering central business district. At the embassy, there is acceptance of military rule. It was so bad before, we are told, that the suspension of democracy and the abuses of human rights, while worrying, are a price that must be paid. We are encouraged to go and see how quiet it all is now in Fatsa.

Ursula Durack, one of our translators, and I left by coach for Amasya in the north. Here we were to meet up with the rest of the observation team: Mario Diaz from Spain, Roger Winterhalter from France, Puis Zisswyer from Switzerland and Benoit Hanquet from Belgium, and our other translator. The coach station is a babel of voices, with coaches leaving every few minutes. Our journey north to Amasya takes about seven hours; we have got the last two tickets for the back row. The man next to me has a face like creased vellum. He is disappointed that he will not be able to talk to me, he tells Ursula, because I have no Turkish.

As we travel north, the landscape changes from foothills to mountains to foothills again. Everywhere is the evidence of an unrelenting battle against drought. The parched earth has in places been relieved by different forms of irrigation. In front of me sits an elderly man, his young wife and a tiny baby. The baby has been brought to Ankara, because there is something wrong with his eyes. The father fills bottles, but the baby cries for most of the way to Amasya.

The driver's assistant moves from seat to seat, pouring cologne into the hands of the passengers, who rub it on their faces. He is also endlessly

209

distributing bottles of water to the passengers. We pass by an intersection of rivers that are almost dried up. Parked in the intersection are about a dozen brightly decorated horse-drawn caravans, with gypsy families gathered around a fire. In a few places, one can see rows of the infamous poppy.

As the light fades, people are moving in from the fields. There appear to be more women than men hoeing the soil. All sorts of animals are being driven home, and everywhere people are on horses or mules. The women's faces are hidden by scarves and their dress is traditional, in striking contrast to Ankara, where most people wear Western-style dress.

We make one stop, and it is near midnight when we arrive. Amasya, surrounded by mountains, is very beautiful. The graves, dating from two to three thousand years BC, that surround the town are like beads in a necklace that has been hewn out of the rockface.

In the morning, at 7.30 AM, we present ourselves outside the military compound in the charge of the Third Army, about ten kilometres from Amasya: the trial will take place in the refectory of this building. After a great deal of hassle, we are allowed to attend, with relatives of the accused and the accused who are not detained. The latter have green identification, and the relatives and ourselves, white.

After being searched, we pass through the barbed wire and enter the main hall. We are divided by a distorting wire screen from about six armed soldiers, who in turn have a screen in front of them. Beyond that sit the non-detained accused. As they need to go to the toilet, their hands are chained and they are accompanied by about six soldiers.

Presiding, under a motto 'Adaket Miiltrun Zemelider' which I believe means 'Justice Is the Greatest Value', sit two civilian and two military judges: the president of the trial process and a uniformed representative of the army. The prosecutor sits on the bench with them. They all wear robes with stiffened collars turned up, rather like the Queen of Hearts. The prosecutor bears a striking resemblance to Napoleon. After a break, we are moved to a position normally occupied by journalists. Now we can really see and hear what is being said.

The procedure was unchanged for the two days that we were there: the accused's names were called and they advanced to a roped area in front of the dais. They answered questions and were asked whether or not they had anything to say other than what was in their statements to the police and to the prosecutor. Practically all said that their police statements had been extracted under duress. This is convincing, as the statements which are then read are long and lack spontaneity. The language of the charges is ideological. In two days, two people are directly charged with shooting somebody. The rest of the charges are for writing slogans, possession of forbidden literature, attending meetings of Marxist-Leninist organisations, participating in boycotts, and so on.

The mayor of Amasya has invited us to have a meal on the evening of the first day of the trial. He is a tall, silver-haired man with very dark eyebrows. He arrives accompanied by two journalists. They are with him as friends, not in a professional capacity, he tells us. We are in the season of Ramadan and wait until the loud explosions signal the time when it is appropriate to eat. The mayor is later to tell me that it has been the tradition for wealthier families to kill an animal and share the meat with the poorer families at the time of the second Ramadan. It is getting more difficult to get a rich family to do this, he says, shaking his head sadly.

He is a retired military man who 'has gone all over the world' testing the effects of rockets on tanks and reporting back for the Turkish army. He came back to Amasya and started a business – an undertaker's firm. When the military regime came to power on 12 September 1980, they suspended the elected mayor of Amasya. Our host was the obvious choice as a neutral, he told us. His predecessor was a communist, he said: in fact, he was a member of Bulant Ecevit's Social Democratic Party.

He questions us about the purpose of our visit. We explain that we are from a non-governmental organisation called the Committee for the Defence of Refugees and Migrants. He talks to us about the conditions that preceded the army takeover. Later in the evening, he invites us to go to the park for a drink. We sit at a table drinking tea and talking of the problems of Turkey. It is late, but everywhere there are children. I ask the mayor what kind of life lies in store for them. He speaks of the problem of birth control: in the town of Mardi, they are sad if you have only eight children; in other towns it is different.

As we walk back, the caretaker of the fire station springs to attention and salutes the mayor. The mayor crosses the road to speak to members of a band, who have been practising and who are now sitting in their minibus about to go home. The driver and assistant spring from the front stand, salute and bow. The mayor smiles benignly and waves them off.

On the second day of the trial, the accused are all from among the non-detained accused. Many are teachers. A mathematician asks how he can teach mathematics in a subversive way. A timid historian claims to have taught nothing beyond the achievements of the former Turkish president Atatürk. An elderly man, a former mayor, must answer for allowing microphones, over which he had control, to be used for subversive purposes – a march – and for playing the castanets at the march.

By now a photographer is taking photographs of us. Obviously these will be used for some propaganda purpose. We were asked earlier by the prosecutor to interview the three prosecution witnesses. One man had had a son killed, another a brother, and the third a cousin. 'Who shot them?' we ask. 'The mayor did most of the killings,' the elderly man replied. He spoke of secret courts. 'How many were held?' we asked him. He did not know. 'How were they set up?' 'It was what people said, and knew,' he replied.

By now I was getting angry at continuously being photographed talking to officials of the prosecution, but at the same time making no progress in our principal task – to get to talk to Fikri Sonmez and the other accused. I had a note translated and passed to the prosecutor, the journalist and the photographer: 'I wish to speak to the accused in private after the session; in particular I wish to speak to Fikri Sonmez. We have been allowed to speak to the prosecution and its witnesses. We have been photographed doing so. Is it now reasonable to speak to the accused?' I handed my note to the various parties. The photographers cease, but I still get no response.

After the hearing, we walk back part of the way while we wait for the bus, with the accused. We explain that tomorrow we will go to Fatsa. Some of the accused give us addresses. So too do the witnesses for the prosecution. We hear of the forms of torture used by the police. A youth of about seventeen years – he was just over fifteen when arrested – tells of electric shocks being administered to his fingertips, toes and testicles. Another speaks of having his eyelids taped open, of being disoriented. Later, another man says: 'I would rather kill myself than go back to the police station.'

That evening, we leave the hotel to have a meal in the centre of the town of Amasya. As we leave, a man with a cart full of melons is asking the chef, through the open window, if he needs any. He sells four. There is a market, full of clothing, cheap jewellery, household items, and lots of fruit and vegetables. We spend a lot of time in the restaurant, which is a covered and lighted yard running up against a retaining wall at the foot of the mountain. There is music coming from the plateaus behind the tombs of the ancient chiefs carved into the rock face. The proprietor gives us fruit as a present before we leave. All through the evening, his children come and chat to the proprietor, sometimes performing small tasks. They move from the kitchens to the makeshift desk, where he makes out his accounts.

Walking back to the hotel, we are filmed by Ahmet, a fifteen-year-old who is going home from his job at the hairdresser's. He began at 8.30 in the morning.

Early next morning we leave for Fatsa. Waiting at the hotel offering to carry bags is Ahmet and his three brothers and a cousin. The children are on their way to town. The youngest will sell round loaves of fresh bread, going from shop to shop. Boys of between six and fourteen will polish shoes. Ahmet's brothers have their shoe-polishing kits slung over their shoulders as they walk to town.

But for us it is onwards to Fatsa.

Hot Press, Vol. 7, No. 14, 22 July 1983

As we walked with the Abaji, as they were called – mostly young children under twelve, who polish shoes for a small amount of Turkish lira – to the bus station to get our tickets to Fatsa, the sun shone warmly and the town of Amasya was already busy.

We boarded the bus at nine and went through about a dozen military checkpoints, four of which involved military personnel coming on to the coach and inspecting the driver's papers, and the passengers. As we approached Fatsa, there was much more evidence of military surveillance.

Our bus arrived in Fatsa at three in the afternoon. We were worried about the shortage of time: we were due to leave in the evening for Ankara. As we left the bus, we were recognised by some of the accused from the previous day. Two of them came and spoke to us, and one joined us for tea. We sat in a park overlooking the Black Sea. After a few preliminary comments, our friend sprang to his feet as two plain-clothes police officers arrived, one holding a walkie-talkie wrapped in a newspaper. We introduced ourselves; they told us they were policemen but added 'We're not like the German police, we behave ourselves.'

We had decided to split into two groups of three, to try to speak to as many people as possible. We had gone only a few yards when we were surrounded by policemen and asked to go to the police station. The chief of police, in a different office, spoke instructions to the man in charge of the station through a two-way radio. 'They've been to see Fikri,' our questioner shouted back. We translated all our documents and answered innumerable questions before we left.

The group, which included Mario Diaz, Benoit Hanquet, our translator, and myself, were followed by a man in a floral-patterned shirt, an undercover policeman. The others were followed by two policemen. One of the most chilling remarks I heard was made by the man in charge of the police station when we left: 'When you are trying a mayor in Europe, we will come,' he said. 'I would certainly hope that you would,' Ursula replied. 'We will hang Fikri!' he continued. 'Surely elementary justice demands that the trial take place before you say such a thing,' Ursula, our translator, said. 'We will hang him!' he said. 'Once he would have liked to hang us. Now it is our turn!'

The fact that we were being followed hampered us everywhere, but the inhabitants knew who we were and why we had come. Many welcomed us.

The day was not without its bizarre moments either. At one stage, our policeman lost us, went racing past a shop where we were, and later found us in a bazaar, where he bought a green balloon, which he kept with him for the rest of the day. On another occasion, he fell asleep next door to a shop where we were buying a few items for our children.

Fatsa is a small town of 23,000 inhabitants, so I suppose it was not so remarkable that we all – two groups of observers and three policemen – ended up in the same restaurant. As we left for the bus station to go to Ankara, we were asked to go again to the police station to answer more questions. An hour and a half later, we got on our bus, accompanied by two policemen, and began the overnight journey to Ankara.

In Ankara, we resumed our round of formal visits. Our most important constant companion was the information minister of the Department of the Interior, Sercun Tarlan, who had been requested to seek permission for us to speak to the detained accused. There was a very close similarity between his presentation and that of the prosecutor who had spoken to us for several hours in Amasya. Their case was that indiscriminate killings were taking place and that the economy had been in chaos until the military takeover. Human rights and democracy could return, but Turkey was not a Western-style democracy – a constant refrain. This was for me the most depressing aspect of our formal visits. So often, a lesser version of human rights and democracy was suggested as being appropriate for Turkey. We relayed our requests, experiences and concern. I hope that future delegations will get to the detention centres; we did not.

I flew from Ankara to Zurich and from there travelled to Basle, where the Committee for the Defence of Refugees and Migrants have their offices – and indeed where they lived, in a most interesting urban cooperative with rooms sometimes being used for sleeping, at other times for office work, and at other times for the communal meal.

In Basle, I was to be given the report of Husseyim Yidirim, a Turkish lawyer who had been in the notorious prison of Diyerkabir: a prison which was built for three hundred and where nine thousand are kept, and where no international agency has been allowed to visit.

This report of torture and harassment in the Kurdish villages, where it has been illegal even to speak Kurdish since 1924, of mass trials, of what Husseyim Yidirim called genocide, should push the West to verify or disprove his account, in the interests of humanity.

Hot Press, Vol. 7, No. 15, 18 August 1983

CHILE

THE GENERAL'S ELECTION

On 5 October 1989, the Chilean people gave a decisive 'No' to the continuation in office for a further eight-year period of the dictator General Pinochet. Since his accession to power, following the murder of the socialist leader Salvador Allende in 1973, Pinochet had ruled with a rod of iron and a barrel of cold steel. In the intervening sixteen years, Chilean society has been completely militarised, with all the functions of civil society being moved to the realm of the military.

While Pinochet himself appointed thousands of mayors to towns and cities throughout the country, without even the vaguest nod towards the concept of democracy or the wishes of the people, an apparently untrammelled military engaged in ruthless acts of murder and violence against opponents of the regime. Chile's trade-union movement had been effectively destroyed in the wake of Pinochet's coup. Many union leaders were among the victims in the immediate blood-letting which the military used as a means of purging Chile of left-wing Allende sympathisers. Others were tortured and imprisoned, and many were forced to choose exile; these latter included Hugo Ramirez, who came to live in Galway and returned to Chile last year. I would spend much of my time in Chile with him.

Yet in the run-up to the plebiscite, a remarkable rainbow coalition of opposition to the perpetuation of Pinochet's dictatorship emerged, with the unification of sixteen opposition parties under the 'No' banner – from the Communist Party, through the proscribed Almeda Socialists (whose leader remained in prison) to the more conservative Christian Democrats.

The campaign was unevenly fought, with state and big-business control of the broadcast media ensuring far greater coverage for the dictator's message – that economic prosperity was possible under Pinochet, and so what if there was not full democracy? – than for that of the opposition. The radio stations anticipated the slogan of the 'Sí' ('Yes') campaign with the suggestion that Chile under Pinochet was 'Our Compromise'.

The opposition, in contrast, were allotted just fifteen minutes of TV time a night, usually after 10.30 PM. Pre-plebiscite polls, however, revealed that the public imagination had been captured by the clever, joyful 'No' campaign and that they were watching their televisions late at night in large numbers.

Looking in on the night of 22 September, I could see that the opposition's concentration on a simple message was effective: 'You can vote for this man, or this man, or this man.' The first picture showed Pinochet in the uniform of Captain General, a rank revived by himself, for himself. The second showed a sunglassed face, the sinister Pinochet of the Salvador Allende period. The third showed the avuncular white elderly leader of the 'Sí' campaign, a grandfather lifting little girls from the ground, being human.

Then came the message: 'No' to dictatorship. 'Yes' to *la alegría* (joy). And there was a song:

> *Chile, La Alegría ya viene . . .*
> *Chile, La Alegría ya viene . . .*
> *Porque digan lo que digan*
> *Yo soy libre de pensar*
> *Porque siento es la hora*
> *de ganar la libertad*
> *Hasta cuando ya de abusos*
> *es el tiempo de cambiar*
> *Porque basta de miseries*
> *Voy a decir que No . . .*

And on it went. 'No to misery. No to abuses. No to the violence of the military. We are all going to say "No".'

The TV campaign was one thing, the popular feeling something else again. The opposition had to discover deep reservoirs of courage to defeat a regime that was intent on retaining its power, by foul means if necessary.

During the run-up to the plebiscite, workers were supposed to be allowed free time between 9 AM and 12 noon to register to vote. Many employers, however, had refused to let them have the time off, and some workers had lost their jobs as a result. In Punto Arenas, down at the southern tip of Chile, the local secretary of the directorate of the 'No' campaign had lost his job after thirty years with the National Petroleum Company. In some remote areas, the intimidation went so far as out-and-out threats, and statements that workers would be sacked if they voted 'No', or even registered to vote.

You could not vote if you did not have your identification card with you. There were sudden delays in the revival of expired cards. There were raids on opposition sympathisers, in which cards were confiscated. Everything, it seemed, was stacked against the opposition.

I arrived in Santiago from Peru, where I had been visiting a friend of mine who worked in El Manton, a town of shanty dwellings which tries, unsuccessfully, to forget the meaning of its title: 'the rubbish tip'. Rejoicing now in the title of 'The District of Our Lady of Perpetual Succour', it is rife with tuberculosis, child poverty, military oppression and police violence.

I, along with other observers, had been invited to Santiago by the Association of International Parliamentarians for Democracy. But the Irish government would not provide funds for our delegation of four: Senators Shane Ross and Joe O'Toole, Workers' Party TD Pat McCartan and myself. The obligation of getting to Santiago lay with us and with representatives of the Chilean community in Ireland, who were very anxious that we should be there.

As 'Observador Uno' – the first foreign observer to arrive – I am scheduled to hold a press conference. There is a huge attendance. Typically, the radio people bushwhack me in the corridor on the way in. Why are you here? Who is paying for your trip? There is great interest in my name: Bernardo O'Higgins was Chile's first president, and the name is on Santiago's main thoroughfare. I get past this with a little judicious explanation. The conference seems to go smoothly, though later in the week *El Mercurio*, the unashamedly pro-Pinochet newspaper of the business sector, attacks the presence of observers, who, it says, will write 'terrible things' about Chile on their return home.

The arrival of French actor Yves Montand creates a stir. He joins the Marche de Alegría, a march of people from all parts of the country. In an emotional ceremony, he lays flowers on the grave of Salvador Allende.

By now Rosa, the fiancée of Luis Tricot, a Trinity graduate who has Irish-born children, has contacted me. Her husband is in prison, but the interest of Irish observers might throw a new spotlight on his predicament. A request to see him is delivered to the authorities on behalf of the Irish delegation. The reply is blunt and unhelpful: such a request was not envisaged under Article 51 and the following sections of the prison regime. Herman Nova Carvajal's signature is a squiggle above his ornate title: Lawyer and National Director of the Gendarmarie of Chile. His reply leaves us empty-handed.

At the entrance to the town of La Hermida is a little shrine to a fifteen-year-old boy whose nickname was Pete. There had been a confrontation here on the day Pinochet was named by the military as their candidate, and Pete had been killed.

His mother, Rebecca, a small woman with striking brown eyes, sits in her neat house under a wall-hanging of Salvador Allende. Every second word she speaks is of oppression. At the edge of the *población* there is a circus of the North American variety. It is a Pinochet initiative directed against the 'subversion' of native or popular culture such as that championed by Violetta Pora as the tortured and executed Victor Jara. Outside the tent a bear is being fed, but most people are watching a condor with a rope around its neck.

The condor is the mystical black eagle of the Andes. An Andean ceremony involves the ritual tying of a condor to a bull's back; when it has gorged itself on the hapless beast, the bird is released and soars to a height of four thousand meters. It is a horrific image, but I cannot get out of mind the parallel with the role of the military in Latin American society – an elite whose prestige and power has been sucked from the life-blood of the people. They are worse than vultures.

As the day of the plebiscite nears, there are more demonstrations. Near the Plaza de Armas, the mothers and wives of the tortured and disappeared – Madres de Los Desparicedos – are placing posters on the wall. When the army arrive, the soldiers pull down the posters.

The women continue to protest. Some are dragged away by the hair. The literature asks: *'Me tortiraron, me asesinaron, me despaeciron, me olvidastea?'* ('Should the tortured, the disappeared, the assassinated be forgotten?') One of the women becomes involved in an argument with two female office workers – *'Momias'* – who talk of discipline. The television cameras are first to arrive on the scene, followed by the tank housing the water cannon, which sprays contaminated water mixed with chemicals and acid on the demonstrators. This is how Pinochet deals with the opposition.

At the Carcel Pública – the public prison – there is talk of a hunger strike. It is just past midday when the gas is released here; we all run into the doorway of a block of flats. An old woman, her daughter and two young children are handing out salt and bits of lemon. The gas is being used indiscriminately, and it gets into everyone's eyes, even those who are some distance away from the main protest.

In the doorway, the photo press are coughing, except for those who have come prepared with World War II–style gas masks. An old woman weeps softly: 'For fifteen years it's the same.' The water tank approaches, the soldiers alight from the truck, and the children are almost knocked down. His mother grabs Jorge, and I carry Lionel up to the landing and out of immediate danger.

Later in the week, I revisit Lo Hermida to talk at greater length with Rebecca and to visit Olla Commones: the communal cooking places, like soup kitchens, from which the poorer families are fed. Last night I heard Pinochet say 'I am middle class, Lucia [his wife] is middle class. The middle class is the biggest class.' I had heard this one before: had Mrs Thatcher, the General's greatest fan, not said something similar? In Rebecca's case, everybody is poor.

Rebecca talks of her son Pedro Mariquo, known as 'Pelluco'. On 1 May 1984, he went to Park O' Higgins, where a demonstration was taking place. He was in good spirits, she tells me. He came home and, after eating, was playing football. Some local youths had lit a fire. A police patrol car came. Four men got out, and one fired three shots. The first bullet lodged in Pelluco's back and the second in his neck; the third grazed his head. By 10.30 PM he was dead.

She relates the events, and her attempts to get justice, without emotion, and also describes the subsequent harassment of her daughter Antoinetta and her son José Christian. She ends firmly with the statement: 'They will never break me.' She is wearing a 'No' badge. I leave her to her work.

I have not been long in the Olla Commone when trouble begins to brew. Word comes that our presence has been reported and that we must leave. We take a circuitous route out and breathe freely when we arrive at a place where we can board a taxi.

The final 'Rally for the No' takes place on the Saturday before the vote. One point two million people fill the streets. La Alegría is coming close. On Sunday, the 'Sí' campaign has its final rally – more a cavalcade of cars. The rich, and those who aspire to be rich, are on the side of Pinochet. Against them are the poor and those who value democracy.

On Tuesday morning, I leave for Punto Arenas, where I will be accompanied by two French parliamentarians. In this town, one in four of those who are employed are part of the military. A policeman was killed in Punto Arenas by his own bomb as he tried to blow up the church. The bishop of the area, Tomas Gonzalez, is an outspoken supporter of the interests of the poor.

I stay in the house of Roberto Lara and his wife Liliana Sougarret Romer. The local doctors and others are co-ordinating the 'No' campaign. I visit the 'Sí' headquarters, where they ask me to write the truth. I promise to do more than that. On the eve of the poll, no political activity can take place, but the preparations are elaborate. Each box of 350 votes will be counted, and computers will be used to draw the local and national results together.

At 7 AM on 5 October, we leave for the polling stations. By 8 AM, the queues are up to a mile long, but the people are not discouraged by the delays. When the polls close after nine hours of voting, the calculations commence. It will be close. The government radio gives out reports from the marginal boxes. Radio Co-operativa is more reliable. At 3 AM, the minister for the interior concedes defeat to the 'No' campaign, though in Punto Arenas we are making slower progress. At 6.50 AM, the count is Sí, 2,389 votes; No, 3,033. By 7.20 AM, it's Sí, 3,879; No, 4,892. It is done . . .

As the day rushes in, I fly back to Santiago and make my way to the hotel. Already the crowds are gathering. There is a confrontation outside the Moneda Palace, where Salvador Allende made his last stand. La Alegría is here at last.

A significant historic victory has been won, securing for the Chilean people the space in which democracy may flourish in the future. In many ways, however, the problems are only beginning for the Chilean people. General Pinochet still holds the reigns of power, and until these have been handed over, in a country where repression has been the norm, anything is possible. The agents provocateurs may be at work even now. For the moment, however, the dictator has been rocked to his foundation. *Viva Chile Libre!*

Hot Press, Vol. 13, No. 25, 28 December 1989

NICARAGUA

TALKIN' 'BOUT A REVOLUTION

The most extraordinary feature of Daniel Ortega is his energy. From the moment of his arrival, standing in the middle of the aisle of the bus, he asked about every aspect of the Irish countryside. Translator Harry Owens was kept busy with the non-stop stream of questions from the Nicaraguan president. What was the housing situation? What use was made of the land in the Golden Vale? What forms of agriculture did we emphasise? What were the populations of different towns?

Ortega has been in Shannon more than twenty times. He recalled a night when few officials were on duty at the airport and a man from Cork presented him with F. S. L. Lyons's *Ireland Since the Famine*. He was familiar with Irish coffee, a drink with which he reacquainted himself on this occasion. He also sampled Guinness, and I was asked to explain the different constituent elements of Guinness and beer.

The arrival of his plane had been delayed until about 5 PM. I was reticent about seeking an interview from him even for myself and *Hot Press*, since some officials in his party were already complaining to me about the crowded nature of the programme. But I had made a commitment to *Hot Press*, and so the interview took place on the road: in his hotels in Kildare and Connemara, and on the coach that left Bishop Casey's house for Shannon, for Ortega's return for Nicaragua.

What was the most important aspect of his visit to Ireland, I asked him? Ireland was due to assume the European presidency in January 1990 and he felt that it was important that it become an activist presidency in support of the Central American peace process. There was, too, the question of European Aid for the reconstruction of the country following years of civil war. Already two of his ministers from the original presidential party to Ireland had had to return to Stockholm, where £50 million had been promised prior to his arrival.

Was he surprised at the British attitude towards Nicaragua? No, Mrs Thatcher was surprising only insofar as the arguments she used were so out of date, he said.

Had Sir Geoffrey Howe, the British foreign secretary, participated in the talks? Hardly at all: he had sat through most of Mrs Thatcher's lecture. But the president was anxious to be positive. He was impressed by one statement from Thatcher: she would not be pressurised by others and would form her own opinions. However, she did seem to accept the descriptions of what was happening in the region from the United States.

It had been decided to stop in the Racket Hall Hotel, at the halfway point on our journey. The president had an Irish coffee and his *compañera*, Rosario, director of the Institute of Culture, had tea and began an affair with Irish brown bread. Rosario and Daniel share an interest in early-morning jogging: during the visit, some members of our security staff had an opportunity of demonstrating their fitness as the president tore along Rusheen Beach.

We were already late, but he insisted on having photographs taken with the children who had gathered and with the kitchen staff of Racket Hall. In fact, everybody seemed to want to have their photo taken with him. Back on board, the discussion turned from the scenery to history and politics. At the back of the bus, Deputy Niall Andrews was available to correct my own more critical accounts of recent changes in Ireland – his version being closer to the orthodox account of success and prosperity. The coach was full, carrying thirty-eight Nicaraguans and members of the Irish Nicaragua Support Group, who had carried out the bulk of the preparatory work for the visit.

At the Moyglare Manor Hotel, the band of the Post Office Workers' Union struck up the Nicaraguan national anthem. Inside were waiting the general officers of the ITWGU and the FWUI, who were hosting a welcoming dinner. They were joined by the ICTU secretary general and a number of general secretaries of trade unions who were interested in, and who had assisted, Nicaragua. Later, somebody was to remark dryly that Daniel Ortega had united, in a day, the Irish Left and the trade-union movement.

The president later described the meeting as one of the most moving of his visit. He spoke at length of the last ten years, which had cost his people sixty thousand lives and $20 billion in economic damage. But still Nicaragua wanted to be a friend of the United States, he insisted. The hour-long speech was merely a *cupla fochail* in Latin terms, as many were to learn.

I had been part of a group working on the trip for about three weeks, since an early-morning call had first alerted me to it its possibilities. Since then, the phone had rung at home practically every two minutes. Everybody wanted to meet Daniel Ortega.

The planning for the visit had gathered incredible momentum. Commitments were being waved at the organising group. Lovely events were planned, but as the advance party of two were explaining, these would have to change. Kevin Dawson of the *Sunday Tribune* was offering to do his interview on the president's morning jog. And there was the question of the Stockholm Conference, which had resulted in two ministers being called away. Also the Local Government and Public Services Union – great friends of Nicaragua – were in annual conference, and Donal Mendez, a leader of the Sandinista Youth Movement, would be flown down to their conference. Groups were ringing about their arrangements, about flags and visits. I had been averaging about three or four hours' sleep a night.

There were four itineraries: one for the president, one for Rosario Murillo, one for development work, and one for Donald Mendez. The INSG power-house had supporting teams and translators – but could it all be kept intact?

By now, the officials of the Department of Foreign Affairs' protocol section were with us. The cars booked for the party had arrived, and we were due at Leinster House at 10 AM. The motorcycle escort sped us through Dublin without delay and the reception was gracious, on Leinster Lawn.

The meeting of Dáil deputies and senators drew one of the largest attendances in memory. In Room 114, President Ortega thanked the Irish TDs and Senators for their all-party support for the Central American peace process. Then it was time for what turned out to be a very warm meeting at Malahide Castle with Taoiseach Charles Haughey and a number of his most senior ministers.

On the way back to meetings with the various political parties, the president had asked for a private period in the afternoon. We had been warned about this in advance. After two meetings, he took a rest before returning to the Dáil for a dinner hosted by the Ceann Comhairle.

On the way back to Leinster House, we discussed some details of his own life. What were the worst moments of his imprisonment from 1967 to 1974? The answer came immediately: 'When we used to hear that one of our comrades had gone missing.' Did he mean 'shot'? 'Yes.' Had he himself been tortured? 'Yes, but so many others had been also.'

He moved on quickly to speak of the work of reconciling the different tactical tendencies opposing the Somoza dictatorship. Different theories of struggle had been debated. Should it be a single-class one? Should it be the movement from the mountain? Should it incorporate anti-Somoza progressives from the ownership class?

There was no simple solution. The president himself had favoured the broader alliance that merged rival and urban opposition groups and formations and was well aware that the United States would seek simply to produce a replacement puppet if the revolution did not incorporate a broad spectrum of support.

Two days before the defeat of the Somoza dictatorship on 19 July 1979, the United States held a meeting in Caracas. The candidate chosen there to become president in a United States–installed government was José Esteban Gonzales. (Gonzales later ran an anti-Sandanista newsletter, the *Dossier Nicaragua*, which carries outrageous assertions of murders, abuses and so forth, allegedly carried out by Ortega's government. One investigation, 'The Contras in Europe', published by the Dutch branch of Pax Christi, concluded that Esteban was purveying 'disinformation about the human-rights situation in Nicaragua, which has been the most important instrument in the anti-Sandanista campaign in Europe'.)

At 8.30 PM, President Ortega was due at the National Concert Hall in Dublin, where he would give one of his most important speeches. The event, which was organised by the Irish Nicaragua Support Group, featured artists such as Scullion, Nancy Bevan, Kieran Halpin, Meristem and Hada-To-Hada Vila, and the poets Tomas Mac Siomoin and Anthony Cronin. It was the main opportunity for the Irish pubic to see and hear the president.

I will never forget the atmosphere in the hall. The event was booked out, and even many of those who had worked night and day organising the visit could not get tickets. Doireann Ní Bhriain and Senator David Norris were the MCs for the night, and I was to introduce Daniel Ortega in three minutes flat!

For me, it was an emotional moment, and a humbling one. I had made many speeches before, but never one that would end with the words: 'May I now introduce the President of the Republic of Nicaragua, Commandante of the Revolution, Daniel Ortega Saavedra.'

I could make no attempt to describe a man whose parents had been tortured and imprisoned, whose brother Camillo had been killed in 1978, and who himself had spent long periods in exile and in prison. Ortega himself spoke about Nicaragua and the gratitude of his people for the work of solidarity from other countries around the world. On stage was Phyllis McGee, holding the Irish flag, and members of the Nicaraguan party holding theirs. Most impressive was the backdrop, designed and made by Aine Phillips of the NCAD. Students' Union. When Ortega's speech was over, the Concert

Hall's foundations were tested by the cheering and the ovation.

Then the concert began. Sitting next to me on the balcony, Ortega asked me about all the music: could I get copies of it for him? He stayed on for the poets but then had to leave. The next day he was due at Áras an Uachtaráin at 10 AM, and there were faxes to be read and answered. My own lift had gone, but I collected some cassettes for him from the artists . . . and the show went on.

On the following morning, President Ortega held a final press conference. The questions were fair, with Panama and Mrs Thatcher by now predictable chestnuts. Ortega said he was pleased with his visit. On the coach across the plains of Ireland, the president asked about the Shannon, and there were more questions about farms, roads and so on. Escorted into Galway, an unbelievable welcome was prepared. The Civic Welcome was so well attended that not everybody could fit in the new City Hall; outside, the Galway Trades Council, LGPSU, Labour Party, Workers' Party, and men, women and children had gathered to provide an extraordinary reception. The St Patrick's Band played the Nicaraguan national anthem. Now, for the first time, I thought that the president looked tired, but he was happy to explain his choice of Galway for a brief one-and-a-half-day private rest, and then we were off to the Connemara Galway Inn. After a brief supper, the fax was going again and I was called to a brief meeting. The consultation between Daniel and his foreign minister, Miguel D'Escoto, would go on until 4 or 5 AM.

In the morning, Rosario restated an edict from the previous day: there must be rest. While the president relaxed, I made plans with the INSG for the thirty-five other Nicaraguans to shop in Galway for last-minute presents. The party ate in The Quays, the capital of alternative Galway. They were in raptures about the food – bean soup, lasagne, salads and Guinness – and the requests for Irish records and cassettes were pouring in. They then filed onto the coach and headed for Oughterard via Spiddal and Sean a Pheistin.

I returned to check on the president. He was already up and about and, after he had expressed a wish to see more of the countryside, officials from the Department of Foreign Affairs were busy whisking him around Ballinahinch, Clifden and Roundstone. When the president returned, he was wearing a beautiful jumper which had been presented to him during his brief foray into north Connemara, and a tweed cap from Miller's of Clifden.

We were due at Bishop Casey's at 7.30 PM, but suddenly Ortega took me aside and said that he would like to visit my own house. Ten minutes' warning to my loved ones was all that was available. By the time we arrived, every child and neighbour was gathered. Moving past the chaotic dining-room table, which serves as desk and parking area for post and books, he sat on a sugán chair in the kitchen.

My next-door neighbour's four-week old baby was presented to him for a kiss. My own children, Alice Mary, Michael Edward and John Peter, gave him flowers, and my son Daniel, aged eight, was lifted in the air by *President* Daniel. While the president had a few sips of Black Bush, Rosario Murillo discussed books on Nicaragua and theatre with Sabina. Our great neighbours, the Thorntons, helped us out. As we left, everybody wanted a photo, and he obliged them all.

We were off to the bishop's. This was a small private working meal. It was characteristically run with great flair by Bishop Casey, who had previously met President Ortega in Managua. Afterwards, as we waited for the coach for Shannon, the Bishop sang a song, and Ortega responded with a poem. Then we were on our way.

En route I resumed our *Hot Press* interview. What would be the biggest dilemma in the process of reconstruction? Undoubtedly asking the people to do without things he would like them to have. They were worn out from the war, he said. And of the elections in February 1990? The FSLN, Ortega's party, would do quite well. What about the polls? They showed a certain amount of consumer dissatisfaction in Managua, but in the rural areas the people would hold fast. What is the most important thing the Irish government can do? Apart from the specific issue of aid, making sure that Nicaragua is understood accurately and assisted fairly by the European Community.

And so, finally, to Shannon, where the night manager of Aer Rianta had arranged not only hospitality but also a lovely presentation to Daniel and Rosario. It was time to go. All the members of the Nicaraguan party and the Irish solidarity workers embraced, and at the foot of the plane they exchanged a last a*brazo*. We and the INDG sang the anthem of the FSLN, 'Avanti Populi', and then the plane lifted into the skies and we all began our journeys home. How wonderful the visit had been, and how different from that of Reagan, where in Galway scarcely a hundred people had watched the window of the presidential car go down three inches, and the presidential fingers protrude. May we remain loyal to Nicaragua even in the face of pressure and manipulation, and may the great efforts of the solidarity workers be matched by others in the heat of the day.

Hot Press, Vol. 13, No. 11, 15 June 1989

It was about 5 AM on the morning of 26 February 1990 when we saw him, sitting on the edge of the kerb, a guitar apparently his only possession. In the streets all around, UNO supporters were already gathering in groups and shouting slogans. We stopped. The man was close to tears. He said he was waiting for the first bus to the terminal, from where he would leave for the mountains. He looked at his feet as he waited. From there, it would be to Juigalpa and who knows what future.

We gave him a lift. He took out his inverted Sandinista notebook and wrote, '*Para mis amigos Irlandeses de Leonel Jenkins las causas justas siempre triumfan*', and signed it, 'Leonel'. He didn't tear the page from his notebook but gave the notebook itself away. A part of his life was over. Who knows what other part was left?

A few minutes earlier, it had been reported on the radio that Doña Violetta Chamorro was inviting a selection of journalists to her house to meet 'the new president of Nicaragua'. At 6.30 AM, President Daniel Ortega Saavedra was almost conceding defeat, even though not all the votes had been counted. 'The FSLN will respect the results of the election,' he stated 'and there will be an orderly transition of functions.'

Some of us had not slept for maybe forty-eight hours. There was no attempt to hide the emotion of what was happening. The count was moving to an inexorable conclusion. By 10.20 AM, UNO – a ragbag coalition of fourteen parties, including the extreme right of the Contra mouthpieces and the extreme left of the Communist Party – had 55.8 percent of the votes for the presidency and vice-presidency, to the 40.9 percent from the Frente Sandinista Liberación Nacional candidates, Daniel Ortega and Sergio Ramirez. Long before the final result would come – 55.2 percent for UNO's candidates, 40.8 percent for the FSLN, and 4 percent for others – it was clear that Violetta Barrios de Chamorro and Virgilia Godoy of the Union Nacional Opositora would be the new president and vice-president of Nicaragua.

The tears flowed. Francisco Espinoza, who drove the car, didn't appear the following day at the scheduled time of 8.30 AM. When he finally came, at midday, he was wearing his Frente T-shirt, his headband, and his scarf of black and red. It was an act of defiance. As we were getting ready to leave for

Daniel Ortega's post-election meeting, I gave him a hug. He shook as he cried. At twenty-seven, with four children, he could remember vividly being on the barricades as a youngster of fifteen, and he could not understand how other people could have forgotten.

At the Olaf Palme Conference Centre, Daniel Ortega speaks after an emergency meeting of the Directorate of the FSLN. He is strong. Bayardo Arce, director of the FSLN campaign, looks broken.

'The people who didn't vote for us are not Contras,' says Daniel Ortega. 'They are not bad people. The are people made weak and desperate by the war and the economic blockade.' There is strength and assurance in the speech. 'We will operate democratically, for, after all, it was we who established democracy.' The crowd are reminded of their achievements against the dictatorship, culminating in the flight of the last Somoza from Managua in July 1979. 'We don't want the return of the National Guard' rings out here and there.

Daniel is continuing about the future of the Frente. 'We will organise from the base, from the *barrios*,' he says, before returning to the necessity of understanding those who could not take the United States economic blockade and its consequences any more. '*Se vendieron*' ('They sold themselves') a woman near me shouts.

'We have lost an election,' Daniel Ortega continues, 'but the revolution is not lost.' Now the cries of 'Do not go!' are ringing out. 'The Frente will defend the constitution of 1986. . . . They will be vigilant as the largest group in the Assembly. . . . There will be no reversal of the agrarian reform. . . . The campesinos will be defended in keeping their land. . . . The social benefit of the revolution will be protected. . . . The professional integrity of the Army and the MINT [the Ministry of the Interior's staff] will be respected. . . . The constitutional and legal position of the productive and credit institutions will remain. . . . The rights of public employees will not be conceded. . . . The right of strike, to organise, to meet, will be defended. . . . '

As he continues, the hours of tears are drawing to a close. It is clear that Doña Violetta and her desperate group of supporters will lack the two-thirds majority required to change the Constitution. An election has been lost, but not the revolution, the Sandinista dream.

Still, Cardinal Obando y Bravo will be pleased. The day before polling day, *La Prensa*, owned by Violetta Chamarro and edited by her son, Pedro, carried a three-quarter-page photo of Cardinal Obando blessing the UNO candidates. 'CARDINAL BENDICE A VIOLETTA Y VIRGILIO' ran the headline, above the subtitle: 'The gesture signifies what will be the future relations between the Church and Government.'

I am contacted by RTÉ radio news for a reaction to the result. I describe how I feel. Later, back in Ireland, this will be described as emotional. I use the word 'heartbroken' which is later seized on by Gerry Barry in the *Tribune*. 'Emotional' has a different meaning in journalistic Dublin than it has in Managua. Nicaragua is lucky.

In tranquillity, my mind goes back over the two weeks I had been in Nicaragua. How could four hundred thousand people have attended a rally in Managua, while UNO could muster only seventy thousand for their final rally – and yet the FSLN still lose the election?

The answer lies in the continuing demands of military service required for the defence of the country against the Contra mercenaries, paid by the United States; the wearing-down of the people by the war of economic attrition; and the dispersal, as it would become clear, of dollar bills in Region VI in the north and along the Atlantic Coast, where the evangelical groups made the cause for finding Jesus sweet with a $10 bill. Jesus and UNO together was worth much more, of course.

When I had left Ireland two weeks earlier, I was retuning to a country that I had known since late 1981 or early 1982. I had known it in its great days of post-dictatorship euphoria. I had known it also after the economic blockade by the United States, implemented in 1985. I had observed the elections of 1984, in which Daniel Ortega and Sergio Ramirez had been eleceted. Those elections were fair, everybody agreed – except the Reagan administration.

In Dublin, back in 1984, I had a copy of the minutes of a United States National Security Council sub-committee, on which Margaret Heckler served, that had as its purpose, well before those elections in 1984 were held, a campaign of disinformation masked under the grandiose title of a 'public-diplomacy programme'.

The chief architect of the lies was roving ambassador Otto Reich. If Contras killed, raped or murdered, Reich would be wheeled out to say that it was not clear, but that the Frente Sandinista had done it. The campaign included targeting 'friendly' parties in Europe, particularly the Christian Democrats, journalists who would not ask too many questions, orthodox Church leaders, the anointed and the lay. The United Sates embassy in Dublin worked hard but with exasperating – at least for them – lack of effect.

Most recently, they had been saying that the FSLN would never hold elections. As it transpired, the elections due in November were actually brought forward to 25 February. Then, they had said that the elections would not be fair. But Jimmy Carter, the Organisation of American States, the United Nations, and thousands of observers, said that they had been fair. Then the United States had said that it would recognise the elections if the results were to their liking!

I knew as I left that Doña Violetta Chamarro had been told in the White House that she could tell the Nicaraguan people that they would be allowed to live, that they would have the economic blockade lifted, and that they would get between $200 million and $230 million in aid. What other country would exercise such moral blackmail on a neighbour's people? I thought of Panama, and the question answered itself.

But for now, I can only think of Leonel, who had gone to the mountains in the throes of the 'day of tears', and who had not heard Daniel's speech. And I am concerned for him and those like him.

Hot Press, Vol. 14, No. 6, 5 April 1990

Since I wrote on the election result in Nicaragua, two pertinent events have taken place: the US administration has lifted its economic blockade and promised $500 million dollars in aid over the next two years, and I have received a letter from my friend and driver in Managua, Francisco Espinoso.

The first event was predictable: the simple delivery of the price of moral blackmail exerted by the United States on Nicaragua. It will be a forerunner of the price Mario Vargas Llosa will pay in Peru, that Patrick Allowyin, president of Chile, will pay, and that Colombia will pay too. As the East–West dialogue progresses, the North–South relationship sinks back into an old patron–client relationship, with the United States turning one Latin American country after another into a dependent colony. No invasion is necessary. Manipulation of trade, aid and, above all, debt will suffice. Behind it all is a subtle racism. Latins are perceived – as U.S. ambassador Dean Hinton put it to me so long ago on the veranda of his house in San Salvador – as 'culturally inferior, economically backward and endemically prone to violence.' Now he is his country's ambassador to Panama!

Francisco's letter is moving. On 25 April, immediately after the election, he lost his job as a driver attached to the president's office. He writes: *'La situación es muy mal.'* On a more optimistic note, he reports that the president is trying to give each of the drivers the possibility of getting a car so that they can set up a taxi co-operative. It is typical of Daniel Ortega that people such as Francisco are high on his list of concerns.

I recall now, thousands of miles away, how I met Francisco's mother. She ran a small kitchen and sold simple food, cooked by herself, but on the night of the election she did not have the heart to cook anything. These relationships will live with me long after I have lost the visiting cards with which I have been showered by those who have never felt, not to speak of never wept, for any cause other than their personal or corporate welfare.

I know, too, that I was humbled by the commitment of the Franciscos of Nicaragua, who will struggle again and again until their country is genuinely free. Franciscos wrote ironically at the top of his letter, *'1990 Año de paz y la reconstrucción'* and, at the bottom, *'Patria libre o morir.'*

Of those I met in Managua, the one who will have been most pleased with the United States' victory is Gilberto Cuadra, president of COSEP, the organisation of the traditional business sector. When I met him in Nicaragua, he spoke English, which he likes to practice, but in whatever language, I don't think I have ever heard such an extreme set of economic opinions. He feels that the children of those who were broken by the economic blockade of 1985 represent a whole new generation of entrepreneurs. Selling single cigarettes and chewing gum will have given them the spirit of commerce.

I put it to him that there was a difference between the tones of Doña Violetta Chamorro, the presidential candidate of UNO, who spoke of 'evening the score with the Sandinista dictatorship'. 'You are a politician,' he replies. 'You should know that the crowd wants the ugly speech even more than the sweet one.' He laughed, and I thought of the old adage that language was the last thing to go before fascism went into the ascendant.

Cuadra was a key figure in the United States' funding of Doña Violetta's campaign, appearing at every embassy function. He was also one of the most dangerous men in UO. If Doña Violetta didn't win – a possibility he would not even consider – 'we will call fraud', he told me, and 'call on the people to claim their victory.' There would be no reconciliation between private capitalism and state capitalism, he told me: 'State capitalism is over. Private capitalism is what we want.' He spoke frankly of getting back to the economic levels of Somoza within five years. But then Cuadra was one of those people who in the past had levied his workers in order to give presents to the dictator.

Driving away after the meeting, I thought of the photographs I had seen of the baptism by Archbishop Olendo y Bravo of Somoza's child, and the party in the swimming pool, with cocktails being served to, amongst others, a corpulent Henry Kissinger.

There were to be many more interviews, including meetings with Lieutenant Colonel Farrell and Commandent Loughnane, Irish officers with the UN's peace force – ONUCA. One pre-election meeting of crucial importance was with vice-minister Orlando Solasomo, who was in charge of economic integration and international economic negotiations. Solasomo spoke frankly of the economic situation. The worst year of the effects of the 1985 blockade was 1988, he told me. Inflation had risen to 3,600 percent, and the United States had spoken of it going to four times that figure before their war of economic attrition had ended. By a process of what he called 'economic surgery without an anaesthetic', the inflation rate had subsequently been reduced to 1,600 percent. But what a price had had to be paid! There were cuts in the most basic items, prices were still rising due to the scarcity imposed by the economic blockade, and public-service pay had to be frozen. We spoke too of the important meeting due to take place on 9 and 10 April, which would decide Europe's relationship to the Central American region.

In the house at Altamira where I and some friends had rested, the companionship of Ramor Dagge and Michael McGaughan was a source of inspiration and strength to me. I travelled with them to the conferring of the award of the Order of Ruben Dario on such artists as Carlos Mejia Godoy. There we danced and met Norma Elena, Daniel Ortega, Sergio Ramirez and Rosario Murillo, on a night when it seemed the FSLN was on its way to victory.

Then came polling day, when, between us, the four Irish observers visited thirty-five polling stations. On the road to Condega, we passed orderly queues of voters, a reflection of the situation elsewhere. The registration process had been fair, the campaign had been fair, and on polling day all was calm. But over those peaceful days hung the shadow of the war of economic attrition, and the more recent blackmail by the United States, to the effect that, if the US administration liked the result, the people of Nicaragua could live without the threat of military intervention, the resurgence of national military service and the pressure of an economic blockade.

That Sunday in Condega, Neil Duggan from Donegal was attacked with a machete. The same day, he told us of the fifteen people who had been murdered by the Contras in the previous two months. His parish of twenty-five thousand people was a regular target for the Contras. They had passed through two weeks earlier, and Neil had buried seven of the dead, including a father and a son. The son had been disembowelled before his father's eyes, and the father had been crucified. These actions were carried out by what the forgetful President Reagan called 'freedom fighters'. I suppose that we should be silent about all this lest we are perceived by the United States as 'anti-American' and we upset public representatives such as Gay Mitchell, or look for equivalent atrocities elsewhere to balance our protests.

On the way back from Condega, we passed the humble shrine to Moses Cordoba Centeno, who was murdered on 7 August 1987. He was known as the most generous man in the region: he gave everything he owned away. The inscription reads: 'Loved by everybody.' His father was a Sandinista, as he was. 'The Contra assassins killed you/ But you are not dead/ You live in our hearts/ Put here by the campesinos of Bramedero and other villages.'

Now the FSLN is moving back to the barrios. It will be a short wait until the red and black flags wave in Managua again. In the meantime, the tasks of solidarity will be even more important. The FSLN will need aid to defend the people and the programme of participation – the literacy campaign, the women's groups, the trade-union enterprises. This support should come now more than ever, as the FSLN plans to open offices in as many European cities as possible.

Hot Press, Vol. 14, No. 7, 19 April 1990

Western Sahara

War in the Desert: Living with the Saharaoui

North Africa is vast in its charms, history and culture, and it is these that remain in the Irish traveller's mind. However, when the news of General Vernon Walter's visit to the Palace of King Hassan in Rabat are flashed on telecasts in Morocco, they serve to underline the fact that all is not well. General Walters is not visiting his sister, who is married to the head of the Moroccan Airlines; he is advising the king on his 'troubles in the desert'.

King Hassan is involved in a war that consumes his people. He has constructed a mound of sand stretching 1,800 kilometres across the desert, punctuated every five to ten kilometres or so with gun-posts. At intervals, these posts are topped with radar installations. The entire set-up is designed to defend the territory the king has grabbed from the Saharaoui people.

The members of the Polisario Front, against whom Hassan is fighting, are dotted in tents in the desert, opposite the wall. They breach this vast edifice at will, and attack it, usually from the side of the occupied territories. Every pebble and grain of sand in the loose ranges of hills in front of the wall are known by these unparalleled experts of the desert. The hills obstruct the radar. The Moroccan soldiers, locked in their bunkers of sand, blaze away blindly with flares and shells in response to carefully placed Polisario mines.

The wall is in reality a tomb of sand, to which a feudal monarch conscripts his subjects. While the king is in his palace in Rabat, they, his subjects, die on it every day and are buried in mass graves next to the wall. No pensions are paid to relatives or dependants, since this would be to acknowledge a level of casualties that is unacceptable to the Royal Palace. The wall is manned by at least a hundred thousand Moroccan soldiers and costs more than $1 million dollars a day to maintain.

Why this royal madness? To answer this question, one must look to the influence of the former colonising powers who still retain the poison of the colonising impulse in their veins. The United States today subsidises Hassan's military exploits. The USSR has signed an economic agreement for thirty years with Morocco, for potash. The French offered technical advice to their puppet at a time when he appeared to be ready to abandon his desert madness.

Above all, however, there is, as in all despotisms, ancient and modern, the motivation of greed. Morocco's king has cut off the Saharaoui people from the sea. The territory he has annexed is rich in fishing grounds. It has minerals. It has been explored for oil and

gas. It encompasses the better part of the desert for simple animal husbandry and agricul-
ture. In short, it is valuable land economically, and King Hassan wants it.

Hotel El-Salim in Algiers is large, its ancient, cagelike lifts exiting to a lobby worthy of Humphrey Bogart and *Casablanca.* Only men are seen in the street. The young men walk in clusters, some in European dress, others in the long cool nightshirts I envy. I do not stay out late, for I have to get my briefing. I am overwhelmed with relief to hear that my suggestion that I leave for the desert twenty-four hours later than planned is likely to be accepted. I can, I feel, listen more easily after a short rest. But at 1 AM my contact rings with the news that I am to be on the flight to Tinduff at six that morning. He will call me at four. 'Of course, of course,' I hear myself saying.

At the central reception area at Simare, where the Saharaoui refugees are accommodated, I am met by Hussein, director of the reception centre, and Buyema, who will act as my translator and companion. I participate in my first tea ceremony and take the first of many naps, as suggested by my companion because of the energy-sapping nature of the heat.

Looking out the window, I see what appear to be little towns of tents, separated by stretches of sand. There are goats everywhere. I think of the model camels on the hills outside Tinduff, proclaiming that area to be the district of the camel. Now it is goats that dominate the landscape around the tents.

I cannot sleep, and run things over in my head. It soon appears to me that the special pattern of the clusters of tents reflects the geography of the lands from which the Saharaoui have been expelled. I am given some lectures on local government and local decision-making from Buyema. But I am too tired to assimilate it all. 'Sleep,' he tells me. 'You will need it.'

The sun blinds me as I wake up. All is quiet, save for the occasional cry of a child from the tents. Lunch consists of products from the experimental Wilaya: marrows, chipped potatoes, stew with a little camel meat, and bread. The juicy watermelon is the pride of our hosts. The meal finishes with mint tea. I have a shower and a walk. At five, I am to begin a round of visits to hospitals, clinics and schools.

The surface of the desert is not in the least as I had imagined it from films. It is hot golden grit, flecked with a black shale. All around, goats forage for bits of paper, cardboard and other waste. My opinion of this animal has been radically altered: it seems to act as a magnificent recycling mechanism of the desert waste.

Visiting the seven hundred children, between the ages of four and thirteen, in their school, I make a list of the materials they need. There is a shortage of tables and school texts. Four black faces pore over an 'Introduction to Mathematics'.

The children come in at eight in the morning and stay until a quarter to twelve; then they rest. Later they work from five until seven in the evening. Their mothers also work. Indeed, it seems that all work in these towns of tents is carried out by the women. The men are at the front – at the wall – where I am headed in a few days' time. There is a great ease here, however. Time is measured, and nothing is hurried.

I sit in a circle in a district governor's tent with his council members. In the corner, tea is being made. Re-used tins house a gas burner and a pot. Into the pot is put the green tea, followed by a profusion of cane sugar, then more herbs and more boiling water. The little glasses are filled from a height to produce a foam. Then again, and again, they empty the contents before handing the glasses round. 'Once it should taste a little sour, for life is hard. Once it should be sweet, for love is sweet. Once it should be soft, that death may be soft.'

On the first occasion, I find the tea sickly sweet, but it is not long before I welcome it. I drink the water from the wells and wonder at the camel, who can travel for fifteen days in summer without food or water, or forty-five days at other times of the year. Everybody looks healthy. I meet a man of almost a hundred, who is fully alert. I am renewed with hope: given that longevity, even Galway West could become socialist in my lifetime!

On my way home on the third night, in a sea of desert, I see a camel driver with his thirty-five camels. We stop, and my companion suggests that it would be a good idea for me to mount the camel. I do so, but the speed with which the venerable animal shifts the saddle sideways indicates a deep-seated distrust of the Irish. I speculate on how the camels' days are changing, with the technological assault of the jeep. Even so, the desert refugees' lives revolve around them: they eat their meat and weave their wool.

Tonight the moon is large, the sky clear. Outside the reception area, the council members sit at ease on the sand. One Mr Suleiman sits winding his turban. He speaks classical Spanish; earlier, he had given me a long dissertation on how Morocco was in breach of international law in relation to Western Sahara. It had never claimed Western Sahara in the past, he points out. The Saharaouis' experience of colonisation was different from that of other colonised peoples. This is not a cessessionist struggle: the Saharaoui, for example, never had a king, as in Morocco, nor had they emirs, as in Mauratania; they were communalists, with a concept of the general will. Their communalism needed no outside ideological props: it is based on their Bedouin culture and history. Mr Suleiman had been in the Spanish parliament in General Franco's time. He speaks of being at 'the court of Franco'.

Over tea and water, we start the discussions. They will continue later over dinner. Later, I hear that my plans are to be changed. Do I really want to go to the wall? If so, the military, with whom I will travel, have left word that I must stay three more days than I had planned. I am beginning to get used to the local approach to timekeeping. The night is long and silent. Sometimes a breeze rattles the shutters or blows sand across the galvanised roof. I will stay for the extra days.

Before dinner, I pack away the stick I was given by the children at the regional hospital. Full of bright colours, it was given to me after a song of welcome by about fourteen black youngsters sitting with their backs to the wall of the dark kindergarten of the hospital. There were songs everywhere today: all the classes at the school sang. But it was during the morning break at the agricultural station that I heard what were, for me, the most interesting songs. Using a petrol tin as a drum, a young girl and her sister sang. Their mother asked me to choose which of the daughters would sing. 'Ask an old woman and there is no delay,' the mother told me. 'Ask a young woman, and you must wait.' But the daughter sings, with the mother ululating. I admire the grace of it all.

Before we reach the tents on the way back, the mounds of sand seem to float like clouds in the distance. The driver is telling me that, if I am here when the Sirocco comes, I must stay still or be lost. A gentle wind whips blasts of sand across our windscreen. It is momentarily white, it seems. But near to Smara I see the red sand that, mixed with water, gives the red coat to the reception buildings. Soon we are among the tents and their cooking houses.

There is a babble of conversation from the bodies stretched out on rugs, propped up on one elbow. The sun is going down, moving like the brush of some demented painter – from gold through burnt ochre, to leave us with a gold-tinged purple that would do the Fellini costume of a Prince of the Church proud. I have, by now, a list of necessary medical equipment and spare parts, and educational needs. But tomorrow my visits will continue to the different sections of the refugee encampment, separated as they are by miles of sand.

*

It is 11 AM, and the sun is at its hottest. A rest is suggested, and the ceremony begins again. Now it is time for mint tea again – by far the best I have tasted. Outside, the children are returning to their tents. They try to speak to me in Spanish. Like the adults, they are better clothed than I am against the sun. *'Como se llama?'* they ask, and giggle. They pronounce my name in Spanish, and pass on.

I continue my walk to the reception area, where I am staying for discussions. We all share a large room for the discussions, with mattresses placed against the wall and many carpets on the floor. The mattresses, covered in floral material, are heaped with long cushions. There is a low table, where our tea is placed. The rectangular room is aired by two very deep, shuttered windows, over which some netting blows. It is cool and comfortable. My companion and I will sleep here when the meetings are over. The other room consists of two sleeping areas, a dining area, a food-preparation area and a set of buildings that house communal toilets and baths. Everything is clean.

I write my notes. This morning I visited a school where, in cool dark rooms, the children are learning mathematics, Arabic, history and Spanish. Then I went on to an experimental agricultural station, where one of Polisario's five engineering agronomists explained their farming endeavours, which revolve around three walls which have been dug by hand. The wells fill a tank, from which rivulets flow to the garden plots. The results have been encouraging.

I was told of the prodigious size of the onions that they had grown. I had eaten the tomatoes and melons, too, but how was the sand made fertile? There is a need for parathion, methyl-parathion or carbyra, I was told. This immediately leads me to think of poisonous fertilisers. Were these not very toxic? In fact, everything is grown organically. The goats' droppings are mixed with the sand to make the soil rich.

The wells are dug manually, to a depth of fifteen meters, with shovels. Crops were rotated, I remember, and the women explain the principles of agronomy in classes. Experience is wasted if it is not transferrable, I had been told. The schools are places where they learn not only techniques but also the story of their people. In class, the old tales are acted out. But during breaks, you can see the budding stars play what they call 'the game of the desert' – soccer.

The Saharaoui concept of community becomes most clear in the tents of the older people. Sitting in a tent with six old men over eighty, I am impressed by their composure. A couple look after their needs. Once a day, a major discussion takes place. The men exchange views on what is relevant from history. One argues that Hassan has taken their territory for economic and strategic reasons. There are rumours of the fishing fleets being invited again by Hassan into the coastal waters of the Republic Arab Saharaoui Democratica. Another emphasises Hassan's statement that the Western Sahara is personal royal property. Another asks: what is the law in it all? This is all at a level of deep, calm intent. There is sadness visible only when Mr Suleiman talks of the camels being killed by aircraft. They say that Hassan regards the Saharaoui as dirt, as brigands, and he bombs their camel herds – a sin against the desert itself. In all civilisations, the most barbaric of actions is the killing of the animals, and the camel is the most sacred symbol of parts of the desert. In the tent of the old women, it is similar. Children come and play, but there will be the one big discussion. Thus the old people of the Saharaoui are kept informed.

The time has come to leave Smara and visit other regions. The dashboard of the jeep is covered with a patterned cloth, with holes cut for the speedometer and the necessary controls. We rattle along for many days. I smile as I notice my first T-junction in the sand. Moving along an apparently endless strip of tarmacadam, we follow a track to the next of the four regions into which the refugees are organised.

This city of the desert, with suburbs of tents, has four small hospitals – one organised with a general section and three with specialities, clinical paediatric and maternity. There is an incredible effort at cleanliness in a region where my guide tells me nobody can live! In these impossible conditions, a republic is being built and a people is being saved.

The hospitals cater for hundreds of people, and the young hospital director speaks anxiously of a battery of tests that is needed for his spectrophotometer, which will be exhausted in a month or less. It is a German machine and it is difficult to get parts for it. I write down the make, the supplier and the model number. Who knows, maybe I can do something when I get back? Water has to be brought here in tankers. There is a shortage of materials for dental prosthesis. French portable dental units are brought out to the schools.

Sick children anywhere are a sad sight. Here I see a few who lie under a damp cloth beside their mothers – sufferers from desert asthma. Others have respiratory and stomach ailments. I leave the Hospital Bachur-Salem knowing that it will not be my last visit to such an area. As in every one of the six villages of each town in each of the four regions, I am awaited; everybody wants to discuss their efforts, their problems, their hopes.

For the Saharaoui women, the most important visit is to the School of 27th February, which is named after the date of the proclamation of the Saharan Arab Democratic Republic. Here, as director Fatheema Emathu explains, women of all backgrounds come for training in military, political and civil matters. Some come for a year-long course, which includes one month's military service. After qualification, a day a week will be spent in military training.

There is a school for teacher training, but women's studies include military, political, cultural, health and agricultural matters. I ask questions, and find no awareness of tradition being challenged by modernity. Such challenges are not comprehensible to the Saharaoui. A woman of fifty does not think like a woman of twenty, I am told, but why should that be a problem? There is a small hospital, an administration office, and a sauna! It is for men and women, and helps them lose weight for military training. Women are prepared for all aspects of life; the Republic regained will be much more for a settled people than for a nomadic, Bedouin people.

I have a strange feeling of returning home as I leave down my bags at Smara. Welcome home, Raul bids. He brings water and lemon drinks. Buyema is busy doing what diplomats do best: changing schedules. He returns excitedly: the Foreign Minister of the SADR National Council has arrived and wishes for me to join him for talks. Meanwhile, I am waiting for the military details about my trip to the wall. We will leave in the middle of the night and travel about a hundred and fifty miles to the tomb.

Buyema arrives with a long scarf for me to wind around my head when the time comes. He will call me when the military car is here. I find it hard to sleep, and gaze at the yellow canvas which covers all the ceilings in this area. The gift of some donor, it has made school bags, mats and ceilings. Raul has left bottles of water and home-made Coke. The *irlandes* who was in Tinduff has left this morning, so for the second time in three years my *Hot Press* column will not be sent – may rejoicing break out among all those who feel it gives them indigestion, and the whiff of a male goat in season flavour their next thousand breakfasts!

The jeep travels at about sixty miles an hour through what my companion calls the cool night. I am as amazed at the number of layers of clothing they wear, as they are at my inability to take long periods of sleep. I have no conception of the sheer organisation of camp life. We break our journey; Hussan, in charge of water and all other human needs, has made a fire. The dead wood is lit and is then removed to two pits, one large, the other small. On the large one is prepared the meal of the few people in our group. On the smaller one, the tea ceremony begins. I am offered a blanket and sleep in the shade of the jeep. Against the jeep lean the Klashinkov M300s of Muhamed Salem and Hakhal.

As we move carefully though the liberated zones, it is explained to me that we will witness three aspects of the conflict. When darkness falls, we will look at the exchanges of fire along a sixty- to seventy-kilometre stretch of the wall. On the following night, I will be brought to within six kilometres of the wall and will be able to see a specific attack. On the final night, they hope to bring me to the wall itself.

The jeeps of the guerrillas move like beetles between camps. I meet Omar, who is in charge of military operations for the region. He is a handsome man of immense calm. He explains the economics of the war to me. I ask how long the conflict will keep him in the desert. 'As long as it takes,' he replies. Together, on that first night in a dugout, we look along the frontier at what seems like a video display. One sound indicates a Polisario attack. The reply, twenty times louder, is the Moroccan reply. I think of those Moroccan soldiers, like mice trapped in a hole. Only half, at most, are professional soldiers; the rest are citizens dying for the aggression of their king.

The yellow flares go up and down the wall. At times, a Bomba de Luz vies with the moon, lighting up a whole stretch of the installations. For about three miles in front of the wall, the area is mined. This does not deter the Polosario guerrillas, who even pick up and relocate the mines.

All the following day, we wait by the tent. In mid-afternoon, the rain of the desert, the Sirocco, whips through the tent. It is hot and uncomfortable. As night falls, we move out until we are close to where the Polisario *guerreros* will strike. Predictably, the night show starts at about 8 PM. Shells land about six hundred metres to our left. Later, we will pass the gouged holes they leave in the sand.

I am more than a little apprehensive. I write notes to myself. Time hangs heavy. Buyema apparently explains that the *guerreros* will clear a stretch of the wall and then I can inspect it. We travel off in jeeps at nightfall. The first jeep is detected on the radar, and a few flashes indicate shells landing about seven hundred metres away. The plan is changed, but the target remains the same. We come to a point about nine kilometres from the wall. From here, we will walk. But first we have tea. Omar contrasts our freedom of movement with that of the soldiers on the wall. I sit and watch as my accompanying *guerrero*, Muhamet Solan, ties his boots. In measured Spanish, he tells me of how these black boots, with their welded soles, are strong enough to defeat the sand. He moves the lace through the twelve eyelets on each side. He rarely wears these boots, which were taken from a Moroccan soldier just over a year ago. Muhamet Solan is twenty-five.

The time has come for us to go, and he walks in front of me giving instructions: keep the time, these are mines, crouch. We move along the sides of the hills. Stop, crouch. Be soft. I take off my shoes. And then I was on the wall. I see the horseshoe of stones, maybe four stones high, where a Moroccan soldier had lain. A rectangular little space, eight boulders high, made the principal living space. Omar grasps my arms and says: 'Now you've seen it. The king's wall.' Somebody appears with a placard. Unbelievably, I hear that they are asking me to place it on the wall. It has a caricature of the king on it. My God, but they begin to clap!

We start the journey home. My legs are moving but all I can think of is water. Hours later, it seems, Muhamet restrains me from gulping back the water from a basin. Gargle, drink only a little, I am told. Back in Smara, it takes me hours to shave. A message comes from the president of the Saharan Arab Democratic Republic. I am still hearing the French of the Moroccan soldiers, intercepted on the radio, in my ears.

The president and I have an extraordinary conversation. 'Tell me about your social problems in Ireland,' he suggests. We spend more than two hours talking about the Saharaoui. He explains how they have no connection with Libya, and how they are not armed by a superpower. How they will continue to ask simply that international law be respected.

He emphasises the Saharaoui's love of peace. He thinks that Ireland should be very interested in his people's struggle. I take copious notes. This is your home now, he tells me.

Late that evening, in a tent on the sand, the Saharaoui entertain a foreign delegation and myself. About a hundred camels are gathered and I, for the second time, mount up. There is singing and dancing and food. I am given a robe to wear.

In the morning, I say goodbye to those at the reception centre. I am at Tinduff, and confusion reigns. Buyema is supposed to travel with me to Algiers. At the last moment, he has no seat. I do not comprehend what is happening. I embrace the driver, but when I look back, Buyema is gone.

Flying home, I go over the details in my mind. I know the legal case; I know what, politically, should be done. Perhaps I have even begun to experience the story of the Saharaoui. I put my hand in my pocket for money, and it strikes me: no money was used for more than two weeks in this society, a society of basic needs in exile. No king will defeat the Saharaoui.

I pick up the Irish papers. Mayo County Council has been consulting with Prince Albert as to how they will make Princess Grace's farm a kind of Republican shrine to their Irish-American princess. A kind of tourist attraction. I think of the desert.

Hot Press, Vol. 10, No. 21, 6 November 1986

SOMALIA

STARVING BY NUMBERS

For several weeks recently, the tragedy of Somalia filled the pages of our newspapers. Tragic pictures of emaciated, dying and dead children moved the Irish people yet again. There has been a generous response. Irish aid workers have as usual underplayed the heroic nature of their work, and the emotional strength that it requires.

Then came the crisis of the British pound. Now the photos were of shirt-sleeved dealers in the middle age of their lives – their late twenties – screaming, a phone receiver clutched to each pale cheek. The fluctuating pound drove the refugee-camp photos from the front pages.

Yet the Irish public's interest held fast, and in schools, workplaces and neighbourhoods, activities are being organised to raise money for the relief of famine in Somalia. I have been getting letters too in response to the much-publicised interference with the distribution of food aid. One letter said simply: 'It is politics that is causing this. You are the politicians. For God's sake, do something.'

The truth is that it is the absence of politics – in the best sense of that word – that makes the present situation as bad as it is. The famine in Somalia, like so many other famines, is made possible by citizens in the powerful Northern economies putting up with the exclusion of the people of the South from politics, from economics.

Indeed, the precarious position of the pound and the Somalian tragedy had this in common: neither event was widely discussed or understood by a public that was largely willing to be kept out of serious discussion. Children, tragically, have to die in front of the television cameras to get a space in public and political consciousness. But no matter how much is achieved in the short term by humanitarian aid, there will be famine again until the public has moved beyond emotion to commitment and participation in politics and economics.

Thinking about the pound should straighten out a few of those lovely neutral 'I'm not a bit political' types. Not a bit political! Just a few days ago, people in Britain were being asked to give up their homes – thirty thousand of them, if necessary – for the welfare of the pound. It was an acute state-ment about contemporary values: living for the exchange rate was more important than living for any moral or social value. The problems of the pound and Somalia also had this in common: both indicated the price to be paid for the fact that there is no real control over unaccountable exploitative economics and the political violence that serves it. In a South African mine, your life is over at forty-five, as your lungs pack in; on the dealer's floor, your life is over at thirty-five.

From an outsider's perspective, the sickening aspect of the tragedy of Somalia is that so much of what is taking place had been predicted. I have in front of me a report dated 26 March 1992 from Africa Watch and Physicians for Human Rights, entitled: 'Somalia – No Mercy in Mogadishu'. The report opens with a quotation from Andrew Natsios, former director of the US Office of Foreign Disaster Assistance. He said that Somalia was 'the worst humanitarian disaster in the world today'. The report stated that last March the International Committee of the Red Cross was spending 20 percent of its entire worldwide budget on assistance to Somalia.

Why then has it taken so long for the world to come to the aid of the Somalian people? Why has it taken the United Nations so long to exhibit even the appropriate concern? The answer is, to go back to where we began, politics – but this time of the worst kind.

Contrast the speed with which the so-called Allies acted during the Gulf war with the lethargy in relation to Somalia. Recently, Erskine Childers wrote that we need 'Operation Moral Storm' much more urgently than we ever needed 'Operation Desert Storm' – and he is right. But is there any hope of that happening?

The reason that there has been such an inadequate response from the UN is given in a Boston-based Physicians for Human Rights paper. The US, the report states, has fought to limit aid to Somalia to humanitarian aid. As long ago as last March, America bitterly resisted moves at the UN Security Council by the African members Zimbabwe, Morocco and Cape Verde to have a political dimension inserted into the resolution on Somalia. But a political dimension is not just required – it is essential. To put it bluntly, the UN mandate on Somalia is inadequate, insufficient and not being pursued with anything like the urgency that is needed.

It is interesting, when it came to Somalia, that President Bush was anx-ious to appease a Congress that expressed concern about the costs of peace-keeping in Yugoslavia, El Salvador and Cambodia but had no such hesitation in relation to Kuwait. If I was an African, I might well ask what kind of international morality is it that puts the restoration of the El Sabahs above the death of children in Somalia?

Here, then, arises an important distinction. The UN on the ground has been found wanting; this is related to the fact that it is the permanent members of the Security Council who decide what is acceptable and what is not.

The tyrannical rule of Mohammed Siad Barre in Somalia from 1969 to 1991 was assisted by the Soviet Union for one decade and the US for another; both were permanent members of the Security Council.

Since Barre was ousted in January 1991, a civil war has raged in Somalia. The country has descended into chaos. The UN stayed away; indeed until recently, when it was shamed into action, the UN has handled Somalia from the safe distance of Kenya. I repeat: the UN's disastrous failures as a bureaucracy stem from its being neutered at the level of the Security Council.

Here, then, is an initiative that should be proposed by Ireland:

§ Sponsor an adequate UN mandate for Somalia, to last for a period of years.

§ Ensure that the mandate will be implemented with an adequate force.

§ Insist on the use of some armed UN forces to knock out the artillery being indiscriminately used against civilians in Mogadishu.

§ Build a dimension into the UN resolution that will enable civil society to be re-established in Somalia, possibly by involving the non-militarised older sources of authority.

Just before writing this column, I have been talking to Joe Feeney, Trócaire's Emergency Officer, who has been in Somalia for the last three weeks. He has been visiting areas outside of the cities where media attention is low and where Trócaire is the only agency on the ground. In the province of Gedo, Trócaire will be assisting seventy thousand people who are in serious need. Gedo is near the north-eastern border of Kenya, where there are fifty thousand people in camps around the town of Mandera. Between thirty and forty people die in Mandera's camps every day. Ninety-five percent of the infrastructure of the region has been destroyed.

Over the years, I have found Trócaire's approach particularly attractive, mainly because of their interest in constructing projects that will not create or perpetuate dependency. Trócaire has got free food, emergency supplies and seeds for distribution in Gedo. In this region, they will distribute forty tons of seed to more than seven thousand families for planting in the next three weeks – and in time to take advantage of the short rainy season.

There will also be a health programme in each of the five districts of Gedo, and a rehabilitation programme. Trócaire's Emergency and Rehabilitation Programme is directed at a province where three hundred thousand people are afflicted by famine, and where they are the sole agency on the ground. They deserve support, as do all the agencies. But the bottom line is that the problem will not be solved by them alone: the political will must be there too.

If there is going to be a visit by President Robinson to Somalia, it will be of undoubted symbolic and psychological value. It would be marvellous, however, if it was also designed to give clear expression to a national resolution to claim back the realms of economics and politics for public participation, social equality and ecological responsibility.

The offensiveness of being asked to live and die for the exchange rate and for the interests of the permanent members of the Security Council will be effectively challenged only when a morally outraged, literate and participating world public demand that things be different. It can be done.

Hot Press, Vol. 16, No. 17, 14 October 1992

There is no experience I have had, in any refugee camp, in any war zone, that could have prepared me for the scale of horror that is Somalia. I find it difficult to describe even now, at a distance of more than a week, as I work through the notebooks I wrote each day.

On a Wednesday afternoon, I decided to go to Somalia. In Nairobi on Friday, I was briefed at a number of meetings on the work of the aid organisation, and in particular by the Irishman Geoff Loan, who is in charge of the International Committee of the Red Cross's impressive work in the field in this devastated region.

Flying north to the refugee camp of Mandera in north-east Kenya, you can see the shattering effect of the drought. The first sight of the camp is like a city of beehives, alongside which lie hundreds of little ridges – the graves of children, women and men. There are fifty thousand people in the camp, more than double the number of people in Mandera itself. One gets an idea of the scale of the refugee problem Kenya is carrying when one remembers that there are four hundred thousand Somalian refugees in drought-stricken Kenya.

In Mandera, food is beginning to be distributed on the scale that is needed, but there is no defence for the bureaucratic delays and the sporadic distribution of food. Seeing this devastation first-hand, I understand the rage, the anger, and the emotion of President Robinson when she gave her press conference immediately after leaving Mandera.

In the eight days I spent in Somalia, I could not get away from the obscenity of the fact that the country was being flooded with weapons at the same time as walking skeletons were moving slowly, staring impassively ahead, waiting to die. How can one not rage at the immorality of the actions of one superpower, then another, in filling a country with weapons and then walking away? The reality of Somalia's terrible vulnerability was known before the despot Siad Barre fled in January 1991.

Again, every day, I thought of the weapons-producing and weapons-selling countries, and of those who are still selling instruments of death into Africa and the South of the planet in general. I thought, too, of the absence of the international media: there was just one North American and one British TV crew working in Somalia, where 1.5 million people are starving and 2.5 million are affected by the famine, out of a population of 7.6 million.

How different it was to the Gulf war, when camera crews competed to bring us pictures of, it seemed, every single rocket as it was launched. How true it is to say that Somalia's plight would be different if it was an oil-rich country.

From its station in Mandera, Trócaire is establishing a project in Gedo Province. Gedo is located in Somalia, near the north-eastern border of Kenya, across from the refugee camp at Mandera.

I stayed in the house Trócaire is renting, where I met field officers Joe Feeny and Kathleen Fahy, and field staffers Zebbe, an agronomist, and Stephen. The house is basic: it has a pit latrine and a bucket hangs in a cubicle, if you have the patience to let the water you have drawn from the well trickle onto you. The rural training suggests that you use a more direct method.

I watched as the elders, who almost certainly offer the only basis from which Somalia's civil society can be reconstructed, handed over lists to Trócaire workers of those who were ready to plant seeds when the short rains came. If the seeds were eaten, they would kill, so Trócaire gives out food with them. They have also been examining the wells which are dotted everywhere, dry and abandoned, and a danger to life. Some of the repairs to the infrastructure are simple: the aim is to have a secure, safe well in every village. Trócaire also has a programme in the five districts of Gedo, training health workers to carry out nutrition surveys and bringing basic health care to mothers and children.

While all this is happening, a new dialogue is being constructed between, and within, the clans that make up the Somalian nation. In Bell Awyo, I met the chief of chiefs and the elders. The chief of chiefs gave a moving speech and was very grateful for Ireland's interest. The night before, an old man had said to me: 'Welcome. It is a holocaust. We have been committing suicide. Thank you for coming.' That feeling was everywhere.

Again and again, I thought of the possibility that Ireland might pioneer an imaginative foreign policy in the developing world. Whatever latter-day revisionists may write, there is in the Irish psyche a memory of famine and of the consequence of colonialism, and a humanistic impulse born of a decent sense of interdependency.

Travelling into the providence of Gedo, we reached the city of Luug, which is controlled by the Islamic fundamentalists. Once a city of maybe two hundred thousand people, it now accommodates just fifty thousand, who have made their way back there. A laboratory technician and a male nurse run the makeshift hospital. Saudi Arabia is willing to fund the rebuilding of the mosque but has not offered to help with the hospital.

The camera crew, including Gerry McGolgan, Ken O'Mahony and Karl Mirren, from EMG are with us. Ken and Karl, on camera and sound respectively, are regular readers of *Hot Press*, and are anxious for me to point out that they have had only one night off in Nairobi, which they spent attending a revivalist meeting and drinking tea with a lay preacher.

Journeying through Somalia, relationships are tested. I felt that the long silences which prevailed at times as we tried in vain to make sense of what we saw were drawing us together in a way which helped us to support each other. I value that and will always remember it.

In the hospital at Luuq, a woman is looking straight ahead. Malnourished, she has a baby at her breast and is trying to care for her sick child of about three years. I can still see her face. I wondered about the act of filming such a person. Her sense of privacy is important – yet she says, through the interpreter, that the world should help and come to know the pain of Somalia and its people.

Travelling to Luuq in daylight took nearly five hours. Coming home through desert tracks in the half-light was more difficult. The journey was broken for the repair of a puncture, as well as for the prayers of the drivers, who took their mat on to a space nearby, positioned themselves, bowed and prayed.

I thought of the question I had been asked in Luuq: who is your prophet? Luuq struck me as an extraordinary place: medieval in its defensive structure, it is surrounded by the Juba river, and entrance is gained through a gateway beyond a protected bridge. Even in the midst of great want and death, women were making and selling tea; as ever, they carry the burden of famine and war.

It is utterly wrong to construct the present conflict between the Mahdi and General Aideed as an indicator of a violence-prone people. When, in the nineteenth century, Richard Burton wrote of Somalia, he spoke, among other things, of their rich oral poetic tradition.

The Somali language was not given written codification until the 1970s, and it was 1976 before the first novel was published here. In the nineteenth century, a person with a new word would travel hundreds of miles for a poetic contest in a village, hoping that a new word, as one man said, would defeat his opponent, who might have defeated him earlier with alliteration.

There was something eerie about travelling the roads, and repeatedly encountering abandoned villages. Everywhere there are burned-out vehicles, skeletons of cattle, roofless huts. The destruction is on an unimaginable scale. Beyond the immediate food aid, there is a mammoth task of reconstruction to be undertaken. Nobody has been at school for two years. Every family has at least one rifle.

In refugee camps, you meet those who have fled from urban areas, such as Mogadishu. They are gathering together along clan lines. From the five basic ethnic units, subdivisions are made, and people have gone in search of their own group.

Those who have not finished their schooling introduce themselves as 'the young intellectuals'. There are older professors too, and it is from a group of these that I received a request that the National University of Ireland help in the task of reconstructing the National University of Somalia.

What I read now in the notebooks makes reference, again and again, to the children. In this country where few live beyond fifty years, the children are everywhere, and they are in very great need.

In Garissa, a hundred and twenty miles inside the Kenyan border, the local bishop, Paul Darmanin, is assisted by an Indian nun and a few others in running a feeding centre. Here five hundred children a day are fed. He is helped by the funding from Trócaire.

In the camps at Mandera and Ifo, the short rains will increase the threat of cholera. If the rains bring hope for the seed plantation, they will also bring even more death to the camps. Hardest of all to witness is the bodies, often covered in sores, their bones bare and brittle. Above all, the beautiful eyes stare out, hopeless. Many of these starving people will need up to three weeks' preparation with vitamin-enriched liquid food before they are able to digest solid food.

Baidoa had the highest reported daily death rate, of two hundred and fifty a day. The journey there will be long and tortuous. One day I meet Goal volunteers Dr Tim Gleeson and nurses Mary Scully and Helen Fitzgerald. Later, I hear of their work in Mogadishu and Afghoi. Indeed, it is worth saying that no words are sufficient to describe the contribution the Irish aid workers are making in the midst of all the horror.

In northern Mogadishu, the Red Cross and the Red Crescent work together in a former prison. Here a man holds lights over a horrifically wounded arm. A little boy is waiting for an operation on his leg. He makes signs to me that indicate that he knows it is to be amputated. They are waiting for his mother to come and give permission for the amputation. His father is dead.

I can still see that little boy, Ali, making his signs. Neither can I forget the haunting face of a dying child in Garissa. We made an attempt to rush him to the clinic. His mother had her dress stuffed in her mouth to stifle a scream. His father was weeping. Two other children were crying as they were led away. We didn't make it in time to save his life. I find it hard even now to write about the children of Somalia.

Something could be learned from all this. As we learned from Dachau and Auschwitz and fumbled towards a version of human rights, could we not take from Somalia an impulse to build food security in Africa, and to prohibit the international sale of armaments?

John Roche heads the Red Cross operation in northern Mogadishu. We attempt to visit the UN office together. We are invited in by a Norwegian officer and an Egyptian colonel. They are unarmed, and a young teenager with a gun barely allows them to return to their own building. They are not allowed to bring us in. The sense of hopelessness deepens.

The youngsters with the guns are chewing qat, pronounced 'gat'; it is a narcotic which is chewed in the month and retained in a ball inside the cheek. When it secretes, it gives the user a high, and by about five in the afternoon its effects are obvious. By evening, however, as the young toters of kalashnikovs, bazookas and rocket launchers on the backs of trucks are coming down, the tension is palpable.

Crossing over to southern Mogadishu, where Concern has its offices, the timing has to be exact, and two separate teams of 'technicals' from the Red Cross are involved. We get a puncture but we make it, and visit Concern, who will bring us to Baidoa.

Passing through the dozens of improvised barriers on the road, it becomes obvious that one is in a war zone. Yet, side by side with this, trading is going on. I remember again the scene near Mandera on the bank of the river that divides Somalia and Kenya: women and children carrying large boxes filled with sachets of curry powder and Rexona, 'for a soft skin'.

As we arrive in Baidoa, there is shooting. The International Red Cross warehouse is being looted. Everything is taken. By the time I reach the town, the Irish media have begun arriving, in preparation for President Mary Robinson's visit. In the Concern house, I share a room with Vincent Browne, who will later deliver a fine piece on Africa in the *Sunday Tribune*. He has the better bed, protected by a mosquito net. The lumps that come up on my hands and legs tell me how useful such protection is!

It is in Baidoa that I see the most disturbing scene: the collection and burial of the dead in mass graves. At about 8 AM, a single-decker bus begins making its way around the collecting points. Occasionally, a body will be wrapped in a blanket. More usually, tied with rags, they look like bundles of sticks. In a vast mountain of earth, the grave-diggers make the space. Several bodies, maybe twenty, are placed in a single grave.

The relatives will not know where in this mountain of the dead their loves ones are buried. In Somalia in the past, when a person was dying the neighbours stopped everything, dressed in white and, for three days, called Tazia, they grieved. On the seventh day, they ate camel or goal meat in celebration of the person's life, in the ceremony of Todobat. Now the dead are being gathered like faggots for a fire. The man laying them next to each other has sacking over each hand.

In the airport in northern Mogadishu, Mr Sahnoun, the UN representative, is waiting for President Robinson. We talk for a while. Then news comes that the plane will be a little late. Mr Sahnoun leaves. The plane comes in on time. David Andrews emerges to stretch his legs and suggests that I have word with the president. I wish her well and thank her for her courage in deciding to come. Anything that can be done to draw international attention to the scale of the horror here is worth doing, I say.

In the Horn of Africa, there are ten million 'displaced' people, who will never be able to return home. Poverty is increasing. Services are disintegrating. Aid is falling. And as Jack Finnucane of Concern put it to me: 'The continent is awash with arms.'

There is hope that, through a congress of elders, Somalian society can begin to be reconstructed. In such an assembly, a legitimacy – however fragile – supported by tradition can be reconstructed. Such a congress might prevail upon General Aideed and the Mahdi to stand down, and thus to create a space in which peace might be established.

The UN will have to get a new, and far stronger, Security Council resolution, and the used of armed forces to protect its food operations – however risky the strategy – seems inevitable. 'Every day here is like a year,' said one Somali to me. There has been too much culpable, immoral decay.

The Irish people, and the aid workers in particular, have shown outstanding generosity and solidarity with a stricken people. It is important that their interest in Somalia be sustained. Our attitude to Africa over the next few years is one of the greatest moral challenges of contemporary history.

Lasting peace will not come easily, however. As I finish writing, the news is bad. Concern are being forced to evacuate its staff from Baidoa, as General Morgan, son-in-law of the ousted Siad Barre, is approaching. The Somalian people will have to suffer even more, if that were possible.

Hot Press, Vol. 16, No. 18, 4 November 1992

ETHIOPIA

AFRICA – APOCALYPSE NOW

My sister-in-law Margaret Coyne works in Mekele, Tigre. She has been in this war zone of the Ethiopian conflict since the early eighties. She and her colleagues run a small eye clinic and a polio clinic there. When we get letters from Mekele, they usually talk about the crops, the rain, the war . . . The difference is that now the eyes of the world are diverted away from Africa. People tell me that they cannot look at the photos of the famine, that the photos are too upsetting.

In the Dáil, I have tried to address the source of the recurring famines in Africa. I proposed an international congress on the causes of Africa's food problems. Gerard Collins, minister for foreign affairs, did not think this was a good idea at this time. Instead, I had to listen to a litany of what the European Community has already done. Within a few weeks, European parliaments will go into recess. While they are so engaged, nearly thirty million Africans will die.

The continuous defence of our inactivity about this unimaginable tragedy will include the suggestion that we have tried before. What about Live Aid? some will ask. The truth is that the size of the debt of those countries threatened with famine is about $160 billion. Interest payments in every year for the last five years have exceeded all aid donated in the same period, including mammoth voluntary efforts such as Live Aid. It is time for action. There is now an urgent need for an international conference on the African debt. Ireland could take the moral initiative by suggesting, organising and offering itself as a venue for such a conference.

Related to the impossible size of the external debt is the issue of the distortion of African economies. It is painfully obvious that concentration on export-crop earnings, paid for in hard currencies, is deflecting energies and investment away from self-sufficiency in food. This is recognised by the international relief agencies and even by the UN. However, such initiatives as have been facilitated by the lending agencies have been geared to market economies of the Thatcherite kind. As primary-commodity prices collapse and import costs rise, African countries have to run faster and faster to stay

257

in the same position on the treadmill of external debt.

The breakdown of the debt also makes for appalling reading, as it reveals the high sums that are being paid to the arms-exporting countries by repressive and undemocratic regimes. Both superpowers have had their fingers in African wars, and all the major arms-exporting countries have equipped such wars. In short, the West has exported death to Africa. Now everybody would like to walk away – and leave the thirty million to die. It is the most significant challenge of our times, a challenge not only to politicians but to us all.

Everybody, it seems, is weary of Africa. Is it not appalling that, when they are shamed into responding to the plight of the Kurdish refugees, some Western countries shifted their food-supply planes from Africa to the Turkish border? And while the long-term issues lie neglected, short-term crises multiply. Food, medicines, blankets, construction materials, seeds, technical assistance . . . all are needed now.

The World Food Programme gives figures for those at risk as follows:

	AT RISK	TOTAL POPULATION
Sudan	7.7 million	23.8 million
Ethiopia	7.5 million	48.0 million
Somalia	2.0 million	7.6 million
Mozambique	1.9 million	15.0 million
Angola	1.9 million	9.5 million
Nigeria	1.8 million	119.0 million
Burkina Faso	1.5 million	8.6 million
Liberia	1.35 million	2.5 million
Malawi	1.0 million	8.0 million

The governments of many of these countries have, for political reasons, denied the existence of famine, among them the fundamentalist rulers of Sudan. The report of the situation there on 16 May by Concern's Aengus Finucane made grim reading:

My recent visit to Sudan sadly confirmed my worst fears. The country is steadily on course for disaster. Hundreds of thousands of Sudanese are walking on very thin ice indeed. People are now dying of starvation every day. How many more will perish between now and Christmas is a matter of conjecture.

Oxfam and Trócaire have warned of this country's problems and about the situation in Africa in general for the last few years. Now time is running out. For many, it already has. I think of Margaret, my sister-in-law, and of her use of reflexology and eye movement – techniques that are used because she often has nothing else to offer a mother who has walked for days with her sick child.

What kind of international order is it that cannot respond? How can half a million people be shifted across the planet for war and yet it be impossible to respond to famine? I have heard no convincing answer to this question. The truth is that, after the Gulf war, there can be no basis to the suggestion that there are insuperable logistical difficulties facing short-term emergency relief. What is required is the will to push it through.

Lest I be accused of naivety, may I acknowledge that there most certainly are political problems. For example, if a country denies the existence of a famine, is this an assertion of sovereignty? I believe that the UN has an urgent responsibility to declare new conditions in which people's lives will not be put at risk by the actions of face-saving regimes.

Political arguments were accepted by members of the Security Council to qualify sovereignty and facilitate action in the Gulf. Political morality requires that the lives of the African people be regarded as sovereign – and a regional UN conference should be convened to deal with this problem.

It is scandalous that the political complexion of a country's leadership should be a factor in the decision about whether to send or refuse aid. The UN has previously passed resolutions on arms sales and proliferation. Should there now not also be a levy on those countries that have fuelled wars between, and within, states? Should armaments not be forced to be purchased back from Africa and destroyed?

I have heard the old tired arguments so often – among them, that so called undeveloped countries are endemically prone to violence. It is a crude rationalisation. All the evidence is that there is a movement towards democracy in Africa that can be powerfully assisted by intelligent politics and aid. The same is true of Latin America.

Hot Press, Vol. 15, No. 13, 11 July 1991

CAMBODIA

RETURN TO THE KILLING FIELDS

On 16 November 1989, the United Nations will be deciding on resolutions in relation to Cambodia. What is said, what is avoided, what is not done through lack of courage, will decide whether or not the Cambodian people will see the return of the Killing Fields.

After the recent Vietnamese withdrawal, the dreaded Khmer Rouge – responsible for the deaths of more than a million Cambodians between 1975 and 1979 – have been making gains. They are estimated, at the beginning of November, to be within thirty miles of Battambang, Cambodia's second-largest city. Further north, they are fighting for Phnow Malat, control of which would give them access to the interior and place the forces of the Cambodian government under pressure.

The Heng Samrin government of the People's Republic of Kampuchea takes its name from the president installed by the Vietnamese after they ousted the Khmer Rouge in 1979. Heng Samrin had been the leader of a faction of the Khmer Rouge that was pro-Vietnamese and, after leading an unsuccessful attempted coup against the brutal regime of Pol Pot in 1978, he defected to Vietnam. Later, he was installed as head of state.

The Vietnamese intervention in Cambodia stopped Pol Pot and the Khmer Rouge. It was at that moment that courageous journalists, notably John Pilger, drew back the curtain of what had happened in Cambodia. The television screens showed stacks of skulls and mass graves on a scale not seen since Auschwitz and Dachau.

Today, the People's Republic of Kampuchea is a country facing immense problems, as the past returns to haunt it. A million people had been killed before the Khmer Rouge forces were driven to the western boarder with Thailand, from which foothold they have continued to do battle with the government of the People's Republic. Medical personnel, meanwhile, had virtually been wiped out for the surviving population, estimated at 6.5 million – this in a country where two out of three children were malnourished, life expectancy was about forty years, one child in four who was born alive died in infancy, and malaria was rife.

Yet the people struggled back from a situation where even basic agricultural implements were unavailable and rice fields had been destroyed, to get to the point where, with a minimum of aid, and above all a security achieved through the initiative of the international community, they see self-sufficiency in food and basic needs as a possibility.

Now they face the return of a regime that has stated that it regards those who assisted the Vietnamese liberation as enemies: the men as potential fertiliser and the women solely as reproducers, as they put it. The world knows this, and on 16 November, the Irish delegation and the United Nations will be called on to respond to a situation which the West has chosen to ignore in recent years.

The scandal of their neglect can be crudely summarised as follows: seated at the United Nations is the representative of the so-called Coalition Government of Democratic Kampuchea in Exile. This group, under the nominal leadership of Prince Sihanouk, is dominated by the Khmer Rouge. And as the United Nations meets, outside its building in New York flies the very flag – red with three yellow towers – which flew over the capital city of Cambodia, Phnom Penh, between 1975 and 1979 whilst a million Cambodians died.

Unlike the situation that prevailed when Idi Amin of Uganda was dislodged by Tanzanian troops, at crippling costs to the brave Tanzanian government, the government of Hun Sen is not recognised at the UN. This is of course connected to the Vietnamese defeat of the United States, who support the Khmer Rouge–dominated coalition.

Because of its recognition of the coalition and its refusal to acknowledge the legitimacy of the government of Hun Sen, the United Nations has provide a ready-made obstacle to all aid from the West for the Kampuchean people. It is vitally important, however, that the work on behalf of the Kampuchean people of such agencies as UNICEF be recognised: they spend $5 million per annum on urgent irrigation schemes, primary health care, medical aid, and a number of child-centre projects. While, at a political level, the UN does not seat the representative of the present Kampuchean government, UNICEF continues with its policy of putting children first. The World Health Organisation also helps. Thus it is essential that the excellent work of those agencies – along with others, such as Oxfam and Trócaire – not be impaired or overlooked in the current debate about who should sit at the United Nations on behalf of Kampuchea.

In 1986, more than twenty of these organisations came together to draw up proposals for relief of the Kampuchean people's tragedy. One of the results was the publication by Oxfam in 1988 of 'Punishing the Poor: The International Isolation of Kampuchea' by Eva Mysliviec. It is the best source of information I know on the whole Kampuchean situation: it gives chronologies of major events, an introduction to the often bewildering 'who's who' of the conflict, an excellent history of events from the 1970s to the present, a thorough account of present realities and, above all, an agenda for action.

Why is November 16 so important? And what is its importance for Ireland? The fact is that Ireland has, up to now, abstained on the question of who should speak at the UN on behalf of the Cambodian people. It was, in its time, a more progressive position than that adopted by other European countries, which supported the so-called anti-Vietnamese coalition representative, but it is no longer good enough.

Furthermore, on the question of aid, the government of Ireland, both at home and in Europe, has, quite simply, disgraced itself. I recall travelling to Dublin to meet three representatives of the government of reconstruction of Hun Sen, who were not even granted interviews with senior officials of our Department of Foreign Affairs.

Today, the way forward is clear. Ireland must vote to declare the Khmer Rouge representative of Pol Pot unacceptable, and the United Nations must give recognition to the government of the Kampuchean People's Republic. If Hun Sen's government (which has promised elections followed by a constitutional referendum) falls to the Khmer Rouge, the UN will be responsible for facilitating such a nightmare. Ireland can, and should, take a leading role in saving the United Nations from continuing to disgrace itself. Of equal urgency is the necessity, at European level and at home, of ending the aid embargo.

There is no point in wringing our hands. It is high time that foreign policy reflected our democratic wishes. So get on the phone to the Department of Foreign Affairs, ask for the minister's office and tell them you want us to recognise the People's Republic of Kampuchea. Tell them, too, that at the very least the Khmer Rouge's spokesman must vacate the United Nations seat, to end the obscenity of a situation akin to Hitler being allowed to represent the Jews of Dachau's death chambers. And if the department suggests something about a common European Community position, ask them what they think of the statement by the French secretary of state for humanitarian action, Bernard Kouchner – that, if necessary, international bridges should be formed to block the Khmer Rouge's return, and that he would be prepared to volunteer for one of these brigades himself!

Hot Press, Vol. 13, No. 23, 30 November 1989

WITHDRAWAL FROM GAZA

CONNING THE WORLD, CONTINUING THE OPPRESSION

Among those taken in by one of the best-managed public-relations stunts in international politics of our times were Jack Lang, former Minister for Culture in France, and Jesse Jackson of the United States – both friends of the Palestinian cause in the past.

What the international media reported was a 'withdrawal' from Gaza of eight thousand settlers. No reference was made to the conditions in which the 1.4 million Palestinians in Gaza lived – 900,000 of them in refugee camps. Two-thirds of the Palestinian population live below the poverty line; unemployment in the refugee camp of Jabaliya is 60 percent, and at around 40 percent in Gaza as a whole.

I recently spent a weekend in Gaza, Israel and the occupied Palestinian lands with Andreas Van Aaght, former Prime Minister of the Netherlands, and six others – three former Ministers, one a former Ambassador of France, one a survivor of Auschwitz. We travelled the routes Palestinians travel and endured for one visit the long, humiliating and degrading ordeal with which Palestinians have to contend on a daily basis.

Gaza is best described as an open prison. After this alleged 'withdrawal', there will not be free movement of persons or goods. The border to Egypt at Rafa, for example, will not be in the control of Palestinians, neither will they have control of the air or the sea.

So what has happened? Twenty-one settlements have been demolished within Gaza, and eight thousand settlers have left. Internal checkpoints have been removed, and replaced by five upgraded military control points on the border. This is to be welcomed. Palestinians in Gaza can go to the sea and move within Gaza with less hassle and humiliation than before.

On the other hand, Gaza is without safe drinking water. The settlers, who used eight times as much water as the refugees per head, used so much for swimming pools, among other things, that they reduced the Gaza aquifer to such a degree that it is now below sea level and has become salinated.

Gaza can never be a viable embryonic Palestinian State. For one thing, it is just 1 percent of historic Palestine and 6 percent of the territory of what was left after the 1967 war, when Israel defeated all its neighbours and drove

Egypt from Gaza, Jordan from the West Bank, and Syria from the Golan Heights.

I first visited Gaza and its refugee camps just under twenty years ago. Since then, everything has deteriorated. Poverty has deepened: 18,000 families in Gaza now get special-needs assistance, including feeding; of these, 3,300 are in Jabaliya refugee camp alone, where the United Nations Relief and Works Agency for Palestinian Refugees in the Near East has been since 1947.

While eight thousand settlers were leaving Gaza, permissions were being granted for new homes for settlers in the West Bank. According to figures released for the twelve months up to September 2005, there were almost thirteen thousand new settlers in the West Bank during this period.

The Israeli government acknowledges that there are more than 250,000 settlers in the occupied West Bank. In addition, more than 150,000 are in new settlements in a horseshoe around East Jerusalem. Israel controls more than 60 percent of the West Bank: this is the context in which all recent events should be construed.

It was in Hebron that the greatest despair, and anger, hit me. I was made conscious of the function of humiliation in the strategy of settler occupation. About four hundred settlers in Hebron are protected by five thousand Israeli soldiers. As for the 150,000 Palestinians, they are forbidden from entering the city's central area.

Contrary to a Hebron accord that dates from the time of the Oslo Accords, a particularly ideologically driven and vicious group of settlers continues to press for the expansion of Jewish settlements and the expropriation of Palestinian property. When these people enter a house illegally, often from next door by knocking through the walls, they change the locks. A confrontation takes place, and the Israeli army moves the Palestinians into custody, for their own protection. Apart from housing, more than 2,500 Palestinian businesses have closed as a result of such intimidation.

We saw at first hand the process of making a settlement. It begins with a simple tent or, more usually, a set of mobile homes. These in time become single-storey dwellings, and later two- and three-storey houses, with red-tiled roofs and swimming pools. In November 1998, Ariel Sharon produced the immortal advice: 'We must all run to the top of every hill. What we occupy, we will keep; what we leave, they will get.' It is on the tops of the hills that the settlements dominate, with their security zone constituting a vast footprint, and the Israeli Defence Forces available as protection.

Walking along the narrow, foul-smelling street that was all that was allowed for the Palestinian market, we encountered the settlers' actions at first hand. The street had a kind of fishing-net cover to protect those trading below. The net was littered with toilet rolls, refuse and waste of all description. Through the net came small stones and gravel. Two Arab women – one with two teenage children, the other with three small ones – subtly attached themselves to us as a means of getting down the street. As we reached the end, a large bottle was sent hurtling down onto a glass table, where an old man and a small child were selling packets of cigarettes. The glass shattered; a serious injury could have occurred.

In 1994, the Mosque, where Abraham, his two wives, Jacob, Joseph and their wives are buried, was invaded by militant settlers. Twenty-nine people were killed in the Mosque at prayer and sixteen in the riot which followed. The response was to divide the Mosque into a Mosque and a Synagogue. Abraham has a wife on each side.

During my visit to Hebron, my thoughts were on a report I had read during the week on a hot, sleepless night. Are children not more traumatised by the humiliation of their parents than by the loss of their parents? I can see this traumatisation in the eyes of the children.

Central to our visit was 'the Wall' – a wall that was adjudged illegal just over a year ago by the International Court of Justice at the Hague. The barrier, which is nine metres high, will shortly encircle Bethlehem. Built on Palestinian land, it robs Beth Jala, Bethlehem and Beth Sahour of all the land available for agricultural use.

In Bethlehem, tourism is already less than 15 percent what it was before 2001. The wall will end all movement without Israeli permission. The Green Line, which divided Israel from Palestine in 1967, is 350 kilometres long; the route of the wall is 670 kilometres. It weaves its way in and out of Palestinian territory, including passing through the middle of settlements, and cuts off communication from the north to the south of the West Bank.

In Beth Sahour, we visited the YMCA/YWCA to re-plant some olive trees which had been saved from the destruction that the building of the wall is creating. We were met by an old man, who had saved a tree that is between four hundred and a thousand years old. Since September 2000, 456,389 olive trees have been destroyed. Each olive tree produces nine kilograms of olives and two litres of oil each year; the trees are important economically.

Moreover, the olive tree has great symbolic significance for Palestinians and, a symbol of peace, is on every peace medal in the world. As the old man put it, the olive tree binds us to our grandfathers.

Jerusalem is being turned into Greater Jerusalem. Twenty-eight villages have been taken in, seventeen Israeli settlements have been built around it, and sixty-four square kilometres has been added to the city's area since 1967. When the wall adds in the Ma'ale Admim, there will be an Israeli majority of more than 70 percent in the city.

The effect of the wall on East Jerusalem will be to cut off seventy thousand people from any form of health service, because there is no hospital behind the Wall. Moreover, 350 teachers will be cut off from the children they teach. There are houses where, in the same family, some of the inhabitants have West Bank–residency-authorised cards and others Jerusalem-residency cards. Exclusion from Jerusalem, apart from religious or political considerations carries the additional impact of loss of what constitutes more than 40 percent of the income of the Palestinian economy.

With the new housing approvals, the settlements, referred to as blocks, are becoming bigger and are stretching more and more to the east, towards the Jordan Valley. The West Bank will be divided along a north–south axis and will become as tightly controlled as Gaza.

Let me make a brief summary:

§   The withdrawal from Gaza was not disengagement. The number of settlers withdrawn, eight thousand, has to be placed in comparison to the 400,000 settlers in the West Bank, and the number of settlements that have been abandoned must be compared to the expansion in the West Bank.

§   Unless the EU and the international community act, there will be a continuance of Israeli breaches of human rights. There will be no possibility of a viable Palestinian state existing in peace, side by side with a secure Israeli state.

§   The ruling of the International Court of Justice in 2004 in relation to the wall has to be brought to the UN, and the decision seen to be implemented.

§   We need a new International Peace Conference on Palestinian–Israeli issues. Otherwise, the recent cosmetic, unilateral 'withdrawal' will be seen as an alternative to the Road Map for Peace. The Quartet – the UN, the EU, the US and Russia – are responsible for the Road Map; unless urgent action is taken, by January it will be dead.

§ The wall must be demolished. It is creating, and will continue to create, incredible new breaches of human rights. Six hundred thousand Palestinians live between the wall and the Green Line; their lives will be made impossible.

§ The international community must insist that their view that Gaza and the West Bank are one unit is respected. If there is to be the slightest possibility of a viable Palestinian state, it must be a contiguous one, enjoying the minimal rights and duties of a sovereign state.

§ If international humanitarian law continues to be broken with impunity, as is happening every day in Palestine, it is not only the Palestinians who will lose. We will all be the losers, now and into the future, in the most fundamental moral and legal sense, as we will be guilty of letting a great wrong continue. Now is the time to act, and to call on those who speak in our name to act.

The Middle East deserves to be at peace. Palestinians have waited too long and there are many in Israel who realise that security will be best achieved when a viable, contiguous Palestinian state becomes their neighbour. We should not look away as we have done for so long. We should be working to bring about peace through solidarity, and support for international law.

Report of a visit to Gaza in August 2005

IRAQ

WHAT IS IT GOOD FOR?

One of the most interesting communications I have received since the Gulf war first threatened was a paper sent to me by a colleague, who had picked it up in Oxford. The paper was entitled 'Metaphor and War', and the author was George Lakoff of the Linguistics Department of the University of California at Berkeley. What was interesting, apart from the excellence of the article itself, was the fact that Lakoff had sent out his paper on a computer network in an attempt to get past the distortions of the media coverage of the build-up to the war.

'We have a chance to participate in the greatest experiment ever conducted in vital, widespread, instantaneous democratic communication,' he wrote. 'Tens of thousands of lives are at stake. During the next two weeks, there is nothing more important that we can send over the networks than a fully open and informed exchange of views about the war.' Unfortunately, the war has begun since George Lakoff initiated his experiment.

Watching Sky News on the morning of the air raid on a shelter in Baghdad, the destructions to which Lakoff directed his attention were obvious. But the destruction extends not only to the war: language too has been decimated. The presenter (let us call her Pru) has a line of patter that defines what we might call 'Skyspeak'.

Interviewing someone who was trying to break the silence on the twenty-seven million Africans threatened with famine and death, Pru interrupted to ask: 'Aren't we in danger of overkill on the topic? Aren't we hearing almost every year now of a famine?' Taking a break from her war videos has made her nasty.

Casually, twenty-four hours a day, the propaganda is churned out. US planes are always described as leaving for strikes against 'military targets'. Ramsey Clark, former US attorney general, was forthright in his condemnation of what he called bluntly 'lies'. He did not last long on Sky. Within hours too, President Bush was throwing mud at him, talking of Saddam being capable only of winning 'a propaganda war'. Ramsey Clark's description of civilian casualties became propaganda for the enemy.

On St Valentine's Day, we were treated to the sight of a phalanx of soldiers in front of a bomber with a St Valentine's Day banner. Even those whose loves ones couldn't write or, instead, who had no loved one, need not worry, we were told: the Kuwaiti government was sending every soldier a Valentine card.

Into all this floats the horrific pictures of charred bodies of women, children and other civilians. Shortly afterwards comes the news that a bus carrying people fleeing from the war zone in Kuwait has been bombed.

One of the many generals trained in PR tells us that it is 'rubbish' to suggest that US intelligence could be wrong in describing the shelter as a military command and communications centre. Why then was it full of women and children? 'Well, we know Saddam doesn't share our values of the sanctity of human life,' he tells us.

George Lakoff's 'Metaphor and War' is invaluable in tracing how the demonology that justifies this war has been constructed. 'Metaphors can kill', is how he opens, describing a metaphor as an image that purports to make complex issues understandable. 'It is important to distinguish what is metagraphical from what is not,' he writes. 'Pain, dismemberment, death, starvation, and the death and injury of loved ones are not metaphorical. They are real, and in a war, they could afflict tens, perhaps hundreds, of thousands of real human beings, whether Iraqi, Kuwaiti or American.'

Lakoff's analysis of how the fairy tale of the 'just war' has been constructed is powerful: Iraqi people are reduced to 'the state of Iraq', then to 'the ruler of Iraq' – evil Saddam. A villain is thus created. The victim is Kuwait. The hero is the US but becomes, for international consumption, 'the Allies'.

To be all-loving is the monopoly of the hero. The language used is of life, defended by the hero, and death, represented by the villain. The purpose of the war, stated as the reinstatement of the emir of Kuwait, would be insufficient in itself for internal consumption. The US public needs to be told that the hero is protecting the 'economic byline' of Western economics and commerce. The quotation from Karl von Clausewitz, the Prussian general, that 'War is politics pursued by other means' is apt.

This grim fairy tale, used to justify the war, buries all the facts, including the background to the original conflict between Iraq and Kuwait, the role of the West, and the building up of arms in the region so as to set Arab neighbour against Arab neighbour. The politics of energy gets buried.

The metaphor of the just war, the heroic war, is primitive. It buries not only the facts of the background to the war but also any sane reflection on the alternatives to war. And there *are* alternatives. The sooner they are used, the more lives will be saved. When this war ends, there will have to be talks. Why not have them now? Why not assist the Soviet, Iranian and Jordanian initiatives for peace?

Even if Iraq is completely destroyed – which would be, in Skyspeak, a heroic achievement – there are huge issues facing the world. What would be the West's response to the Arab nationalism of Iran? Right now, both are facilitators in the Hero's journey to destroy the Evil One – but what about later?

The endless attempts at pretending not to understand why many Arabs refuse to condemn Saddam are pathetic. Understanding the Arab viewpoint requires suspending a number of Western assumptions, such as the identification of a people with a state.

The state boundaries recognised by the West do not have the same resources in the Arab world as they have in the West: for many Arabs, they are the arbitrary legacy of the coloniser. There is a real feeling of Arab humiliation. Not for nothing does the Arab proverb run: 'Better be a cock for a day than a chicken for a year.' Buried in this saying, of course, is the concept of male strength and female weakness. But there is also a concept of brotherhood stronger than the loyalty to state or ruler. And there is a concept of dignity.

If there is no attempt to understand the Middle East and its people, this war that has been unleashed could carry on for generations in one manifestation or another. Meanwhile, actions of quiet intimidation against those who dare to question the war are growing. Phone calls are being made suggesting that to be against the war is to be pro-Saddam. (And here I must repeat that, when I condemned Saddam's massacre of the Kurds, few voices in the West were raised in support. Instead, the West continued arming him.)

Now is the time for Irish people to come out in support of an end to this war. Now, not later. After the war, when international teams visit and count the bodies, what then will our reaction be?

There are immediate practical alternatives to the death and destruction. Troops could be reduced in number, and rotated. They could be put back to a defensive level while the withdrawal of Iraq from Kuwait takes place. The holding out against discussing regional peace is simply not acceptable, given the level of casualties from the war.

The only groups gaining from the war at the moment are the armaments manufacturers and their messengers of death in the Gulf and in Africa. Is it not a fact that, if the arms level of the Gulf countries had not been built up by the West, the present war would have been far less likely? Now the stores are empty, but they will be filled again unless a view prevails that arms production and sales in the shadow of famine is a blot on the face of humanity.

The war must be ended, and Ireland has a role to play. We should ask our representatives where they stand on the issue. The demonstrations for peace need our support. It is not a time for Skyspeak; it is a time that demands moral action.

Hot Press, Vol. 15, No. 4, March 1991

IRELAND SHOULD CALL FOR AN END TO THE ECONOMIC SANCTIONS

AGAINST THE PEOPLE OF IRAQ

In 1982, I was asked to consider writing a regular column for *Hot Press*. I remember well the shock I felt. Armed with past issues of *Hot Press* and *NME*, I considered the madness involved with all the strange material spread across a room over a weekend in Cork.

From 1982 until 1993, I contributed to the magazine. My motivation, I suppose, was to some degree influenced by the fact that I could write about topics that were current and reach an audience I did not normally reach either in formal politics or through lecturing at UCG in sociology and politics. It was thus a robust and vulgar exercise in the best sense of those words. My contact with young people who read the column was often at night: 'There's your man . . . ' I would hear, and a conversation would ensue about Pinochet or General Evren, or whatever I had been writing about.

In 1993, when I became minister for arts, culture and the Gaeltacht, my life changed in terms of how my days and nights were spent. The spontaneous conversations seemed to be swamped by tasks that were important, urgent and time-consuming, be it in film, broadcasting or the Irish language.

Like *Hot Press*, I had changed format, and I was a reader of the magazine now, not a contributor. I missed the street encounters and the contacts with a generation that was vitally interested in the world, from El Salvador to East Timor. Yet while I missed the contact at a personal level, I continued to be interested in the lives of young people. My own children were after all in their late teens, heading for their early twenties.

I have in these years of reflection been quite shaken by the sudden, intense increase in the exploitation of young people, the filling of their lives with stress, fear, anxiety and pressure from peers. I note the banality of those who speak of and to young people. Phrases like 'There are a lot of them out there', as if they were on planet Mars, are often used. Such a phrase denotes an important rupture. 'Out there' is a space of less than personal concern. It is over the wall of self-interest and a personal version of the economy. So many of the attachments to society are being commercialised, and so many have been discarded. So many idealisms have been broken through bad faith that life has become a lonely one for a person who is young in the nineties. Time has been shortened, space contracted, context obliterated.

Yet there is a space of indomitable humanity. I remember how moved I was a short while ago at the messages young people were writing on the wreaths at a funeral of one of their friends, who had been killed tragically young in an accident: phrases like 'You were always there for me', denoting the loneliness in the modern world. The invitation of the nineties seems to have moved from belonging in the world to attacking it.

A recent advertisement states 'The Celtic Tiger needs more claws', and an educational leader tells graduates that they are 'the cubs of the Tiger'. More interestingly, a recent MRBI report suggests that only 6 percent of respondents between eighteen and twenty-four are interested in world events. Life, it seems, has become constricted to the sensations purchased as a consumer rather than an invitation to any solidarity offered and shared as a citizen.

Yet my own experiences tell me that much more than 6 percent of young people are interested in Iraq, Palestine, world debt, aid or the neo-imperialism of the World Trade Organisation. Even so, the depolitisation of an entire generation is a matter for concern. What is undoubted, however, is that everything has changed in just a few years in Ireland. Now we are invited to work very hard at creating an unhappy, disconsolate public that is not very informed by ethical imperatives.

I have all these thoughts in my mind as I try to write of issues such as the effect of the UN economic sanctions on the Iraqi people. Nine years ago, I was in Baghdad with David Andrews and Paul Bradford in an attempt to secure and speed the release of Irish medical personnel regarded as 'messengers of peace' by the authorities in Iraq on the verge of war. They were, as their relatives in Ireland saw it, 'civilian hostages'. They were home before the bombing of 17 January 1991.

I wrote about my visit in *Hot Press*. Now, nine years later, when discussing my visit of December 2000 on a radio station, I am asked the question, by a reasonable interviewer who felt he represented the callers, why, with so many problems at home, is Michael D. going halfway across the world to ask about children dying in Iraq? In the last nine years, Ireland has become quite a morally shrunken place. One is back before the early sixties in terms of having to make a case for an interest in rights, justice, equality or plain decency in human relations.

And yet there are so many who are still interested. It is more than habit that brings those over sixty, those grown old with principle, to campaign against Plan Colombia or Iraqi children dying, at the gates of the US or British embassies. It reflects on their part a moral consistency in bad times of both a rising intolerance and of a declining capacity to think or live reflectively in the world. In education, utility is central. Everything is preparation for an infinite economic growth. Yet some young prisoners of the economy escape to such occasions of moral concern as protests and public meetings. When they arrive, the faces of older people light up. There are those, they think, who will assert the prophetic, the radical, the just and the truly human. I have seen it in recent times. It is a glimmer of human expression at a time when the culture carries a new mark of aggression and violence.

In answering the question on radio, I said that, in my experience, precisely the same people are agitated about poverty and an unjust society at home as are interested in issues of human rights, aid, trade and world debt. Precisely the same people who are not interested in anything beyond themselves at home also don't give a damn about world issues such as poverty or the absence of human rights.

Preparing to leave for Iraq on 9 December, I reflected on the courage of such exceptional people as Ramsey Clerk, former US attorney general and human-rights campaigner. His book *The Fire Next Time* stands as one of the great testaments to legal integrity and moral courage, to an engaged jurisprudence and scholarship. That work detailed the war crimes committed by the US during the Gulf war. The questions he raised will not go away. Was it right to bury soldiers who were in retreat in the desert sand? More importantly, was it acceptable to bomb long lines of civilians on suspicion of there being weapons among them?

The previous genocidal actions of Saddam Hussein against the Kurdish population were raised by me in the eighties in Dáil Éireann, with little general interest, I have to say. The victims were Kurds, and the mustard gas came from a country within the European Union. Insufficient attention too has been given to the deaths of between thirty thousand and sixty thousand of the Shia population who rose against Saddam with US and British encouragement in March 1991 and who were later abandoned. Neither should we forget that Saddam's weapons of the years of destruction before 1990 came from the West.

Such activities as those of Saddam Hussein, however, do not and can never justify the use of the civilian population of Iraq as pawns in a game that began over oil and that continues as a feature of a geopolitics where there is only one global player, and where interests have replaced morals at the centre of foreign policy.

Above all, nothing can justify the loss of children's lives as a result of sanctions that, far from achieving their stated objective, have secured Saddam in power and indeed converted his status to that of a regional hero. It is morally indefensible, it seems to me, to use the civilians of Iraq as tools of opposition to Saddam Hussein's administration. The preceding and succeeding genocidal actions of Saddam Hussein, I repeat, do not justify what is now taking place.

An academic argument is now taking place in some of the journals as to what the true figures for child deaths and malnutrition are. Some academics, it is claimed, take Iraqi health statistics at face value and lend themselves to become big victims of propaganda when a figure of 7,500 child deaths per month is used. No estimate from any agency or source is less than two thousand per month. There is no denying that between sixty and seventy Iraqi children die needlessly every day. The academic argument, I have to say, puts me in mind of the arguments about the Irish Famine and the number of deaths attributed to starvation.

Of course, it would be useful to have a benchmark figure not only of the number of children dying but also of those suffering from the various forms of malnutrition: child hunger, stunted growth and wasting of bodies. To the Iraqis, as our delegation was told, the gathering of health statistics is a domestic government function covered by considerations of sovereignty. To the coalition against Iraq – particularly Britain and the US – it is an attempt by the Iraqi government to use child deaths as propaganda for consumption by a gullible international humanitarian community.

To me, the important fact is that the children are dying needlessly. The sanctions, far from working as intended, are killing civilians, including children, and are tearing the heart of whatever civil society might be possible for the Iraqi population. Indeed, I often think of that evening when the bombing began. The Irish public, like others dominated by the journalistic cynicism and sycophantic militarism of Sky TV, watched on at the destruction not of military targets alone but of the infrastructure of a country from which most of the major belief systems of the world's religions had sprung. The war was a video game. Television covered the events less as news than as combat television entertainment. Later it would be the Kosovo video game and the destruction of life there. The victory of militarism over diplomacy would merge seamlessly into entertainment. Even our Taoiseach and his partner on a visit to our peacekeepers in the Lebanon donned military fatigues for the photos.

What is left after the television trail of 'intelligent' missiles? A devastated landscape. Broken pipelines. Leaking reservoirs. Waterborne diseases. Much of this would go unnoticed if it were not for a deadly paradox that haunts the victors, if one can use that word, in the Gulf war: the medical consequences for their own soldiers of using depleted uranium. As different countries of the alliance assess the state of health of their own soldiers, it becomes possible that the rise in Iraqi children's death rate from leukaemia might merit consideration: child leukaemia in certain parts of Iraq has trebled.

The parliamentary delegation which visited Jordan and Iraq, and of which I was part, consisted of David Andrews, John Gormley and Senators David Norris and Michael Lanigan. All had an exceptional interest in the Middle East and the effect of the sanctions on Iraq in particular.

Unlike the previous time I visited Iraq, it was not possible to fly into Baghdad because of the bureaucracy attending the sanctions. We travelled by jeep from Amman in Jordan 1,100 kilometres along a highway through the desert to Baghdad.

One could not but be struck by the continuous traffic of oil tankers between Jordan and Iraq. The vehicles are old and they leak. The sides of the road are blackened with spillages. Travelling through the grit of the desert past deposits of blackened rock lava cooled from old volcanic eruptions in the north, one can see old trucks parked alongside the Bedouin community's tents. Unrepaired pipelines make the vehicles necessary for an endless cycle of transportation.

The foyer of the Al Rasheed Hotel has a new mosaic at the entrance. It is a gesture of defiance. It is of George Bush over the message: 'GEORGE BUSH – GUILTY OF MURDER'. The hotel itself is showing signs of the sanctions but still has an occupancy rate of around 20 percent.

Thinking back on what the Iraqi people have suffered in recent decades, one is conscious of why the population is weary. It is showing the effects of a war against Iran that cost between 250,000 and 300,000 lives, a Gulf war that cost more than 100,000 lives, the Kurdish and Shia revolts of 1991, which cost thousands more, and now economic sanctions. Households sell their books, the inner doors of their houses, their carpets – all in order to live.

It is an extraordinary achievement that life can continue. Yet the force of the statement made by a US commander during the Gulf war – 'We will drive you back into the dark ages' – rings in one's ears. It is hard to avoid the conclusion that the economic sanctions are about the pauperisation of the Iraqi middle class, the humiliation of a people with a cultural history that goes back to at least 12,000 BC. That is how the Iraqi people see it. That is why the sanctions, combined with the loss of life in Palestine, have the capacity not only to ignite a catastrophic regional war but also to provoke a global conflict between Islam and the West.

Many delegations from Ireland have gone to Iraq in the past – mostly to sell beef. On the Security Council, we will be expected to be interested in the people of Iraq. How is the war to be ended? How will we know when it has ended? What guarantees will be created for eliminating weapons of mass destruction? Whose interests are served by the exhaustion and replacement of military stocks?

So many questions. So much real politics to be discussed. So many connections to be made. After all, is it not better to have envisaged an alternative to militarism than to have been a pawn of what one's heart and head feels to be wrong? It is a time for involvement and activity rather than passivity, or selfishness based on ignorance and moral indifference.

Hot Press, Vol. 24, No. 24, December 2000

I welcome this opportunity of finally debating the situation in Iraq in wider terms than simply responses to meetings such as the European Council meeting or meetings of the Security Council. I want to use the time I have available to deal factually with matters that I believe have been made unnecessarily complex in the course of this debate.

In relation to legality, this House and the Irish public are entitled to a straightforward answer to a very direct question. Where do they stand in relation to the principle of pre-emptive action? Kofi Annan is very clear on this issue and is often quoted by the government. His opinion is straightforward: pre-emptive action is outside of the United Nations' Charter and is illegal. None of the ministers and deputies who have spoken so far have answered that question. When will the Irish government state that pre-emptive action is outside the United Nations' Charter and is illegal? In relation to Resolution 1441, the Irish government suggests that there is a legal ambiguity in the interpretation of the resolution. In fairness to the minister for foreign affairs, when Resolution 1441 was passed in November, he stated that it was 'an alternative to war'. He was speaking at the end of a complex process in which it had been admitted by many of the participants as they worked on Resolution 1441 that it was almost impossible to achieve a unanimous decision.

In relation to the passing of a resolution, I wish to deal with fact. The United States ambassador to the United Nations, John Negroponte, stated at the UN that Resolution 1441 had no trigger for military action. Less than one week later, the British foreign secretary made a similar remark in the House of Commons and, two days later, in a lengthy interview, the deputy secretary for foreign affairs stated that Resolution 1441 did not have a trigger for action, although he would have wished it otherwise.

Let us be fair to Resolution 1441. In the limited time available, I can only deal with some matters of substance in it. As the minister for foreign affairs is well aware, the operative paragraph, paragraph 12, explicitly states that it is the Security Council that will take a decision in relation to evaluating compliance with Resolution 1441. Much has been said about the previous sixteen or seventeen resolutions passed in relation to Iraq. I am familiar with all of them. Nearly all of them open with a statement recognising the sovereignty of Iraq, thereby acknowledging the legal problem with regard to an invasion, and go on to use an important formulation of words: 'the Security Council will remain seized of the situation'. The Council occupied the field, stating that it alone would deal with the issue of evaluation, which was envisaged as involving a four-fold process: the elimination of weapons of mass destruction would be dealt with; inspectors would look at the process and report to the Security Council; a conclusion would be reached as to whether or not a material breach had occurred; and, at that point, a decision would be taken on appropriate action.

When, on the first page of his speech, the Taoiseach stated: 'I will limit myself to its defiance of the United Nations', he could have been referring to the United States or the United Kingdom, or both. However, he spoke exclusively of Iraqi non-compliance with resolutions: it was a one-sided speech, as were so many others. With respect, I thought that his speech could have been written at 10 Downing Street – and that is a compliment, because I might have said that it could have been written at the Pentagon, which would be even worse. I refer to an extraordinary statement on page three, in relation to the terrorist threat:

> The attacks of 11 September demonstrated that the world had entered into a new and dangerous era. The optimistic suggestion put forward in the aftermath of the cold war that we had reached the end of history proved to be seriously premature.

If one wishes to deconstruct that statement, I suggest that there has been an outbreak of severe existentialism in the Fianna Fáil Party. In trying to make sense of it, I was encouraged to reflect on what it might mean. Having immersed himself in the work of Francis Fukuyama, the Taoiseach might have wandered on to the writings of others who have invented and crafted the source of the new US foreign policy. I believe the strike we are now witnessing in Iraq was envisaged very clearly from about 1997 onwards in statements made by some of those who now advise the US president – Donald Rumsfeld, Paul Wolfowitz and others. In the founding principles of Project for a New American Century, posted on their website on 3 June 1997, they wrote:

> As the twentieth century draws to a close, the United States stands as the world's pre-eminent power. Having led the West to victory in the cold war, America faces an opportunity and challenge: Does the United States have the vision to build upon the achievements of past decades?

Does the United States have the resolve to shape a new century favourable to American principles and interests? Our aim is to remind Americans of these lessons. . . . We need to increase defence spending significantly if we are to carry out our global responsibilities today and modernise our armed forces for the future. We need to promote the cause of political economic freedom abroad. We need to strengthen our ties to democratic allies and to challenge regimes hostile to our interests and values. We need to accept responsibility for America's unique role in preserving and extending an international order favourable to our security, extending our prosperity and implementing our principles.

That is a clear signal from Dick Cheney, Elliot Cohen, Mitch Dexter, Paul Dobransky, Steve Forbes and, indeed, Francis Fukuyama – the Taoiseach's intellectual and moral source – as well as Donald Kagan, Peter Rothman, Paul Wolfowitz and many others. Moving on from 1997 to April 2002, those sources made a clear link to the Palestinian–Israeli question. In this regard, the leading signatory was William Crystal, who stated:

Nobody should doubt that the United States and Israel share a common enemy. We are both targets of what you, Mr President, have correctly called an axis of evil. Israel is targeted, in part, because it is our friend and, in part, because it is an island of liberal democratic principles – American principles – in a sea of tyranny, intolerance and hatred. As Secretary of Defence Rumsfeld has pointed out, Iran, Iraq and Syria are all engaged in 'inspiring and financing a culture of political murder and suicide bombing against Israel, just as they have aided campaigns of terrorism against the United States over the past two decades.' You have declared war on international terrorism, Mr President. Israel is fighting the same war.

I use this quotation not to be anti-American but, rather, to be very strongly pro-American. That illustrates the distance between, on the one hand, the particular mindset created in 1997 by that small group of people now in the White House, which viewed the Middle East in a particular way and needed a war with Iraq, and, on the other hand, people like former President Carter and Senator Bird, dean of the United States Senate, who have spoken against the war, and the many millions of people in the US who oppose the war.

As a previous speaker mentioned, there is a context and a particular world-view which has implications for United States foreign policy when we relate it to the long history of UN resolutions in relation to Iraq. When I listened earlier to the rhetorical reference by the minister of state, Deputy de Valera, notably her phrase 'This is a man . . . ' and so on, I was tempted to add, 'to whom former Taoiseach, Charles Haughey wrote: "We are looking forward to closer relations in culture, economics and politics" and added the compliment: "You are the leader of a country that is the cradle of civilisation." That was after Halabja. Let us deal with the facts and the tragedy of Halabja, directed against the Kurds, who were caught in the middle of the Iran–Iraq war, with chemical weapons being supplied to the Iranian side by Western governments and mustard gas being supplied to the Iraqi government, also by Western powers.

Time does not allow me to review all the older sources. Specifically on the legal issue, with regard to Resolution 1441, there is a mechanism which could have determined whether legal capacity exists in Resolutions 678 and 687. It is as clear as day. The British attorney general, Lord Goldsmith, is on his own, and our attorney general is off the wall in terms of his opinion as conveyed in the Taoiseach's speech. That opinion was given in the context of Article 28.3, but he refused to combine the obligations of Article 29. One cannot decouple Article 28.3 from Article 29. When I say that Lord Goldsmith is on his own, I am referring to the sixteen independent international lawyers – and I stress *independent* – located at Oxford and Cambridge and owing loyalty to nobody, who, in the *Guardian* a few days ago, published an opinion that there was no legal basis for a strike in Resolutions 678 and 687. The suggestion that there is confusion as to whether or not there is capacity in the previous resolutions to make a strike against Iraq is merely used as a cover: there is not. In that regard, it is appalling that the confusion that has been sown has been used by the government to refuse to answer my first, fundamental question on where it stands with regard to the principle of pre-emption and unilateral action outside the UN Charter. . . .

Why did the government not come to the House to explain why the goalposts were systematically changed? Members should remember being told that the project was the elimination of weapons of mass destruction, something with which we could all agree. The project suddenly became the admission of the inspectors, with which we all agreed. After that, however, a time-scale was introduced.

Why, after twelve years, did a time-scale become urgent? Why could Hans Blix not be given the extra time he sought? In that was sown the basis of the US project to deliberately defeat the actions and the intentions of the other permanent members of the Security Council. We, by our actions, are siding with those who have damaged the Security Council. The French position at the Security Council was against war 'at this time', as the French foreign minister explicitly stated, and as his ambassador put on the record at the United Nations Security Council. That too was distorted.

There was a suggestion that, because certain countries were not going to get the resolution they wanted, the veto had dislodged the six countries in the middle. The veto has been used seventy-five times in thirty years – some fifty times by the United States. It was used on 19 December 2002 against a mild resolution criticising Israel for its actions in the Occupied Territories and Palestine. That is the issue with regard to the veto.

One thing will remain the same with regard to the problem in 1991 and now. We will rely on courageous and independent journalists who have not embedded themselves in the military. We will still be looking at obscenities, such as Sky Television reducing the death of innocent people to a video game. We anticipate that it will be a war that will not be covered. No more than we saw the six thousand people who were ploughed into the desert with ploughs mounted on the front of tanks near Basra in 1991, we will not see the civilian casualties in this war either.

The first six months of the war will cost $56 billion. UNICEF has given a figure of $135 million for all the humanitarian relief needed for six months, and just 35 percent of that is on offer. The military strike is against a people, half of whom are under the age of fifteen, in which there are one million malnourished children and 3.3 million people immediately affected, and where there is an expectation of 100,000 immediate casualties and 400,000 secondary ones. The humanitarian relief for those casualties and their relatives may be undersubscribed, but the military strike on them, in an illegal action, is fully subscribed.

Bishop Kirby is correct that we are at a turning point in history, international relations and foreign policy. We are also at a moral moment for ourselves in regard to accepting violence in our lives. The violence includes that against the United States troops who will die, some 35 percent of whom are recruited from minorities and 20 percent of whom are black. The United States is reduced by fear to a life less than one fully lived as people invent terrorist attacks. People have been traumatised since 1997 in a systematic creation that suits military expenditure, military action, and acts of a violent kind, and works against the much more difficult and slower task of creating non-violent strategies for the resolution of conflict.

I have often stated and written about the humanitarian consequences of this. I have met people in Baghdad who are different from those of 1991. In 1991, seventy thousand tons of explosives rained down on Iraq in forty-eight days. The sky went black when the refinery was burned. On this occasion, the people have been through twelve years of sanctions; they will not be leaving their houses. The Republican Guard will use them as human shields. They will be used by Saddam and abused by the person coming, allegedly, to liberate them.

This is an obscenity, and it was avoidable. No reasonable person can suggest that, given more time, more resources and more co-operation, the elimination of the weapons of mass destruction could have been achieved by the inspectors. Importantly, had that model of decommissioning of weapons of mass destruction been established in Iraq over a longer period, it would have been available for use in other countries. Instead, there is unilateral, pre-emptive action outside international law.

With regard to Shannon, there is a notion that one can give an opinion based on Article 28.3 of the Constitution while closing one's eyes to Article 29. While we are not at war, we are facilitating it. The International Court of Justice, established in 1950, could have ruled on the fundamental issue of whether capacity exists for a strike in regard to Resolutions 678 and 687. It could also have ruled on other matters, as that is what it is there for: it is a United Nations institution, mentioned in the Charter, for inter-state resolution and for giving what the Charter calls a learned opinion.

We did not seek to find out where the law lay. We simply drifted in the shadow of those who say: 'Well, if it is going to happen, and the planes are going to be flying over somewhere else and landing somewhere else, we should forget that they are landing in NATO bases and might as well make a bit out of it the same as anybody else.' I find that shameful.

Bishop Kirby is right. The United States will spend $396.1 billion on defence expenditure in 2003. I realise that I am rejected by those who say that we do not live in an ideal world, that there is no point in creating utopias, and that we must be practical. However, I am still free to imagine this: what if the most powerful country in the world, instead of spending $396.1 billion on armaments, was willing to spend a fraction of that on relieving world poverty?

The minister for foreign affairs was at Monterrey when the Millennium Development Goals were established to reduce world poverty by half by 2015. This House should, considering the deflection of human resources and intellectual resources into an unnecessary and illegal act of war against one of the poorest nations in the world, take a stand and say: 'We are sorry: no facilities will be available to those who act illegally and who wage war against a country in these circumstances.' There should be no excuse that we will urge or beseech people to observe the position of civilians or children. That is the law.

We have not heard so far what we will do practically to vindicate the Geneva Conventions. Sadly, I must say this: we are lessened at home and abroad by allowing ourselves to be complicit in an outrageous action.

Speech in the Dáil, 20 March 2003

LEBANON

IS THIS THE BEGINNING OF THE END FOR INTERNATIONAL LAW?

The protection of and respect for the welfare of civilians and civilian infrastructure in times of occupation are two of the fundamental principles of international law in recent history. These principles are enshrined in the Geneva Conventions. The response to the atrocities of concentration camps, the destructive consequences of war, and the threat of nuclear annihilation were a powerful impetus in driving the movement for human rights forward. Recent events in Lebanon represent such a significant departure from these principles as to suggest that this is the beginning of the end of international law and its protections.

Those of us on the Left who have condemned the Hezbollah action as one which, given experiences to date, would draw a reaction as unlawful as it would be indiscriminate, and which is having a disastrous impact on the civilian population of Lebanon, are clear in our support for the international legal protections for all civilians. This has been the basis of our demand for an immediate ceasefire, as well as calls for respect for the sovereignty of Lebanon, a commitment to the political process, and sustained and realistic involvement by the international community.

The destruction of the lives of civilians, be it in Israel or Lebanon, must be condemned unequivocally. Parties of the Left have consistently rejected terrorist actions not only because of their impact on civilians but also because of the response they call forth from the powerful who abuse their position and are unlikely to be restrained by norms of law or basic decency.

The response of Israel, supported by the most powerful country in the world, is outrageous in terms of both the killing and injuring of civilians and the destruction of civilian infrastructure, which is occurring in such fashion as to make impossible even the delivery of humanitarian relief by the United Nations and its agencies.

Such destruction should not surprise the international community, however. Israel has followed this policy for decades in Gaza and the occupied territories of the West Bank. At the heart of the policy lies the principle of collective punishment of civilians, denial of human rights, and destruction of a way of life. In full knowledge of this, the European Union has remained silent, refusing to implement the human-rights clauses of its own agreement with Israel, despite being called on to do so by the European Parliament.

The Quartet, comprising the United Nations, the United States, the European Union and Russia, has consistently neglected the issue of the expansion of illegal settlements in the West Bank, the absorption of Palestinians into a new ghetto in East Jerusalem, the illegality of the Wall, and sustained breaches of human rights by Israel.

Ncither have the parties to the Roadmap for Peace recognised the distinction between the Hamas voice coming from Syria, and the evolving views of the Palestinian Hamas movement, which has formed a government after free elections. These elections were monitored by observers from the countries comprising the Quartet, and indeed by former president Jimmy Carter's Institute, all of whom described them as free and fair.

Tragically, in its failure to respond to the eighteen-point proposal by prisoners representing four factions – a plan that had the support of Mahmoud Abbas and is likely to have the support of the vast majority of Palestinians – the EU carries a large responsibility for what has taken place in recent weeks in Gaza. In effect, it has handed the Middle East to the militarists.

If the Irish government is to recover anything of its credibility, it should use its influence to call for a return to talks on a comprehensive settlement within the framework of international law. Such talks must deal with all the issues of illegal settlement and their expansion, the denial of human rights, the expansion of East Jerusalem, the release of prisoners, and meaningful security. It must examine all the issues rather than calling for a version of security predicated on the simple demand for demilitarisation on the part of those who can point to the neglect by the international community, and the EU in particular, of all the abuses that flow from illegal occupation.

The European Union must talk to the Palestinian government. It should recognise also that cutting off aid to that government was a disastrous decision that has visited suffering on the Palestinian people. There was never any likelihood that alternative structures existed to distribute aid or pay salaries.

The refusal of the United States to agree to talks with Syria, or to an immediate ceasefire, is reprehensible. Its policy in supporting the continuing loss of life and destruction of civilian infrastructure in Lebanon by Israel as a collective punishment of the Lebanese people for having Hezbollah in their midst is such a breach of international law as merits its being brought before the international courts.

Tragically, the stance of the US is more likely to mark the beginning of the end of the disciplines of international law itself. At such a moment, practitioners and supporters of a genuine global security based on such universal principles as the Geneva Conventions must speak out and call on their governments to state where they stand on the basic protection of civilians under international law and on such a basic principle as the sovereignty of Lebanon.

With regard to media coverage of events, it is past time that space be allowed for a genuine consideration, which will include all the elements of the present killings and destruction, to take place. Indeed, the fact that Israel is a nuclear power that is not within the disciplines of the Nuclear Non-Proliferation Treaty, with all the implications for the region that this represents, is rarely referred to in the accounts we have seen thus far. Actions that will endure and bring the best prospects for the region require such an analysis.

The Irish Times, 27 July 2006

TO LIVE REFLECTIVELY

Europe has the benefit of two fine reports on the importance of culture: 'In From the Margins' of the culture committee of the Council of Europe, published in 1997, and 'Our Creative Diversity', the report of the World Commission on Culture and Development published by UNESCO in July 1996. In 1998 in Stockholm, representatives of eighty-four nations attended a World Conference on Culture and Development, at which UNESCO sought to advance proposals for a Charter on Cultural Rights.

I will refer to just some aspects of these two reports and the World Conference, as time does not allow the fuller summary that would well be merited. I regret such a limitation all the more insofar as I believe that these reports and proceedings have been neglected in the politics of the European Union and its member states.

'In From the Margins' described its purpose as: 'The central themes are two interlocking priorities – to bring the millions of dispossessed and disadvantaged Europeans in from the margins of society and cultural policy in from the margins of governance.' It had nine general suggestions:

1   Culture will have to be brought into the heart of public administration.

2   There is a need for a consistent theory of cultural policy which accepts that culture has its instrumental uses, but also recognises the limits to which this can be applied without endangering it.

3   A new social ethic, obliging cultural organisations to adopt inclusive rather than exclusive policies, would help to ensure access to, and participation in, culture for all.

4   A more holistic approach to education is needed by transforming schools into culture-centered environments and enabling them to become foci of cultural life in their local communities.

5   It is time to restore the natural links between the arts and sciences which were broken in the eighteenth and nineteenth centuries. Centres of technological innovation would help to heal the long-standing schism in the industrial world between the so-called 'two cultures', as would a substantial technological investment in informal education and the availability throughout adult life of retraining opportunities.

6   While recognising the difficulties some governments have in agreeing standard-setting instruments in the field of cultural rights, the need at least for a European Declaration on Cultural Rights appears stronger now than ever.

7   A new ethical approach to the heritage is called for, which recognises the destruction of one's community's heritage is a loss to Europe as a whole. The creation of a European Heritage Bank, funded by public and private contributions and devoted to financing capital investments and providing loans, should be explored to help communities where the burden is greatest.

8   The establishment and maintenance of a healthy 'third sector' of voluntary associations and communities of interest which enable individuals to negotiate with one another and with public authorities. It is logical to seek measures, sometimes short-term, to ensure that there is a 'level playing field' of opportunity for European cultural producers. Governments should note the growth in the celebration of the local which is a natural response to globalisation and is often driven by the apparent cultural renaissance of image-conscious cities. The nurturing of creativity is essential if this is to be sustained – cities do not regenerate themselves spontaneously or at the behest of politicians.

9   Recognition by the international agencies that their programmes of support should be re-oriented from the current lottery of one-off projects towards schemes which promote more sustainable cultural relationships. National governments need to review their international cultural policies to reflect more adequately contemporary cultural practice and the changed political environment in Europe.

Among the most valuable comments of 'Our Creative Diversity' were those on cultural freedom. It was seen:

§   As a collective freedom.

§   As a guarantee of freedom as a whole.

§   As something that, by protecting alternative ways of living, encouraged creativity, experimentation and diversity; and finally

§   Freedom is central to culture.

The report saw these aspects of cultural freedom as threatened by global pressures and global neglect. I would like therefore to reflect on the present position in the European Union on the eve of European elections.

As a former minister for culture and a former president of the Council of Culture Ministers, I note with increasing sadness the failure to move culture in from the periphery of European concerns. We are living through a period where culture is seen as 'soft', where economics is 'hard': everywhere it is most macho to be at the new-technology end of the economic Europe.

There is no doubt whatsoever that the European Union, which for a number of reasons has no reference to culture in its founding treaties, is quickly assuming the character of a market with people attached. An unthinking approach to deregulation driven on by the Maastricht Treaty has already observable consequences in the cultural area. Europe, for example, is a commercial province of Hollywood in film terms. It exports cultural expression, audio-visual trade, and jobs to the US at an alarming rate.

We are drifting towards an unfreedom that can best be summarised as the transition from a concept of citizenship, with implications for interdependence, transcendence of the self, solidarity, and indeed justice, to a concept of consumerism which is market-driven, individualised, privatised and insatiable of satisfaction. Such a transition promises us a homogenised future, our tastes commodified, our experience of communications changed from one of active symbolic exchange to one of being passively entertained. There probably never was a time when we needed more the capacity to be reflective, to consciously articulate philosophical options. Yet Europe has never been weaker in terms of philosophy and public intellectual discourse. The speed of technological changes has been immense. For example, convergence of the technologies of the personal computer, the television and the telephone has created the shape of a digital future. However, insofar as the social model of the delivery of science and technology has not been debated, such a digital future promises an unaccountable technology rather than a democracy exerted through deeper and wider communication.

Standing alongside the current fetish with information technology is the practice of the media itself. The nature of the narratives that accepted the responsibility to inform and educate, as well as entertain, has been abandoned in the pursuit of advertising revenue. For example, the decontextualising of news from any historical, cultural or ethical setting is not accidental. From monopolised sources comes a standard product – news that could come from anywhere at any time, cynically strung out between voyeurism and fantasy. It is frequently presented within a mode of cynicism – a cynicism, however, that is as different from Diogenes as it is from an ironic critique that might make a critical comparison of the ideal and the actual. It is not a cynicism of resignation, either, but is a corrosive cynicism of alleged expertise within a hot medium that knows no space, time, or culture of affiliation. Yet a decision has been taken by the European Commissioner with responsibility for competition to have no directive on concentration of ownership but instead to leave such matters to the marketplace for resolution. That a Europe of citizens is entitled to such regulation as would create a diversity of editorial views within a theory of culture and freedom carried no weight. Cultural diversity is a term, suffice it to note, that at present is within a discourse that, at best, is in exile from the existing disposal and discourses of power in the European Union.

Among Europe's citizens, however, there is, I believe, an ineradicable yearning for authenticity. I use the term as it is used by the Canadian philosopher Charles Taylor. This yearning for authenticity, for a critique that would return to the promise of modernity rather than to its delivery, represents a source of hope. It seems to retain a faith in human creativity, in the ability of such creativity to correct a misplaced trust in the neutrality of technology – in reason itself.

Standing in contrast, too, to the combination that enjoys a hegemony in the European Union, a combination of market hubris, technology and cynicism, stand 'the artistic impulses', the creative expressions that comprise a mosaic of differing cultural influences. From their actions comes a call for respect: for the integrity of memory and the freedom of the imagination. It envisages a tolerance that is beyond the minimalist recognition of pluralism. It speaks of multiple stories as pasts not yet imagined. It makes space for the futures of an unlimited imagination. Yet the political space has been deprived of such an ethical contribution. Many artists have abandoned the political space in pursuit of their own version of cynical reality.

It is the present, then, of the European Union that is shallow, that is economically defined to the point where so many of all ages wish to fly from it in so many different ways. Changing that present would require a recognition of the cultural space that is not now available in Europe. There has never been less of a contribution from what Jacoby would call public intellectuals.

In the Council of Europe report 'In From the Margins', we read in the chapter entitled 'Is There a Future for European Culture?' of four great themes which they see as permeating the complexities of the European scene:

The first of them concerns cultural identity as the peoples of the Continent came to terms with the project for European integration and the rise of local and regional aspirations. Secondly, the cultural landscape of European society has become more diverse, but this has been accompanied by social, cultural and economic fragmentation and exclusion, reinforced by policies unable to accommodate diversity. Thirdly, the relation between the state and the individual is changing. Government expenditures on welfare provision are under pressure, and the cultural role of the state is undergoing change. The maintenance of thriving civil societies depends on a proper balance between the public, private and voluntary sectors. Fourthly, a global culture, riding high on the back of the information revolution, and newly invigorated regional and local cultures are set on a collision course, so creating the possibility of a so-called global squeeze.

With the greatest respect, this is a profound simplification of the problem. How can one so readily define local, regional, national or global culture? Within the cultural space, there are layers of meaning, of assertion and response, of authority and resistance, and these layers exist at both formal and informal level and constitute both public and hidden transcripts. Their purpose may be to serve the illusion of authority, to mock it, or indeed to subvert it. It is also painfully easy to see how culture, even in recent times, can be used as a mask for repression, violence, domination and hate.

We are forced back, I believe, in the sense of Samuel Beckett's characters, to the rawness of our selves. The achievement of cultural diversity and a respect for a diversity of culture is much more than an administrative matter: it is a matter of morality made immanent and consensually established. It has to do with values that define our humanity. We have to face the reality, of course, that some universalists still long for an absolute answer. Existentialists will live for the question, yet between them there is a shared category of the human that has to be negotiated. On that fragile soil we must build. The yearning for an authenticity of the self is accompanied by an acceptance at a more general level of the requirement of transcendent living. From this flows community and the related ideas of solidarity, justice and trust.

Our most immediate threat, however, comes from the unaccountable and anti-democratic version of the developed economy we have inherited: there are ways in which a corrosive cynicism, an absence of political will to intervene in the market, the homogeneity of a commoditised life, the search for authentic expression gone wrong, a distorted memory, and a future of fear can make a deadly cocktail of violence.

In building an alternative to drift and acquiescence in the unfreedom of the market, we should remember that to live reflectively is still the greatest challenge. We live in a flux that carries sometimes little or no potential for the experience of humanity. We go on in expectation that it will carry more, that history has not ended but is still capable of being made.

Finally, I suggest that we may have much to learn from those who have had to construct lives out of the flux, namely exiles and immigrants. Theirs is a life of transience. Their spaces are never lasting. Home is both a memory and a project of return for them. They are not of their place of origin, nor of their destination, but are transients in the space of in between. Yet it is there that heroic survival and great generosity takes place.

Without the trappings and securities of bundles of commodities and memories, we all become as bereft, and as free, as Beckett's tramps, and as spiritual in our taking note of each other. Just that.

Delivered as part of the symposium 'Regions, Nations, Union: In Search of the European Identity', convened by the European Commission Forward Studies Unit, Brussels, 22 January 1999

PART V

THE FUTURE

The Importance of Reflection

Is There a Basis for Hope?

The past of a political party might be constituted as a narrative. This lends itself to drawing on the roots and history of a political party; not merely as a source or validation, of past struggle but, much more importantly, also as a source of renewal in terms of the basic values of the political party or movement in question.

This narrative, however, is not written in stone but has to be flexible. History demands that it be such. Fundamental values have to be restated and recast to deal with new circumstances and challenges. Again, the narrative has to envisage the shape of the future. This last is an exercise in imagination. It also, crucially, requires the shape of the narrative of the future – the alternative narrative – to be made manifest. It has to be articulated.

Beyond such articulation, there is a need to connect the values and principles at the heart of a political party with the political discourse of the day. This requires the conversion of the narrative into policy, around which support can be mobilised.

Such a policy programme has to be expressed within the specific conditions of time and space, and indeed culture, in which a political party is mobilising, agitating and seeking support. Part of the policy programme may be achieved in one period of government, but the overall vision remains intact as a strategy for change.

Parties that prepare for participation in government or coalition frequently create the impression that they are approaching these challenges for the first time, rather than drawing on previous experience or the experience of others. Again, some theorists of coalition go so far as to suggest that a relationship of trust between the parties in government requires such a merging of identities that the parties in question become indistinguishable from each other during the period of shared government. This, in certain circumstances, can be little less than a disaster for the parties concerned. It is also more honest for parties to share candidly a programme for a definite period of time and to be willing to react with consideration of each other in regard to external events while at the same time respecting the differences in the medium- and long-term visions that each party holds.

The concept of narrative is an enabling one. It is particularly valuable to parties of the Left, which have an ideological departure point, as opposed to parties of the centre, which have a history of short-term, pragmatic reaction to events. Narrative in effect empowers parties of the Left: the concept of continuous and flexible narrative stands in contrast to the suggestion that history must be rejected, and old values abandoned, in favour of contemporary reaction. The concept of 'Old Labour' and 'New Labour', in the UK and elsewhere, can be exposed as little other than vulgar populism: at best, opportunist in seeking to recruit outside the fundamental values of a political party or movement and, at worst, offensive to those who may have given their lives towards the creation of a society which they believed to be ethically and morally desirable but unattainable in their own lives, but nevertheless worthy of defence as an option for future generations.

What, then, of these fragments, which have been, as it were, half-buried in the ashes of the times – embers that need the stirring of a renewed affirmation, the prod of a restatement, a belief that the possibility remains of something truly human, in its capacity for joy, and for celebration in communion with all life on our planet? It is hard not to recall an image I have used on more than one occasion in my poems: the image of an abandoned house, with its roof broken down. The fire has gone out, and the rainwater mixed with the ashes speaks of abandonment and loss.

The act of raking the coals, then, is the choice of life over the ashes. The new sparks come from that which has been retained, and yet they point to what is yet to be. There is thus never a single moment for the birth of the possible, rather an infinite raking over of what has been spent, for the making of the future.

Rio: Still a Mountain to Climb

> We must nurture our children in order to preserve out planet, and we
> must preserve our planet in order to nurture our children.

This was one of the concluding remarks made by James P. Grant, executive
director of the United Nations Children's Fund, when he spoke recently in
Rio de Janeiro in Brazil. He was one of the people I interviewed for a series
of television documentaries on the United Nations Conference on
Environment and Diversity – or the Earth Summit, as it was popularly
known. Bits of those interviews come to me now as I try to unravel – for
myself as much as for any other reason – what was attempted, what was
achieved, and what was lost in Rio.

After the two main preparation sessions to UNICED – which, on paper,
was somewhat dramatically described as 'Twelve Days to Save the Earth' –
there existed two agendas. The first concerned a small range of matters on
which there was agreement. This was called 'clean text'. The second concerned the much larger number of matters about which there had been dis-
agreement, even down to the language of competing propositions. This was
designated 'bracketed text'. In that first week at Rio Centro, officials worked
to eliminate the 'bracketed text' level so that, when their nominal leader came,
there would be the least amount of distraction within the spectacle. Indeed,
the second week was pure spectacle.

At Rio Centro, the conference centre, Greenpeace was particularly well
organised. Not only had they preceded the conference with a challenging
publication, 'The Greenpeace Book of Greenwash', they then published
single-page issue briefings in their press pack, which were just what journalists – inundated with paper – needed.

At Rio Centro, a quiet battle of public relations was going on. Everybody
was in favour of the new concept, 'sustainable development'. If in 1972, in
Stockholm, the phrase 'Spaceship Earth' was given to the world, Rio spawned
'sustainable development' as its equivalent mantra. In fact, as a concept it has
been around for a few years, particularly in the context of the development
reports of the UN. Where publications like those of Greenpeace provided
an edge was in challenging the notion that such a concept could mean anything – to transnational corporations, for example.

The Business Council for Sustainable Development, which at Rio Centro was sitting side by side with government, is chaired by Swiss billionaire Stephen Schmidheiny. He has considerable interests, both personal and familial, and sits on the boards of companies that sell nuclear reactors and operate steel mills. Indeed, he is on the board of Nestlé, long famous for its attempts to reduce breast-feeding among mothers in the Third World, with consequent effects on infant mortality and survival.

Here, there was a straightforward conflict. The Business Council for Sustainable Development was arguing that, not only have the leopards found it necessary to change their spots, but, as they put it themselves, we are beyond the Third Industrial Revolution. Now, government and business must co-operate in 'sustainable business practice'. The Bible of this new thinking was widely available: 'Changing Courses: A Global Business Perspective on Development and the Environment'.

Greenpeace was quick off the mark to draw public attention to the fact that the advertising agency Burson-Marsteller, which had been hired to present the new image, had previously specialised in advising corporate clients on how to face down local protest groups. Meanwhile, working closely with the Business Council for Sustainable Development was the International Chamber of Commerce. Their specific aim was to ensure the least governmental or international interference with the transnational corporations in the operation of what they called 'free market' principles. So, while everybody talked of 'sustainable development', it meant different things to different groups – groups which had widely differing agendas.

Weeks later, I find bits of paper with notes for pieces to camera scrawled in large letters to myself, and I recall the chaos of the press, TV, radio and film presence. Nerves taut owing to helicopters appearing from nowhere every few minutes, presenters smoothed their pulchritude – or facial destruction, as the case may be – and gave their daily report.

In week two, anybody remotely like a leader – that is, if they floated rather than walked – was rushed by camera crews. Brian Mulroney of Canada worked on a family image, holding hands with what appeared to be an entire extended family.

The leaders were confined to seven minutes for their speeches to the plenary session. The buzz around the place was that Fidel Castro would never stick to this limit. He did. He spoke for five minutes, during which there were several ovations, even in the press rooms, where monitors were relaying it.

To understand the reaction to Castro's speech, you would need to think of the issues about which nobody spoke in the days before he came – issues such as debt, trade, aid and world hunger. When the assembly heard the words 'Let us pay the ecological debt, not the international debt', they were glad that at least somebody was addressing the issue of the annual transfer of $50 billion from the South of the planet to the North. When they heard 'Let us attack hunger, not the human person', another point of moral evasion had been uncovered.

The speech was electrifying precisely because it exposed the lost agenda of UNICED at Rio. If, up to that point, many in the group known as G7 were silent, now they were applauding. The lost agenda, about which hardly anybody spoke, was the issue of debt primarily – but militarism too. These are some salient facts:

§   In 1989, the global economy was valued at $20 trillion.

§   In 1989, Developing World debt was $1.3 trillion.

§   This debt amounted, on average, to around 44 percent of the GNP of that part of the world.

§   The unequal access to trade, finance, and labour markets costs the developing world $500 billion annually.

§   Thirty percent of aid goes to the highest military spenders, and 66 percent is spent on the donor's own products.

§   Thirty-nine percent of US aid goes to Israel, Egypt and El Salvador – 1.2 percent of the world's population.

§   Less than 7 percent of US aid finds its way into popular education, health care, water and family planning.

On these matters, there was silence in 'Bracket Land'. In our Taoiseach's speech, there was not much evidence of any great pain about such issues.

At the Global Forum – the alternative summit, if you like – where five thousand non-governmental organisations were gathered, issues of debt, trade and aid hardly surfaced either, except for the very important discussions which produced thirty alternative treaty statements.

These treaties, the Women's Tent, and individual performers were the high points for me of the Global Forum. I sensed, however, not only a hostility in certain quarters to economic themes but acceptance of right-wing thinking in the most unexpected places. An Indian speaker lectured us on 'self-reliance' while he waited to introduce Ted Turner, who, having asked for all the media – excluding CNN – to go to the back of the marquee, proceeded to give a trivial address, insulting in its banality: 'Seven years ago, I made up these Ten Commandments . . . it was seven years ago . . . but here goes.' Accompanied by Jane Fonda, who apparently gave a thoughtful speech elsewhere at the Forum, Mr Turner was the worst speaker by far.

These star turns at the Global Forum revealed something else also, something that one might call 'the Andy Warhol factor'. Before each speaker had finished, long lines of strategically seated questioners would form up in order to ask questions or, more often, to offer earnest little speeches. The most popular topics were themselves, love, themselves, the planet, and themselves: 'I'm Mary Beth from Minnesota and I've been relating to the process of the happiness of mosquitoes and sunflowers for two years now . . . '

The Dalai Llama and Jacques Cousteau were the most visionary and most sought-after speakers, according to popular evaluation. Present too, and speaking very practically about pesticides being distributed abroad that were barred at home, was Bianca Jagger.

Pelé also made an appearance, but my family's soccer loyalties had to take second place to a man I was interviewing (unsolicited) on the importance of boring a hole at the North Pole within the next five years, with US assistance, so as to release air bubbles and clear water.

Twelve days, and one day off. . . . It wasn't just that there was a huge gulf between North and South: between Rio Centro and the Global Forum, there seemed to be an unbridgeable gap – between the logics and the languages of heart and head. And the gap was there *within* both too.

Towards the edges, groups like the United States Heart Foundation gave sessions on bio-dance and, in the evening, massaged, co-counselled, rubbed, loved, related and shared.

I am far from cynical, but there was an uncomfortable missing agenda. Nor was it clear whether or not the problem of global development had been understood in its full complexity. It was not that the planet's precarious position had not been noted. It was not that the problem of the crisis of consciousness and, within it, the problem of language having become arbitrary, alienating and oppressive had been missed.

There were exceptions, such as Marcos Arruda, who could move with ease from the immediate problems of sheet-metal workers, through geology, to issues of economics and democracy in the age of globalisation.

Moving in taxis between the two worlds that did not speak a common language, I saw posters in Brazilian Portuguese announcing a new kind of eco-tourism. Beyond the nineties, Rio would be remembered as much for UNICED as for the tango. But where were the children? They had been gathered up into schools and institutions, the streets made clear for the eco-concerned and the leaders. The odd one appeared before the 15th, and then they were back in numbers.

Carrying in one's head facts, such as that between 1982 and 1990, the new transfer of capital via debt from South to North was $418 million; knowing that, on average, more than twenty economies of the South are 60 percent more indebted in 1992 than they were in 1982; sensing the gap in language; looking straight at the child of the streets – being conscious of such realities would make it difficult to go on.

'Capture the atmosphere,' somebody said. But in truth, I don't know what to say. I found no exciting new connections between science, technology, and society; they continue to be linked primarily by a set of power relations. To dance to the sun might be indulged; to speak of power or decision-making beyond the individual would invite derision.

It was not the planet's physical constitution, it was consciousness that was shrinking. On a rock-and-roll stage, a famous Brazilian singer/dancer is replaced by an American who screams on Copacabana Beach: 'I'm American and I've been part of this process for two years.' Alongside me, two Brazilian vendors of beer argue about a returned bottle.

The saddest interviews I conducted were closest to the *Rainbow Warrior*. Here I spoke to representatives of the 5.8 billion people who live on that sixth of the planet known as the Pacific, maybe twenty-five nations all told. They were denied the right to tell their own story. Their imperial powers did it for them.

Some occupants of atolls know that the rising sea level is not an academic issue for them. By 2000, many communities will be gone. Meanwhile, the French have just announced a year's moratorium on nuclear testing on Moruroa and Fangataiya atolls. This after twenty-three years of protest. Into the Pacific communities' lives have been fired every kind of missile test and every form of toxic waste. And the scandalous exploitation continues.

In East Timor, since the illegal annexation by the Indonesian government in 1975, two hundred thousand people have died. Yet our partners in the European Community, Britain, are getting ready to sell an additional fifty Hawk fighters to Indonesia.

When John Major gave his first press conference at Rio Centro, he referred to some adverse commentary on the British position as 'ungracious', a nice word from one of the nice new people of politics selling instruments of death to the military dictatorship that is the Suharto family.

So, Rio was about consciousness: about what was left unsaid and undone:

§   It left the issue of CO_2 emissions without a definite set of commitments.

§   It dropped the issue of militarism.

§   It neglected the issues of trade, aid and debt.

§   It allowed the transnational corporations to walk away without any new obligations.

§   It abandoned the indigenous peoples of the world, constituting them, insultingly, as 'a dimension'.

§   It avoided the issue of population, claimed by Cousteau to be the key problem.

§   It left biotechnology to the marketplace for regulation.

§   It did not curtail the dumping of nuclear waste.

§   Its Agenda 21 hangs around an initiative called 'The Global–Environmental Facility', in which the World Bank and the International Monetary Fund call the shots.

§   It gave credence to the most dangerous myth with which to finish this century – that the marketplace and economic growth, as we have known these things, can lead to environmental health.

There is a need indeed to look closely at the thirty Environmental Alternative Treaties. There is an even greater need to advance their thinking into public consciousness. And we should remember the Tao: 'You cannot stop the birds of sadness flying over your head but you can stop them from building nests in your hair.'

Hot Press, Vol. 16, No. 13, 30 July 1992

Imagining the Future

A Global Perspective

Many people today experience a great longing for authenticity. They sense that, at a personal, community and global level, theyhave experienced a frustration at best, and perhaps even a violence, that condemns them and others to a life far short of their capacities at an ethical or creative level. Such a statement is very particular to this present age but it is also one that has engaged scholarship in different centuries in a powerful way. For example, there is a particular moment when the spiritual gives way to the rational and the Enlightenment arrives, and there is a particular moment when modernism arrives. But what one can detect in the present period is a deep search for authenticity and a sense of frustration that it is not being realised.

One of the distinguishing characteristics of the present time is that there is a greater intolerance towards the discussion of such a contradiction than at any time in recent years. It is a time of narrowness. It is a time of extreme intolerance and, to my mind, very reduced scholarship. I list, therefore, a set of issues I propose to deal with that I have been thinking about since I was contacted to give this paper. I will give a summary of what I am suggesting and then return in more detail to some of them.

I am suggesting that we cannot live fully conscious lives unless we question the inevitabilities that are suggested to us. This involves developing both the personal and the social consciousness necessary to create a critical capacity so that we might truly experience freedom and choice, and moral responsibility for the consequences of our actions. Second, I suggest that, in dealing with that kind of challenge, we will find no automatic solution in retreating to old certainties. This does not mean that the certainties have been discarded. I am simply suggesting, philosophically, that they are insufficient. For example, I spent time as a young student in the 1960s and 1970s in the United States, Britain and Ireland, when we were told that the Western World was an advanced world and that it was only a matter of time before the rest of the planet lost its backwardness and could become modern and developed just like us. Of course, this set of assumptions constituted a model that was ethnocentric amd culturally insufficient. In sociological terms, as a theory of change it was unacceptable in its assumptions, in its methodology and, above all, in its conclusions. Historically, it also lacked credibility – a fact that did not seem to bother many people, however. It spawned a host of works, and a kind of scholarship that was unilinear, evolutionist, and accepting of political and economic structures that were in political, economic and cultural terms dominating, exploitive and manipulative.

It is very interesting the way in which waves of intellectual ideas return. I recently met a person I knew in the 1960s and 1970s while studying in the United States. I met him on a plane and he was heading to what was the Soviet Union before 1989. As he put it, he never thought that those old files would be useful again. He had dug them all out, and here he was peddling the modernisation model all over again. The basic ideas, which had been provided in a series of studies known as the Princeton Studies, between 1958 and 1963, were being recycled uncritically. That is what I mean when I say that some contemporary scholarship is shabby.

I turn now to the need for questioning certainties that are not necessarily sufficient to deal with the angst of our times. I think the way people handle the problem is very interesting, but escapist. I say this with great respect. People change beliefs, and have always done so in the history of ideas, through the construction of myths. The nature of a myth is such that you suggest that something is so obvious that it is natural for it to be taken for granted – rather like modernisation, a powerful myth. Everyone who studied at post-graduate level in the United States from the end of the 1960s to the end of the 1980s was reared within this myth. Globalisation is a contemporary myth. When you look at the assumptions of globalisation – that you have a single model of the economy, to be prosecuted in a linear way, market-led and so forth, private- rather than public-driven, with no notion of involvement of the state, and unmitigated by social protection – one can see that globalisation too is a myth. The difference between it and the modernisation myth is that it is being implemented through institutions which were not originally set up for such a purpose, such as the IMF and the World Bank. Where such a myth is most dangerous is in its capacity to dull people's critical capacity.

What does one do when invited within twenty-four hours to deliver a paper? Certain books will select themselves. I found myself reaching for Carl Jung's book *Modern Man in Search of a Soul*. When I reflected on the Jungian thesis in this work, it suggested to me something that is also in my poems, the notion of exile. The past from which we have come is embedded in us – in our psyche – in a way from which we cannot totally distance ourselves. We also look to the future, as to how we might see it as containing promise or

306

hope. But how do we handle the present as we take ourselves from the past and face the future? In the discussion where Jung makes his critique of Freud and Adler, he suggests a crucial difference between them. Freud approaches this problem almost as if our condition was pathological. In the case of Jung, he leaves the possibilities of consciousness there for our realisation. The concept of consciousness is incredibly important, I suggest.

In relation to my opening statement, that we experience a longing for authenticity, consciousness tells us that it doesn't matter enormously where this authenticity is institutionally located, simply that spirit cries out for a version of the self and of the world, and for the capacity for creation, which is not being met by our present circumstances. We have to answer that problem through an integrated scholarship that is not easily available to us any more. It is as though we try to see these problems through a broken glass, through pieces and shards of experience. Thinking it through raises a question about the role of culture – a culture which is at once inherited and being re-created, but also fundamentally charged, and never static. Creativity is not something that is located randomly and vicariously in individual people, as those phrases 'she had it in her' or 'the piano will stand to her' suggest. The alternative view is that we are all potentially creative, if we are allowed to develop. Genius may be more randomly and vicariously distributed.

Accepting the necessity and power of creativity has implications for our discourse on the economy. I have been at many conferences on the knowledge economy, and I repeat something that I have taken to repeating in the hope that it would lodge somewhere: that the creative society makes possible myriad forms of the knowledge economy but that, if you change the society to one form of the knowledge economy in a short period of time, you not only damage your capacity economically but also dislocate the creative society and diminish the capacity for a vibrant citizenship. This has to be taken seriously because it has wider implications, such as the relationship of education to the economy at every level through the economy. If today you state that you are, as an academic, in favour of reflective scholarship, this somehow or other is to confess a disability in the current times in relation to funding. I was an academic for most of my life. I have taught in the university system in America, in Britain and here in Ireland. I am distressed at what I see as a lack of confidence in the possibility of hope at an intellectual level.

In previous decades, scholars seemed so much more morally engaged. If I were to go back to Jung's work , published in 1933, scholars were trying to envisage a time where we would never have war again. Then, through the nineteen sixties and seventies, an immense debate arose about what you might call the framing of technology and science. There was a debate about the Bomb. There was a debate about the use of physicists in creating instruments of war, about whether science was neutral, and about its relationship to technology.

The story, of course, is not a black one entirely. One of the greatest developments of the last twenty-five years has been an increasing interest in ecological responsibility, Even at the UN Conference in Rio, you had the Business Council for Sustainable Development deciding that sustainable development was an unavoidable concept.

Looking back at the origins of a dangerous hubris, the high point of an uncaring science was perhaps when Francis Bacon said, 'I lead to you nature and all her children in bondage for your use' and, again of nature, 'We must gouge out her secrets.' Bacon, at the beginning of a period of empire and colonisation, was supplying a rationalisation for these forces and a relationship to the environment which would be tragic in its consequences. It was a frame of mind, a paradigm, a governing myth. So we are searching, therefore, for a new paradigm in which we might enframe science and technology, and at the same time discover, or rediscover, points of continuity from the past and be able to face the future without fear.

The problem is one of having an instinct for what ought to be, what might be, and finding it contradicted. In this regard, I suggest that it is worthwhile to consider the concept of prophecy. In one of the poems in my new collection, *An Arid Season*, I deal with this concept of exile. We are in exile, I suggest, from the different and perhaps better versions of ourselves. It is rather like the situation in the Psalm, when a person cries out to God and asks: 'Why do you not answer?' It is that we have in ourselves a hunger for a better version of ourselves, and a need to have that better version of ourselves made available. Our cry is perceptible, but we wait for the answer. Whether you call this a longing for utopia – a better place or, strictly speaking, a different place – or whether you call it, in a theological sense, prophecy, it is a cry out of exile for a possibility that has not been rejected, even if it appears unattainable in present circumstances.

It is interesting that Martin Luther King, who was not to see the full realisation of his dream in the United States, described his vision spatially – 'I have been to the top of the mountain' – and then prophetically: 'I have seen the promised land.' My poem 'Too Close to the Ground' concluded that the resolution of our problems has to be achieved by ourselves.

One of the most important aspects of change in our lives today has been the change in the relationship between the economy and society. Our attitude to work and leisure has been crucially changed. A new discourse has been invented to justify our subservience to the economy. Issues of personal and social development have given way to ones of utility. We rarely hear such questions as: What would you really like to do with your life? Where do you think your interests really fit? On the other hand, we are instructed on a daily basis as to what we must do with our lives, and our children's lives, to sustain 'the needs of the economy'.

Our society is under pressure for time. Voluntarism is declining. There is little time for community. Time previously spent with neighbours is now spent in traffic jams. We earn more, but everything costs even more. The relationship between the generations is fundamentally changed, with care of the elderly, for example, now being discussed almost entirely in terms of institutional provision. We now have 65.1 percent of women and 1.5 percent of people above the age of sixty-five in the workforce. There is hardly anybody else to be sent into the economy.

If you contrast the present discourse to that which prevailed when I was appointed first in 1969 in UCG, as it then was, we were being endlessly invited to attend seminars about the leisure society, and what we were we all going to do when there was so much free time: take on hobbies, learn languages, travel? People were to prepare themselves for retirement. I remember quoting Oscar Wilde's phrase: 'Work is for horses.' The working life was to be shorter; the working year was to be shorter; the working day was to be shorter. Then, suddenly, there was no free time. Now it is a disloyal and near-traitorous act not to work endlessly. You are letting the economy down if you retire at seventy. When you consider the time spent either at or travelling to work, there is very little free time left.

A solution to our form of economy has to be structured across the spectrum of space and time. It has to take into account the issues of income, but also issues of quality of life. The challenge is to sustain the economic version you desire while at the same time finding a way to realise your ethically unrealised self.

We began most of our lives when the concept of citizenship was being widely debated. With citizenship came notions of universal rights. Surely people should be entitled to clean water; surely people should be entitled to education; surely people should be entitled to good housing; surely people should be free from insecurity in illness or old age. But now we listen to lectures about how we should purchase our own security in every one of these areas. We are becoming consumers of services that will more and more be provided to us by the market, rather than as rights we are entitled to under a concept of citizenship.

Such a world as I have described has been accepted as inevitable. This world, sustained by the myth of globalisation, is a world about which we have to ask ourselves a fundamental question: Do we have the critical capacity to subject it to critique? We have in our consciousness actually shifted to being consumers rather than citizens. This is accompanied by the commodification of more and more aspects of life, and has created an alienation that has masked itself as the sole desirable lifestyle – a lifestyle that invites us, I suggest, to move towards a life of being consumed in our consumption. The interdependency which was at the basis of citizenship is recognised, but it is devalued by an aggressive and, at times, vicious individualism. Indeed, I notice that our language itself has changed. People rarely speak about 'the personal' any more, but instead of 'the individual'.

Market fundamentalism is accepted as the single paradigm of economic development and its imposition as the sole strategy for development and poverty alleviation. This, I suggest, is disastrous, and not only in the poorest countries or transition economies, but also in the so-called Developed World.

We have as consumers experienced such a dulling of our consciousness as blocks our capacity to engage critically with our world. If we take the media as an example, we are affected by fragmentation of audiences, concentration of ownership, and a drive towards cultural homogeneity. We should be honest and accept that the concentration of ownership in the media internationally, with its stress on commoditised entertainment on television in particular, plays a crucial role in the limitation, even destruction, of our life-world. Our scholarship has become apologetic and accommodating, rather than critical. We are, as Charles Taylor, the Canadian philosopher, puts it: 'acquiescing in our own unfreedom'. We are 'drifting', as he says, to our 'unfreedom'.

This broken world appears to us in shadows through shards of experience; some of the most insightful and ethical responses that do engage with this condition, do so on a single-issue basis. I found, for example, that several of my friends, who became communitarians in the eighties in California, did not want a strong role for the state, the bureaucracy. Let's all do it – make the changes, from the bottom up, they said. Ronald Reagan, as governor of the state, clasped his hands and said thank you for helping me. He closed the parks. Nettles grew where flowers had grown before. Some well-meaning reformers had assisted the agenda of the Right without thinking about it.

Again, one of the fastest areas for growth in bookshops, not only here but all over Europe, and particularly in North America, is the self-help genre. This raises the question: can you heal yourself? The answer in such writing is, of course, that you must heal yourself first and then deal with the wider world. I suggest that much of this is a very insufficient response to the kind of problems which I have been describing. Of course, it is important to recognise the significance of personal integration so as to survive in a broken world, but we need to attend to the urgency of an integrated approach to our shared, interdependent planetary existence. We have, to invert a Raymond Williams phrase, become the targets of consumption rather than the arrows of a deeper, more extensive and more humane communication. We have the technological capacity to widen and deepen our communication, and engage with all the issues of the world and with other people from different cultures. Instead of such a project taking place, the technology has been turned against us. Even in the production values of television programmes, context is eliminated and a distrust of narrative is obvious. There is a distrust of the possibility of democratic extension. The world, in the new value system, is one whose complexity is amenable solely to expertise. The view it sustains is that such expertise is separate from ordinary democratic discourse. Ordinary people, it is suggested, don't understand. From this assumption, it is a short distance to the dangerous views of Leo Strauss, with his notion that the public may have to be deceived and the development of the concept of the 'noble lie', as adopted by the neo-conservatives in the recent history of the United States.

I remember writing a poem once which reflected on authoritarianism in the church in rural Ireland in the 1950s, when people accepted that priests often had to read books for the benefit of the general public, who were unable to understand them. Many people objected to that, of course. Nobody, however, objected in the nineteen eighties and nineties to people asserting that economists have to tell you what the state of the economy is, for your sake, because you don't understand it. The structure of a television programme on the economy in that period was to interview members of the public, who could be assumed to give a simplistic view of a particular problem. Then, when they were finished, the three or four eminent people who understood the economy were wheeled out. They summarised it for you and told you how it really was. The Church in Ireland in my lifetime was never as unaccountable as today's spokespersons for an unacceptable and morally disinterested economics such as was emerging then, and would come to prevail.

It is appropriate, therefore, to ask what kind of world we inhabit. Why do we accept it? What are the consequences of appearing to recognise an interdependency that we are forced to contradict? As we discard ethics for a narrow, market-led vision of fundamentalism, can social cohesion survive in such an atmosphere of exclusion and market fundamentalism? In Mrs Thatcher's Britain, one of the fastest-growing sectors was private security. You had very wealthy homes in gated communities which, their owners felt, needed protection because of the perception that the underclass were coming up the road and, as the new rich put it, 'they want what we have and we are protecting ourselves against them'.

The acceptance of a world so divided, a planet that is not sufficiently respected for its diversity, places much at risk. It has a numbing effect. People regularly say to me that they are not happy about this or that and they want to do something about it, but they lack the moral resources and the courage to actually debate it. All I want at the present time is simply to raise some questions that I feel to be important but that are neglected. Going back to Jung's work, he spoke about the unconscious and then about the practical consciousness that enabled one to do tasks, and, more importantly, he spoke of a discursive consciousness, which was one where you allowed yourself to ask the questions: Why am I doing this? What are the reasons behind this?

In Jung's example, Westerners thought it absurd and unnatural that tribespeople in parts of Africa believed that, if you shot an animal, a dying person in a neighbouring village may be robbed of his or her soul. Yet how much more ridiculous and unnatural was it for visitors to be overdressed in the tropical heat and to require their servants to wear white gloves over their black hands?

So there is a problem about what is natural. That phrase – 'what is natural' – purports to describe what is inevitable and makes the myths by which we live. I have been to many places where there are huge problems with poverty, disease and malnutrition. The question digs itself into you. How often do we have to see this, and experience it again and again on television? Does it not contradict any ethical or moral impulse we claim to have within us, when we insist that many things repeat themselves as if they were inevitable?

In 1994, the late and brilliant Erskine Childers, an assistant general secretary of the United Nations, wrote in his book *Renewing the United Nations* that:

One point four billion people now live in absolute poverty, 40 percent more than fifteen years ago. Nearly one in every four human beings alive today is only existing on the margins of survival, too poor to obtain the food they need to work, or adequate shelter, or minimal health care, let alone education for their children. . . . Overall, for the poorest among human kind, the thirty years between sixty-four and ninety-four have been like trying to go up a down escalator.

Our structures of aid, trade and debt, and our neo-liberal market model, assured the continuity of these divisions. In 1960, the richest one-fifth of the world's population enjoyed thirty times more income than the poorest fifth. By 1989, the richest fifth was receiving sixty times the income of the poorest. Aid has been falling every year for the last ten years. In relation to trade, wealth is being transferred from the South to the North every day. I say this in relation to debt. If debt had been cancelled in 1997 for the twenty poorest countries, the money released for basic health care could have saved the lives of about twenty-one million children.

Zambia, for instance, in 1989 paid in debt service a sum that was 13 percent of its gross domestic product – or more than the country's combined health and education budget. For every 1 percent that was transferred from debt service to the combined health and education product, you would have been able to save the lives of children at the level I have mentioned. In that country, life expectancy owing to HIV and AIDS has fallen from forty-three years to thirty-three years, with half a million children out of school and the education system in a state of collapse.

We created an agenda in September 2000 through the eight Millennium Development goals, about which there should be no backsliding. At the present time, one of the eight Millennium goals that deals with Africa and HIV and AIDS is at about 42 percent of what was hoped for in terms of funding – or something like $42 billion short of what is needed to address that problem.

I want to finish by saying this about our unquestioning acceptance of the world in which we live. If we had wanted to live fully conscious, critical lives, if we had wanted not to be the target, if we had wanted not to have the arrows directed at us, as consumers, if we had wanted, as Raymond Williams put it, to be the arrow not the target, would we have accepted so much of the monopoly I mentioned earlier in the media?

Between 1987 and 1989 the ubiquitous Rupert Murdoch, through his News Corporation, earned $2.3 billion. He paid no corporation tax, and in the whole world, for all his operations, he paid less than 6 percent tax. Do we regard that as a good thing? Why do people put up with this? Well, the historian R. H. Tawney speculated once about why tadpoles put up with their miserable existence: 'Maybe it is because they live in expectation that one of their number will sprout a jaw and leap to earth and become a frog.'

There is a suggestion in our society that, through some kind of individual miracle, we can escape from our condition. What is needed is a return to questioning the inevitabilities by which we live, and looking at some of the certainties that have been discarded: critiquing the myths by which we live, concentrating on the critical capacity that scholarship and public debate require, encouraging consciousness, and respecting prophecies.

The capacity to change the world still exists, and we can create a new world rather than remain the victims of history. One of the most inspiring phrases in Raymond William's last book, *Towards 2000* – 'Once the inevitabilities are challenged, we have begun to gather our resources for a journey of hope' – reminds us that we too can take our first steps towards a new world.

From Imagining the Future, eds. Father Harry Bohan and Gerard Kennedy,
Veritas, Dublin, 2005

TOWARDS A RIGHTS-BASED APPROACH TO THE ECONOMY

I would like to address three very basic issues, issues that once lay at the heart of economics but that are now not only neglected but almost unacceptable in economic discourse and the media – and indeed in political and some trade-union circles. Such issues include: How are basic needs to be defined and met by the economy? Do they include housing, health and education? What is to be the role of the state? Should the state provide services as a principle of universal general access or should it regard itself as a partner with the private sector within a market model? I suggest that the market model is the very antithesis of a rights-based approach and that a rights-based approach is what the trade-union movement must demand.

It is essential that, even in the short term, housing, health and education be regarded as matters where minimum targets, expressed across a time-scale no longer than five years, are set. These minimum demands should be regarded as social and economic rights, as the requirements of citizenship, not conceded as the crumbs of growth made available, after a struggle, to a lesser form of consumer – the consumer of public goods. A rights-based approach begins with the recognition of human rights, their location in basic needs, and their extension along a line towards meeting that which is necessary to live a full and creative life.

When future historians come to write of the period of high economic growth experienced in Ireland in the 1990s and beyond, they will ask some fundamental questions, ones that are not being sufficiently addressed in our own time – questions from which we cannot run away. How could the public accept such speculation in housing as would transform society for the worse, tear the heart out of the economy, and create a mountain of debt for a future generation of young couples? The issue is not what happened to the average mortgage repayment during the period of the Partnership for Prosperity and Fairness. The issue is what happened to the price of houses, and why?

Again, in relation to education, how could the highest period of growth end with the deepening of inequality, with, for example, a pupil–teacher ratio above the European average, dilapidated school buildings, and a generally unhappy society of parents and teachers. With regard to health care, inequality in our two-tiered health system has been deepened and is set to be extended, with public taxation being directed into private medicine, built on the back of publicly funded medical education, staff, and laboratory and services provision.

How could the highest growth in any economy in Europe be squandered in such a way as to leave housing lists nearly doubled, hospital waiting lists our of control, and basic school buildings in disrepair? Part of the answer lies in the politics of how the growth was used. The fruits of growth were distributed disproportionally to the top two-fifths of the society. Certainly no attempt was made to accept, not to speak of extend, a rights-based approach to social protection. The disgraceful rejection of a rights-based approach to disability was perhaps the most blatant example of the government's thinking. Indeed, we come out of our period of growth as one of the least socially protected peoples of Europe.

The trade-union movement has always faced a particular challenge when it comes to health. Traditionally, health was seen as falling within the private rather than the public realm. Health was also understood as the 'absence of disease'. The first laws containing health-related provisions go back to the era of industrialisation. The Moral Apprentices Act (1802) and the Public Health Act (1858) were adopted in the United Kingdom as a means of containing social pressures arising from poor labour conditions. The 1843 Mexican Constitution included references to the state's responsibility for preserving public health.

The evolution towards defining health as a social issued led to the founding of the World Health Organisation in 1946. With the emergence of health as a public issue, the conception of health changed. The WHO developed and promulgated the understanding of health as 'a state of complete physical, mental and social well-being and not merely the absence of disease or infirmity'. It defined an integrated approach linking all the factors related to human well-being, including the physical and social surroundings conducive to good health.

Current trends suggest that 'the enjoyment of the highest attainable standard of health', which the WHO describes as 'one of the fundamental rights of every human being', is seen almost as a by-product, as something that will trickle down to the bottom at some time in the future. There is a long way to trickle before this fundamental right reaches those who are destitute (currently one-fifth of the human race), those who survive precariously in the informal sector, or those whose access to health care is limited by their age or their disabilities, or by armed conflict. And while seven out of ten of the world's poorest people are female, women's health needs are wide-ly neglected, whatever their background. Yet, if development is not for health, what is it for – and who can expect to enjoy it?

With the establishment of the WHO, for the first time the right to health was recognised internationally. The WHO Constitution affirms that 'the enjoyment of the highest attainable standard of health is one of the funda-mental rights of every human being without distinction of race, religion, political belief, economic or social condition.' Over time, this recognition was reiterated, in a wide array of formulations, in several international and region-al human-rights instruments.

The Poor Law inheritance is still present in some public discussions of health. The alternative to a public-health system based on universality, with general access, is a private, unaccountable investment in the 'sickness indus-try'. It is this latter which Finance Minister Charlie McCreevy assists with tax breaks at the same time as he underfunds the public system.

Turning to housing: our housing policy has been designed by market fun-damentalists whose influence is indicated by such evidence as the vastly increased proportion of housing owned by speculators. In reply to a Dáil Question from me on the amount of tax foregone under Section 23 of the Finance Act, the following emerged:

> Figures of loan interest allowable on borrowings taken out for invest-ment in house property are not separately identified in tax statistics, and it is not therefore possible for the Revenue Commissioners to estimate accurately the cost of the availability of interest relief to the landlords of rented residential property. The only indicative information available on the cost of the tax relief are tentative estimates which were compiled when the relief was abolished in 1998 and restored in 2002. It was ten-tatively estimated at the time of its abolition in 1996 that removing the relief would provide a saving to the exchequer of €33 million in a full year, while its restoration in 2002 was estimated to cost €50 million in a full year.

It seems that Minister McCreevy was so anxious to reward speculation that some of the concessions allowed were not even fully costed before being introduced.

The number of claimants and the estimated cost of tax relief for rent paid in private rented accommodation has increased from 33,100 in 1996 to 103,700 at the end of 2001. The estimated cost of tax relief has risen from €9 million to €32.3 million. The number of individuals and companies with rental income and estimated tax yield was 60,200 individuals, yielding €174 million, and 4,320 companies, yielding €101.6 million. These figures are for 2000, the last full year for which statistics are available. Put simply, our housing sector is a speculators' paradise.

As to a rights-based perspective in housing, I suggest that a further direct challenge has been thrown down to trade unionists in that Ireland has not ratified Article 31 of the Revised European Social Charter, which states:

> Article 31. Right to housing: with a view to ensuring the effective exercise of the right to housing, the Parties undertake to take measures designed:
> 1 To promote access to housing of an adequate standard.
> 2 To prevent and reduce homelessness with a view to its gradual elimination.
> 3 To make the price of housing accessible to those without adequate resources.

The Irish government's refusal to accept Article 31 is as much based on an unwillingness to give information on the scale of the housing crisis as it is on the rejection of a justifiable right to housing.

We need a property ownership survey now. I can tell you that those who owned two or three houses in Galway years ago now own more than a dozen. It is a fundamental demand that we know who have, thanks to tax inducements, become the new landlords – the least-regulated landlords in Europe, with the most-unprotected tenants.

The result, of course, has been to place housing out of the reach of couples on moderate income, with both partners forced to work. The result is a massive increase in time spent commuting, the strain of an inadequately funded child-care system, and the widening gap between disposable income and debt service. One of the consequences of speculation being promoted by the government, actively through tax concessions and passively by the failure to establish land banks or introduce windfall profits tax on rezoned and hoarded land, is that a huge gap has opened up between capital accumulation and real wages.

Neither should we forget what the Boston model of the economy favoured by one of the parties returned to government means. It is one of reduced social protection and an unregulated labour market. Workers should reflect long and hard on Professor Michael Dunford's review of the position of workers in the US in his chapter of Ronan Palan's *Global Political Economy*.

Between 1973 and 1993, real wages in the US of the unskilled fell by 30 percent. From an increase of one-third in wealth, 20 percent gained. In fact, workers in the US, Professor Dunford tells us, have to work 245 hours more in order to keep their living standard at the same level as it was in 1973.

What sources, then, might we quote for our demand for a rights-based approach to the economy? A good starting point might be the 1948 Universal Declaration of Human Rights, which states:

> Everyone has the right to a standard of living adequate for the health and well-being of himself and of his family, including food, clothing, housing, medical care and necessary social services, and the right to security in the event of unemployment, sickness, disability, widowhood, old age or other lack of livelihood in circumstances beyond his control.

Then again, Article 2 of the International Covenant on Economic, Social and Cultural Rights, signed by the Irish government, states:

> Each State Party to the present covenant undertakes to take steps, individually and through international assistance and co-operation, especially economic and technical, to the maximum of its available resources, with a view to achieving progressively the full realisation of the rights recognised in the present covenant by all appropriate means, including particularly the adoption of legislative measures.
>
> The States Parties to the present covenant undertake to guarantee that the rights enunciated in the present covenant will be exercised without discrimination of any kind, of race, colour, sex, language, religion, political or other opinion, national or social origin, property, birth or other status.

The present developed version of the economy stands in contrast to such a rights-based approach.

Trade unions have in recent times been, and are now again, invited to discuss economic indicators as if they were separate from any social, political or indeed moral values. Employers ask for children to be educated for the economy rather than the economy serving the rights of children. Workers are asked to prolong their working lives in conditions of increasing insecurity and shrinking real incomes.

Insisting on a rights-based approach will mean embarking an a new journey for trade unionists. It is an invitation to be profoundly human, to restore the moral relationship between life and work.

Such a society will of course be more productive in every way. Growth, far from being threatened by a cohesive society, will be enabled rather than inhibited. The mediating institutions, such as trade unions, have a positive and valuable role in a society working to a rights-based agenda. In an unregulated market, by contrast, they are driven out of existence.

A rights-based approach is fundamentally based on citizenship. Is not a society with an enhanced sense of solidarity, within the framework of citizenship, not more cohesive and happier? If faced with a choice between an open-ended, neurotic consumerism and a citizenship built past the satisfaction of basic needs, and moving towards the creative use of increasing free time, would not the trade-union movement choose the latter?

Not only through wage advances and fair taxation but also through the vindication of rights can the trade-union movement create the basis for the alternative society that is waiting to be born.

Delivered to the Biennial Regional Conference of SIPTU, Corrib Great Southern Hotel, Galway, 1 November 2002

The Task of the Left

Towards a Politics Beyond the Self

The tasks which will face an ethically driven left-of-centre government seeking to displace the present government, which accepts inequality as a principle, will neither be simply technical nor will they be managerial in nature. Any new government will have to tackle the profound alienation of many from their lives and society. It will have to implement a strategy for inclusion and reconnection.

The public have been reduced to the level of spectators as the economy is analysed as something separate from society. The question that arises at the end of many a weary and frustrating day is: How can the economy be described as doing so well, yet so many people be left short of the social protections that are basic in so many countries, and regarded as rights in many?

These are contradictions which have to be addressed. Tackling the alienation that now exists through a set of strategies based on the politics of fear would be a disaster. The wellspring of ethics that goes beyond the self is still there among the public, even if it is devalued by a current politics that asserts an aggressive individualism over the social, and that speaks of the need for inequality as a principle.

A left-of-centre government will have to have a new discourse for times it must make different. The difference between genuine personal freedom achieved within the social and the prevailing unlimited individual greed will have to be established.

Faoi scáth a chéile is not how we now live. Yet the indications are that there is support for a genuine citizenship based on such necessary conditions as solidarity, participation, equality of provision, security and justice. There is much evidence that such an impulse to life beyond the self underpins the pursuit of universal human rights, shared ecological responsibility, fair trade and an end to famine, child labour and war.

The issues I wish to raise are moral, ethical, political and social. Politics has been severely damaged, trust has been destroyed, and the image, created by our right-of-centre government, of contemporary Ireland is of a greedy country consumed in its consumption, one where, as the loudest mouth of the present government puts it, 'inequality in society is necessary as a spur to achievement'.

The radical, individual acquisitive greed that is at the centre of this government's thinking has led to their trumpeting a version of Ireland as manipulative, speculative, ostentatious and grossly vulgar in its flaunting of wealth, which strikes at the very basis of responsible and inclusive citizenship. The present alliance in power has allowed housing speculation to tear the heart out of the economy, while not seeing any contradiction between their boast of being the second-richest economy in Europe, and having the second-lowest level of social protection in Europe.

The thinking of the Right is that such social expenditure must come after the needs of the depeopled economy have been served. The benefits of economic expansion are overwhelmingly distributed to those who speculate, and accumulate ever-greater fortunes, not from producing any real wealth, but from the speculative opportunities provided by the government parties, which they support and fund.

In every area of current government policy, there is an exploitation of the politics of fear and an abandonment of a politics that might be built on what transcends the self. Why do I say this challenges politics itself? It does so because the capacity to go beyond oneself, towards others, to take their needs and lives into account, is the prerequisite of all human solidarity and the viability of society. It is the only real definition of citizenship.

Of the commitments to competition and cohesion in the Lisbon Agenda of the European Union, only competition is acknowledged by those who feel they can impose a neo-liberal model in every circumstance at home and abroad. This model stands for an extended and stressful working life from which the basic guarantees won by generations of struggle have been stripped. In the name of labour-market flexibility, new forms of exploitation emerge, often directed at the most vulnerable of employees, in particular migrant workers. All this in a country that calls itself a Republic!

What, then, is the test of the Left and of the Labour Party? We must, above all else, insist on a return of values to politics and make the 'values debate' a central part of our election campaign. The campaign cannot simply be about changing the managers of a system that is exploitative, unfair, dismissive of ethics and, by any standards of public provision, immoral. We must invite the public to reject what the extreme individualism of the Right has done: the destruction of the social that continues, and that promises to blight future generations. Any party with which we might cooperate, in or out of government, must realise that there are bedrock values upon which Labour will not compromise.

One of the most important aspects of change in our contemporary lives has been the change in the relationship between economy and society. Our attitude to work and leisure has been crucially changed. It is not simply that a single version of the economic – the neo-liberal model – has dominated the social. It is rather that a new discourse has been invented to justify our subservience to the economy.

Issues of personal and social development have given way to ones of utility. We rarely hear such questions as 'What would you really like to do with your life?' and 'Where do you think your interests really lie?' On the other hand, we are instructed on a daily basis as to what we must do with our lives to sustain 'the needs of the economy'.

Our society is under pressure for time. Voluntarism is declining. There is little time for community. Time previously spent with neighbours is spent in traffic jams. We earn more, but everything costs even more. Indirect taxes and charges mask the true cost of living. The relationship between the generations is fundamentally changed, with care of the elderly, for example, now being discussed almost entirely in terms of institutional provision.

In the 1970s, there were endless seminars about the leisure society. What were we all going to do when there was so much free time? Take on hobbies, learn languages, travel? People were to prepare themselves for retirement. I remember Oscar Wilde's phrase 'Work is for horses' being quoted. The working life was to be shorter; the working year was to be shorter; the working day was to be shorter.

Then suddenly there was no free time. Now it is a disloyal and near-traitorous act not to work endlessly. You are letting the economy down if you retire at seventy! For young couples there is very little time left after the massive increase in the time taken in going to and coming back from work, which is demanded of both partners.

A solution to our current form of the economy has to be structured across the spectrum of space and time. It has to take into account issues of income but also issues of quality of life. The challenge is to sustain the version that we want of the economy, while at the same time making progress towards that which I have been describing by way of realising our ethically unrealised selves.

Most of us began our lives when the concept of citizenship was being widely debated. With citizenship came notions of universal rights. Surely people should be entitled to clean water? Surely people should be entitled to education? Surely people should be entitled to good housing? Surely people should be free from insecurity in illness or in old age?

But now we listen to lectures about how we should purchase our own security in every one of these areas. We are becoming consumers of services increasingly provided to us by the market, rather than as rights we are entitled to under a concept of citizenship.

Such a world as I have described has been accepted as our inevitable world, sustained by the myth of globalisation. It is a world about which we have to ask ourselves a fundamental question: do we have the capacity to subject it to critique? To say that globalisation is a myth is not to say that it does not exist. It is rather to say that all forms of imposed change have sought to describe themselves as natural and inevitable. The issue is to critique, control, and direct the process of global change.

Indeed, those who speak of what they call an 'ethical globalisation' must answer the question: do they speak of making the process ethical, or of wrestling with the consequences of a new global capitalism so as to wring some ethical crumbs from them?

We have shifted to being consumers rather than citizens. This is accompanied by the commodification of more and more aspects of life and has created an alienation that masks itself as the sole desirable lifestyle – a lifestyle that invites us towards a life of being consumed in one's consumption. The interdependency which was at the basis of citizenship is recognised, but it is devalued by an aggressive and, at times, vicious individualism. Indeed, I notice our language itself has changed. People rarely speak about 'the personal' any more, but speak instead of 'the individual'.

Market fundamentalism, I have suggested, is accepted as the single paradigm of economic development and its imposition as the sole strategy for development and poverty alleviation. This is disastrous, not only in the poorest countries or transition economies, but also in the so-called developed world.

As consumers, we have experienced a dulling of our consciousness, which blocks our capacity to engage critically with our world. For example, to take the media, we are affected by a fragmentation of audiences, a concentration of ownership, and a drive towards cultural homogeneity. We should be honest and accept that the concentration of ownership in the media internationally, with its stress on commoditised entertainment on television in particular, plays a crucial role in this limitation, even destruction, of our lifeworld.

President's Address to the Labour Party Conference
Dublin City University, 1 April 2006

Vision and Action Will Shape Labour's Future

The Labour Party is the oldest political party in Ireland. It was founded, we should never forget, in the year before one of the greatest confrontations between labour and capital. What was then a poverty-stricken and vulnerable movement of labour was seeking to organise against a version of capitalism that refused the most basic rights, including that of organisation, to workers. That confrontation required courage, tenacity, solidarity and, above all, a commitment to class and history beyond the short-term challenges. We are the beneficiaries of their struggle, and in our generation we must lay the foundations for future achievement.

Out of the most extreme conditions of 1912/13, there emerged a vision that dealt not only with the immediate problems of working people but also with a vision for the changes that were necessary in the structures of the economy, the society and the political system.

What is required of the labour movement into the future is no less than these values of courage, tenacity, solidarity and commitment. Much of the energies of the labour movement in the intervening period between 1912 and the present moment have concentrated on the protection of workers in a hostile environment. These protections have had to be won through negotiation, and more often in the past through courageous confrontation. In the period into which we are now entering, it is clear that this task remains.

There will be an attempt in the next few years to erode many of the gains made by the trade-union movement in Europe as the tyranny of the neo-liberal model of the economy is sought to be imposed in Europe by parties of the Right. There is no doubt that, in the name of alleged labour-market flexibility, hard-won securities for workers will be challenged. Many of us who favoured the protection of workers in the applicant countries to the European Union under a social model are aware of the potential for abuse of such countries. The existing social protections are being challenged as a condition for foreign direct investment. They are being forced to accept a US model of very limited worker protection.

However, the challenges facing the Labour Party and parties of the Left in Europe go far beyond such a protective role. Our party and other parties have to push on and make the case for a rights-based approach to the economy, the society and the political system, within a comprehensive theory of citizenship. The recent war has opened up a huge gap between the citizens of countries and their administrations on the issue of militarism. The citizens who rejected their governments' support for militarism are also against unfair trade, crippling debt, tied aid and economic exploitation, cultural domination and political oppression.

There is as great a gap between the public support for fair trade, untied aid and debt relief, and their political representatives and governments, who refuse to question the devastating consequences of a single paradigm of economics – the neo-liberal agenda – with its devastating consequences at home and abroad, as there was between militarism and its alternative – peace.

It is beyond time, too, for the Left to question the popular assertion of the Right that, after 1989, the moment of socialism has passed. Neither the legacy of Stalinism nor the collapse of the Berlin Wall, nor the horrific events of September 11, discredit the powerful liberating humanism of the socialist vision, and this should be stated loudly, clearly and everywhere Labour members gather.

While Labour members must have the courage to acknowledge past distortions of socialism, and even failures to criticise these distortions, it is even more important now to restate the values of socialism for a generation that is carrying the marks of the legacy of Thatcher–Reaganism, with its extreme individualism and greed, so well represented by the Progressive Democrats and the Fianna Fáil Party.

A rights-based approach to the economy and to society is not a burden too great for the manifestos of parties of the Left. It does not demand that you do that for which you do not have the resources. The template is accepted as a solemn commitment to be progressively realised. Legislation is tested for its progress to the rights-based goals, in relation to housing, health, education and special needs, and there is total transparency. The parties of the Right, with their version of the limited state, are willing to abandon the most basic human needs to the logic of the market. Parties of the Left have to oppose this at every level.

The Labour Party and like-minded parties of the Left, while they have to respect the complexity of the real circumstances of the economy and the society in which we find ourselves, are not required to capitulate to the version of the economy or society which the Right suggests is inevitable. The Left will be judged much more by its adherence to principle than by its competence. Both are important, but the principles and vision are the most important.

When Raymond Williams suggested that it was only when the inevitabilities were questioned that we had taken our first steps in a journey of hope, it is required of us that we not only question the inevitabilities but that we develop the alternative, based on our values, which we must have the courage to advance at every level.

Far from socialism being out of date, it is more necessary now than ever. What is old-fashioned is the eighteenth-century version of greed and selfishness being imposed upon us within a neo-liberal model of the economy that wreaks death and destruction in the developing world and that deprives citizens at home of their most basic rights in health, education, housing and special needs.

Our tasks, then, in the next few years are only minimally ones of a managerial kind. Rather, they are of a radical kind. We have to accept the responsibility of producing a wide range of policies derived from a vision for which we are willing to campaign and on which we will be opposed by the riches of capitalism and a monopolised media.

This will require courage, commitment and responsibility. We should be proud of what makes us different, committed to speaking publicly about it, and in our relations with each other should put into practice the values we are advocating for the larger society.

There is a great need for Labour's vision. There is a great future for the Labour Party. That future, however, has not only to be crafted, it has to become a matter of belief and, based on a vision, delivered into action. That is our challenge.

President's Address, Labour Party Conference, Killarney, 10 May 2003

NOTES

NOTES TO 'THE LIMITS OF CLIENTELISM: TOWARDS AN ASSESSMENT OF IRISH POLITICS', pp73–96

1   Basil Chubb, 'The Government and Politics of Ireland', Oxford, Oxford University Press, 1970. This work pioneered the study of the phenomena referred to within the framework of political culture.

2   Chubb does not use these terms technically, as the formal literature on patronage and brokerage uses them. He writes of them in an empirical sense as networks of influence.

3   Chubb, *op. cit.*, 76.

4   Mart Bax, 'Harpstrings and Confessions' , Amsterdam, Van Gorcum, 1977, 183.

5   *ibid.*, 7.

6   *ibid.*

7   Paul. Sacks, 'The Donegal Mafia', New Haven, Yale University Press, 1976. This work is a study of machine politics in County Donegal.

8   *ibid.*, 7.

9   Peter Gibbon and M. D. Higgins, 'Patron age, tradition and modernisation: the case of the Irish "Gombeenman" ', *Economic and Social Review*, Dublin, 6, 1974, 27–44.

10   *ibid.*, 44.

11   George Russell, in a letter to the *Galway. Express*, 7 September 1910.

12   'Gombeenman' is derived from the Irish *'gaimbín'*, which carried a pejorative meaning associated with usurious dealings. The derivation is discussed in an excellent article by Tomas De Bhaldraithe, in *Eigse: A Journal of Irish Studies*, 17, 1977–78, 109–13.

13   Sacks, *op. cit.*, 92. Sacks presented a table giving a councillor's diary for a month.

14   Sacks, *op. cit.*, and Sax, *op. cit.*, are the field studies referred to.

15   The author is here drawing on notebooks dealing with his constituency work, being kept for a wider study of the Irish political system; these will, where appropriate, be referred to simply as 'Author's notebooks' in later references.

16   D. Turpin, 'Achieving a single service', *Administration*, Dublin, 2, 1954, especially 82–87.

17   J. F. Zimmerman, 'Role perception of Irish city and county councillors', *Administration*, 24, 1976.

18   Author's notebooks.

19   I am not sure of the origin of this phrase, but it occurs regularly in my notes as the usual description of such a personal advantage.

20   Chubb, *op. cit.*, 284.

21 Fine Gael (translated as 'Kith and Kin of the Gael') is the second-largest party in Ireland, whose founders supported the Treaty which ended the War of Independence: it has in recent times been in power from 1973–77 and again in 1981, with the support of the Labour Party. The party in power for most of the modern period has been Fianna Fáil ('The Soldier of Destiny'), which draws its origins from opposition to the Treaty. It has regarded it as an important aspect of its identity to ostentatiously speak of republicanism. In recent years it has drawn support from the more recent speculative capitalism.

22 Author's notebooks.

23 *ibid.*

24 *ibid.* In one of the counties under study by the author, a councillor made allegations of inefficiency against local-authority officials and had co-operation with the staff withdrawn from him for a very long period, in which time the work of the local authority itself was impeded. The matter was resolved through mediation after several months.

25 F. G. Bailey, *Stratagems and Spoils*, Oxford, Basil Blackwell, 1970.

26 Author's notebooks.

27 Irish governments over the years have been nervous of using the word 'planning'. for fear of offending. the Roman Catholic Church's position on 'the principle of subsidiarity', which saw. state activity as being justified only when individual and corporate action had been exhausted as options. Thus in the late fifties, the word 'programme' was used in the title of 'The First Programme for Economic Expansion 1958–63'. A deep hostility exists to the public service today, which, in fairness, is not due to Church influence but to a business-orientated and business-controlled media.

28 A phrase used to describe a representative forced to choose another constituency due to the revision of constituency boundaries.

29 Author's notebooks.

30 *ibid.*

31 'Dáil Debates', Dublin, for 10 March 1981.

32 Author's notebooks.

33 Local newspaper reports and the national press were commenting on the inevitability of an election right through March and April 1981. The election came in June.

34 Luigi Graziano, 'Patron-client relationships in southern Italy', in Steffan W. Schmidt, Laura Guasti, Carl H. Laude, and James C. Scott (eds), *Friends, Followers and Factions: A Reader in Political Clientelism*, 360–378, but particularly in a paper presented to the European Consortium for Political Research's Workshop on Clientelism, Florence, 25–30 March 1960. Graziano's work has impressed the author as demonstrating powerful parallels between the experience of southern Italy and the Irish Republic.

35 The author' s notebooks contain the following phrase from the occupant of a major position in one of the political parties: 'What are we doing with all these policies with glossy covers and expensive paper that nobody is interested in? It's votes that count.'

36 This abuse was covered by all the Irish papers, local and national, at the end of July 1981.

37   Gibbon and Higgins, *loc. cit.*, especially 28.

38   David E. Schmitt, *The Irony of Irish Democracy*, Lexington, Mass., Lexington Books, 1973, especially 77–80.

39   J. C. Russell, *In the Shadow of Saints: Aspects of Family and Religion in the Rural Irish Gaeltacht*, San Diego, University of California, 1979.

40   Conrad Arensberg, *The Irish Countryman*, London, Macmillan, 1937; followed by his revised work with Solon T. Kimball, *Family and Community in Ireland*, Cambridge, Mass., Harvard University Press, 1966.

41   P. Lynch and J. Vaizey, *Guinness Brewery in the Irish Economy, 1759–1876*, Cambridge, Cambridge University Press, 1960, is the classic exposition of this model of the Irish economy.

42   Gibbon and Higgins, *loc. cit.*

43   *ibid.*, 43.

44   *ibid.*, 43.

45   *ibid.*, 44.

Notes to 'The Gombeenman in Fact and Fiction', pp97–118

1   A version of this paper was first read to Dublin History Workshop on 11 March 1978. I am indebted for the opportunity to receive many helpful comments on that occasion and from its participants in later correspondence. Some of the arguments as they affect an evaluation of the literary contribution of Liam O'Flaherty and Peadar O'Donnell are summarised in my 'Liam O'Flaherty and Peadar O'Donnell, Images of Rural Community', the *Crane Bag*, Vol. 9, No. 1, 1985.

2   Becker, Bernard H., *Disturbed Ireland*, London, Macmillan and Co., 1881, 207–208.

3   De Bháldraithe, Tomás, *'Gaimbí, Gaimbín, Gombeen'*, *Eigse: A Journal of Irish Studies* Vol. 8, Part I, 109–13. I am indebted also to Dr P. L. Henry for his useful comments in correspondence on the origins of the word.

4   Arensberg, Conrad and Solon T. Kimball (1968); 2nd edition, Cambridge, Mass.

5   See particularly: Carleton, W., *The Black Prophet*, London, Lawrence and Bullen, 1899. O'Flaherty, Liam, *The House of Gold*, London, Cape, 1929. O'Donnell, Peadar, *Proud Island*, Dublin, The Wolfhound Press, 1975.

6   'Two Lovely Beasts' was first published in *The Bell*, Vol. XIV, No. 3, December 1946.

7   Coulter, H., *The West of Ireland: Its Existing Conditions and Prospects*, Dublin, 1862. Becker, Bernard H., *op. cit.*

8   Coulter, H. *op. cit.*, 195–98.

9   *ibid.*, 201–2.

10   *ibid.*, 23.

11   Becker, Bernard H., *op. cit.*, 208–12.

12 Donnelly, James S. (Jur.), 'The Irish Agricultural! Depression of 1859–65', *Irish Economic and Social History*, Vol. III, 1976, 33–54.

13 Donnelly, James S. (Jur.), *op. cit.*, 51.

14 Lynch, P. and Vaizey, *Guinness's Brewery in the Irish Economy, 1759–1876*, 170.

15 Lynch, P. and Vaizey, *op. cit.*, 163.

16 See Gibbon, Peter and Michael D. Higgins, "Patronage Traditions and Modernization: The Case of the Irish Gombeenman', *Economic and Social Review*, Vol. 6, No. 1, 1974, for the initial statement of our position, and Kennedy, Liam, 'A Sceptical View of the Reincarnation of the Irish "Gombeenman" ', *Economic and Social Review*, Vol. 8, No. 3, for the allegation of contributing to a 'demonology', and Gibbon, Peter and Mchael D. Higgins, 'The Irish. Gombeenman, Reincarnation or Rehabilitation', *Economic and Social Review*, Vol. 8, No. 4, for our reply.

17 Carleton's work has already been referred to. Kyril Bonjiglioli is the latest to contribute to the fictional treatment of this figure. ' "The Gombeen Man" New Irish Writing', the *Irish Press*, 20 May 1978.

18 Carleton, W., *op, cit.*, 56–57.

19 *ibid.*, 63–66.

20 O'Flaherty, Liam, *op. cit.*, 1946.

21 *ibid.*, 18–20.

22 'The Agricultural Labourer', Vol. 4, Part IV, in the report of the Royal Commission on Labour, HMSO, 1893: The report by Mr Arthus Wilson Fox (Assistant Commissioner) upon the Poor Law Union of Westport (Mayo) is the one to which reference is made. See particularly page 70, where the account of G. H. with B. C. Grocer and General Dealer is presented.

23 Patrick J. Sheeran, *The Novels of Liam O'Flaherty*, Dublin, Wolfhound Press, 1976, quotes Father Flatley's evidence. The quotation comes from the Royal Commission on Congestion in Ireland, Appendix to the Tenth Report (Dublin, 1908), 16–17.

24 Chubb, Basil, 'Going About Persecuting Civil Servants', *Political Studies*, 1963, is a little known but valuable indicator of what was to be Chubb's consistent version of political explanation. It is quoted by Sacks in his *The Donegal Mafia*, Gale University Press, 1976. Mart Bax's study of Irish politics is published under the title *Harpstrings and Confessions, Machine Style Politics in the Republic of Ireland*, Van Gorcum, 1976.

25 Chubb, Basil, *op. cit.*, 1963, 273–79.

26 Bax Mart, *op. cit.*, 1976, 55–56.

27 Sacks, Paul M., *op. cit.*, 1976, 124.

28 Gibbon, Peter, 'Arensberg and Kimball Revisited', *Economy. and Society*, Vol. 2, No. 4, 1973.

29 Patrick F. Sheeran, *op. cit.*, 1976, 42.

30 *ibid.*, 39–40.

31 Patrick F. Sheeran's work has been of great value to the writer. His work is invaluable towards an understanding of the social context of O'Flaherty's work. It falls short of a literary theory in social terms. It is, however, a useful corrective to the

prevailing: literary mode, which stresses the separateness of explanation in Anglo-Irish literary studies.

32   O'Flaherty, Liam, *op. cit.*, 1929.

33   *ibid.*, 90–91.

34   *ibid.*, 152–64.

35   I made this point in my review of Hugh Brody, *Inishkillane: Change and Decay. in the West of Ireland*, London, Allen Lane Press, in *Hibernia*, Dublin, September 1974.

36   O'Flaherty, Liam, *Shame the Devil*, London, Grayson and Grayson, 1934, 43–44.

37   O'Flaherty Liam, *op. cit.*, 1929, 24.

38   *ibid.*, 163.

39   *Connacht Tribune*, 1 December, 1934.

40   *ibid.*, 8.

NOTES TO 'THE THREAT TO THE ENVIRONMENT'S MARVELLOUS SYMMETRY', pp 124–127

1   Bateson, Gregory, *Steps to an Ecology of Mind*, Paladin, 1973.

2   Dickson, David, *Alternative Technology*, Fontana, 1974.

3   Habermas, Jurgen, *Towards a Rational Society*, Heinemann Educational Books, 1968.

PUBLISHERS' ACKNOWLEDGEMENTS

The publishers would like to acknowledge the following, in whose publications versions of chapters in this collection first appeared: *Hot Press* magazine, for 'Building the Black and Green Alliance', 'The Trial', 'Darkness on the Edge of Town', ' "We Will Hang Fikri" ', 'The General's Election', 'Talkin' 'Bout a Revolution', 'We Have Lost an Election – But the Revolution Is Not Lost', 'Back to the Barrios', 'War in the Desert', 'Starving by Numbers', 'A Season in Hell', 'Africa – Apocalypse Now', 'Return to the Killing Fields', 'What Is It Good For?', 'Ireland Should Call for an End to the Economic Sanctions Against the People of Iraq' and 'Rio: Still a Mountain to Climb'; the *Irish Times*, for 'Is This the Beginning of the End for International Law?'; Brandon Books, for 'The Delivery', 'Katie's Song', 'Collecting' and two extracts from 'Brothers', all from *The Season of Fire* (1990); Salmon Poetry, for 'Dark Memories', from *The Betrayal* (1993); Veritas for 'Imagining the Future: A Global Perspective', from *Imagining the Future*, eds. Father Harry Bohan and Gerard Kennedy (2005); Townhouse for 'My Education', from *My Education*, ed. John Quinn (1997); and Cambridge University Press, for 'The Limits of Clientelism', from *Private Patronage and Public Power: Political Clientelism in the Modern State*, ed. Christopher Clapham, 1982. The publishers have made every effort to trace holders of copyright material and would be happy to correct any oversights in this regard in future printings of the book.

INDEX

Italicised page ranges refer to chapters.